Everyman, I will go with thee,
and be thy guide

William Shakespeare

TWELFTH NIGHT

Edited by
JOHN F. ANDREWS

Foreword by
ALEC MCCOWEN

EVERYMAN
J. M. DENT · LONDON
CHARLES E. TUTTLE
VERMONT

Text © 1991 by Doubleday Book & Music Clubs, Inc.

Textual revisions, revisions to notes, introduction, note on
text, chronology, and all end matter © J. M. Dent 1994 and
Charles E. Tuttle Co. 1994

First published in Everyman by J. M. Dent 1994
Published by permission of GuildAmerica Books, an imprint
of Doubleday Book and Music Clubs, Inc.

Photoset by Deltatype Ltd, Ellesmere Port, Cheshire
Printed in Great Britain by
The Guernsey Press Co. Ltd, Guernsey, C.I.
for
J. M. Dent
Orion Publishing Group
Orion House
5 Upper St Martin's Lane, London WC2H 9EA
and
Charles E. Tuttle Co.
28 South Main Street, Rutland,
Vermont 05701 – USA

British Library Cataloguing-in-Publication Data is available
upon request

ISBN 0 460 87518 3

CONTENTS

ACKNOWLEDGEMENTS

The editor and publishers wish to thank the following for permission to use copyright material:

Associated University Presses for material from Stephen Booth, 'Twelfth Night: The Audience as Malvolio' in *Shakespeare's Rough Magic*, ed. Peter Erickson and Coppelia Kahn, University of Delaware Press, 1985;

Ralph Berry for material from 'In *Twelfth Night*: The Experience of the Audience', *Shakespeare Survey*, 1981;

Charles and John Van Doren for material from Mark Van Doren, *Shakespeare*, 1939;

Folger Shakespeare Library for material from L. G. Salingar, 'The Design of *Twelfth Night*', *Shakespeare Quarterly*, 1958, and Jean E. Howard, 'Crossdressing, the Theatre, and Gender Struggle', *Shakespeare Quarterly*, 1988;

Modern Language Association of America for material from Porter Williams, Jr., 'Mistakes in *Twelfth Night* and Their Resolution', *PMLA*, 76, 1961;

Oxford University Press for material from Bertrand Evans, *Shakespeare's Comedies*, 1960;

Princeton University Press for material from C. L. Barber, *Shakespeare's Festive Comedy*. Copyright © 1959, renewed 1987 by Princeton University Press;

University of California Press for material from Stephen Greenblatt, *Shakespearean Negotiations: The Circulation of Social Energy in Renaissance England*. Copyright © 1988 The Regents of the University of California;

Every effort has been made to trace all the copyright holders, but if any have been inadvertently overlooked the publishers will be pleased to make the necessary arrangement at the first opportunity.

NOTE ON THE AUTHOR AND EDITOR

William Shakespeare is held to have been born on St George's Day, 23 April 1564. The eldest son of a prosperous glove-maker in Stratford-upon-Avon, he was probably educated at the town's grammar school.

Tradition holds that between 1585 and 1592, Shakespeare first became a schoolteacher and then set off for London. By 1594 he was a leading member of the Lord Chamberlain's Men, helping to direct their business affairs, as well as being a playwright and actor. In 1598 he became a part-owner of the company, which was the most distinguished of its age. However, he maintained his contacts with Stratford, and his family appears to have remained there.

From about 1610 he seems to have grown increasingly involved in the town's affairs, suggesting a withdrawal from London. He died on 23 April 1616, in his 53rd year, and was buried at Holy Trinity two days later.

John F. Andrews has recently completed a 19-volume edition, *The Guild Shakespeare*, for the Doubleday Book and Music Clubs. He is also the editor of a 3-volume reference set, *William Shakespeare: His World, His Work, His Influence*, and the former editor (1974–85) of the journal *Shakespeare Quarterly*. From 1974 to 1984 he was director of Academic Programs at the Folger Shakespeare Library in Washington and Chairman of the Folger Institute.

CHRONOLOGY OF SHAKESPEARE'S LIFE

* It is rarely possible to be certain about the dates at which plays of this period were written. For Shakespeare's plays, this chronology follows the dates preferred by Stanley Wells and Gary Taylor, the editors of The Oxford Shakespeare. Publication dates are given for poetry and books.

CHRONOLOGY OF HIS TIMES

Year	Literary Context	Historical Events
1565–7	Golding, Ovid's *Metamorphoses*, tr.	Elizabeth I reigning
1574	*A Mirror for Magistrates* (3rd ed.)	
1576	London's first playhouse built	
1578	John Lyly, *Euphues*	
1579	North, Plutarch's *Lives*, tr.	
	Spenser, *Shepherd's Calender*	
1587	Marlowe, *I Tamburlaine*	Mary Queen of Scots executed
1588	Holinshed's *Chronicles* (2nd ed.)	Defeat of Spanish Armada
1589	Kyd, *Spanish Tragedy*	Civil war in France
	Marlowe, *Jew of Malta*	
1590	Spenser, *Faerie Queene*, Bks I–III	
1591	Sidney, *Astrophel and Stella*	Proclamation against Jesuits
1592	Marlowe, *Dr Faustus* & *Edward II*	Scottish witchcraft trials
		Plague closes theatres from June
1593	Marlowe killed	
1594	Nashe, *Unfortunate Traveller*	Theatres reopen in summer
1594–6		Extreme food shortages
1595	Sidney, *An Apologie for Poetry*	Riots in London
1596		Calais captured by Spanish
		Cadiz expedition

Year	Age	Life
1597	33	Buys New Place in Stratford
		The Lord Chamberlain's Men's lease to play at the Theatre expires; until 1599 they play mainly at the Curtain
1597–8		*The Merry Wives of Windsor* & *2 Henry IV*
1598	34	*Much Ado About Nothing*
1598–9		*Henry V*
1599	35	*Julius Caesar*. One of syndicate responsible for building the Globe in Southwark, where the Lord Chamberlain's Men now play
1599–1600		*As You Like It*
1600–1		*Hamlet*
1601	37	*Twelfth Night*. His father is buried in Stratford
1602	38	*Troilus and Cressida*. Invests £320 in land near Stratford*
1603	39	*Measure for Measure*. The Lord Chamberlain's Men become the King's Men. They play at court more than all the other companies combined
1603–4		*Othello*
c.1604	40	Shakespeare sues Philip Rogers of Stratford for debt
1604–5		*All's Well That Ends Well*
1605	41	*Timon of Athens*. Invests £440 in Stratford tithes
1605–6		*King Lear*
1606	42	*Macbeth* & *Antony and Cleopatra*
1607	43	*Pericles*. Susanna marries the physician John Hall in Stratford
1608	44	*Coriolanus*. The King's Men lease Blackfriars, an indoor theatre. His only grandchild is born. His mother dies
1609	45	*The Winter's Tale*. 'Sonnets' and 'A Lover's Complaint' published
1610	46	*Cymbeline*
1611	47	*The Tempest*
1613	49	*Henry VIII*. Buys house in London for £140
1613–14		*The Two Noble Kinsmen*
1616	52	Judith marries Thomas Quiney, a vintner, in Stratford. On 23 April Shakespeare dies; is buried two days later
1623		Publication of the First Folio. His widow dies in August

* A schoolmaster would earn around £20 a year at this time.

Year	Literary Context	Historical Events
1597	Bacon, *Essays*	
1598	Marlowe and Chapman, *Hero and Leander* Jonson, *Every Man in his Humour*	Rebellion in Ireland
1599	Children's companies begin playing Thomas Dekker's *Shoemaker's Holiday*	Essex fails in Ireland
1601	'War of the Theatres' Jonson, *Poetaster*	Essex rebels and is executed
1602		Tyrone defeated in Ireland
1603	Florio, Montaigne's *Essays*, tr.	Elizabeth I dies, James I accedes Raleigh found guilty of treason
1604	Marston, *The Malcontent*	Peace with Spain
1605	Bacon, *Advancement of Learning*	Gunpowder plot
1606	Jonson, *Volpone*	
1607	Tourneur, *The Revenger's Tragedy*, published	Virginia colonized Enclosure riots
1609		Oath of allegiance Truce in Netherlands
1610	Jonson, *Alchemist*	
1611	Authorised Version of the Bible Donne, *Anatomy of the World*	
1612	Webster, *White Devil*	Prince Henry dies
1613	Webster, *Duchess of Malfi*	Princess Elizabeth marries
1614	Jonson, *Bartholomew Fair*	
1616	Folio edition of Jonson's plays	

Biographical note, chronology and plot summary compiled by John Lee, University of Bristol, 1994.

FOREWORD TO
Twelfth Night

So many memories of *Twelfth Night* . . .

At the Royal Academy of Dramatic Art, aged sixteen, being cast as an unlikely Sir Toby, and my pride in my first stage-belch before saying 'A plague o' these pickle-herring!' At school I had never dreamed that I would be asked to display this talent. Belching for a living? An actor's life for me!

The first time I saw *Twelfth Night*, in 1946 at the Birmingham Rep when I was twenty-one. I still remember leaving the old theatre under a spell of enchantment – convinced that I had discovered a masterpiece single-handed, and that nobody else had ever realized its magic.

When I was about twenty-four, being asked at short notice and with no rehearsal to play the Second Officer, who has to come on and say, 'Antonio, I arrest thee at the suit of Count Orsino.' When I entered, I realized I didn't know which actor was playing Antonio and whispered to a fellow Officer for information. In this same production there was no time for a costume fitting, and the crotch of my tights was embarrassingly level with my knees. Luckily this was a single performance at the Battersea Town Hall or it might have halted my career.

The thrill of being cast as Malvolio in a lovely production at the Old Vic in 1960. In order to imagine and duplicate the Steward's passion for his Mistress, I pretended to myself that Olivia was actually Vivien Leigh, with whom I personally had been besotted for years. Then one night Vivien Leigh came backstage to congratulate me – and I was too tongue-tied to confess that she had been my inspiration.

Playing Malvolio again in the BBC Television Shakespeare series, and watching Fabian emerge as a leading character under the skill of the young Robert Lindsay.

But perhaps best of all is my memory of a recital of Shakespeare pieces given by a group of us when we were on tour in Russia with the Royal Shakespeare Company. We were invited to an Old Actors' Home, which was located in a grand palace in Leningrad (now St Petersburg). I was to open the recital with Malvolio's famous letter speech. The old actors were in their seats and an interpreter came on to explain the plot to them. Suddenly I heard indignant shouting. 'What's happening?' I asked a Russian guide; 'it sounds like a riot!' He said, 'They are shouting "We *know!* We *know!* We *know* the plot of *Twelfth Night!* Don't tell us! We *know!* Get on with it!" ' They were a wonderful audience, and I got my laughs.

Twelfth Night is a deceptively simple play. It reads, and can be performed, without effort. And yet Shakespeare has created an entire world of madness, and an entirely original cast of beguiling characters. It is a comedy; but the comedy will only work against the background of the cruelty and danger in the play.

Feste is desperate to keep his position as Clown. Maria is quietly desperate in her love of Sir Toby. Sir Andrew is gulled and robbed. Orsino, Viola, Olivia, and Antonio are sickeningly in love. And the treatment of Malvolio is monstrously cruel. But at the end of it all, we have visited an enchanted world – a world we somehow recognize, a world that is forever lodged in our dreams.

And as well as all the wonderful poetry within the play, the heart-catching lyricism, there is the best retort to all the killjoys and puritans: 'Dost thou think, because thou art virtuous, there shall be no more cakes and ale?'

Alec McCowen

ALEC MCCOWEN, one of Britain's leading actors, made his New York stage debut in the role of the Messenger in *Antony and Cleopatra*. His wide-ranging Shakespearean roles include Hamlet, Malvolio in *Twelfth Night,* the Fool in *King Lear,* and Antipholus of Syracuse in *The Comedy of Errors*, in which he toured Europe, the United States and the Soviet Union. Among his diverse acting credits are the title role in *Hadrian VII,* Professor Higgins in *Pygmalion* and Martin Dysart in *Equus*.

EDITOR'S INTRODUCTION TO
Twelfth Night

Twelfth Night, or What You Will, is commonly referred to as the last of Shakespeare's 'festive' comedies. From all indications it was completed in late 1601 or early 1602, though cogent reasons have been offered for placing at least the initial phases of its composition in 1600, and the first performance that can be dated with certainty occurred at London's Middle Temple Hall on 2 February 1602.

In ways that hark back to *The Comedy of Errors*, a product of the years before 1595, and look forward to the tragicomic romances with which Shakespeare would round out his theatrical career between 1608 and 1613, *Twelfth Night* conveys an aura of 'Wonder', an enigmatic confluence of 'Chance' and 'Destiny', which serves to counter any temptation we might have to presume that 'What You Will' is altogether a matter of human choice. Like most of Shakespeare's works, it compels an audience to consider the problematic relationships between the 'real' world the drama imitates and the 'play' world it conjures into the charmed circle, the 'Wooden O', in which its staged events were originally presented to a theatregoing public. In the process it prompts us to ponder the elusiveness of such concepts as Fate and Freedom, Wisdom and Folly, Sanity and Madness, and Nature and Art.

The principal catalyst for the metamorphoses that constitute the comedy's action is an ingenue named Viola. In keeping with her name, she proves to be an instrument of harmony. But when we gauge her movements in terms of the kinds of initiative that define a heroine's part in earlier plays such as *As You Like It* and *The Merchant of Venice*, the maiden whose fortunes we follow in *Twelfth Night* seems comparatively docile. Like her Shakespearean predecessors, she resorts to male disguise; and like them, she realizes that she must rely upon her wits to survive, let alone prevail, in circumstances that force her to function as a displaced person. Unlike Rosalind, however, who enters the Forest of Arden of her own volition and who then proceeds to work a special kind of 'Magic' in the green world of *As You Like It*, and unlike Portia, who manifests even more assertiveness than Rosalind when she assumes the persona of a 'learned Judge' in the tension-filled courtroom of *The Merchant of Venice*, Viola finds herself in a strange land that appears to be at the mercy of influences beyond her comprehension and control. To a degree that is unusual among Shakespeare's resourceful female protagonists, she entrusts her lot to Providence, and only through what Wordsworth was later to term 'wise passiveness' is she finally able to negotiate her way from the coast of Illyria to the metaphorical Elysium with which her quest concludes.

For Viola's story the playwright drew upon a prose romance, Barnaby Riche's tale of 'Apolonius and Silla' in *Riche his Farewell to Militarie Profession* (1581). It is possible that Shakespeare took some details, either directly or indirectly, from an anonymous Italian comedy, *Gl'Ingannati* (*The Deceived*), which was published in 1537, and from two Italian plays named *Gl'Inganni*, one (published in 1562) by Niccolo Secchi, the other (published in 1592) by Curzio Gonzaga. He may also have consulted adaptations of *Gl'Ingannati* in Matteo Bandello's *Novelle* (1554) and in Pierre de Belleforest's *Histoires Tragiques* (1579), the two antecedents for Barnaby Riche's rendering of the narrative. But as Middle Temple law student John Manningham remarked in the earliest extant account of *Twelfth Night* (1602),* the ultimate source for the play's love-plot was the Roman playwright Titus Maccius Plautus (254–184 BC). Shakespeare had already borrowed from Plautus's *Menaechmi* (a farce about identical twins) when he wrote *The Comedy of Errors* several years previously, and it is likely that he repaired both to the *Menaechmi* and to his own updating of Plautus when he began thinking about *Twelfth Night*.

More important for the play's atmosphere than any specific

---

* See the opening paragraph of 'Perspectives on *Twelfth Night*' for a quotation from Manningham's diary.

literary or dramatic model, however, was the mood traditionally associated with Twelfth Night (the evening of 6 January, the twelfth day after Christmas), when the Church celebrated the Feast of the Epiphany. On this occasion Christians commemorated the appearance of the Saviour to a world in need of pardon and deliverance, and in accordance with New Testament exhortations to seek 'peace' and exercise 'good will' (Luke 2:14) Elizabethans engaged in a form of carnival release that liberated them from many of the restraints that governed their lives for the rest of the year. Festus, the Lord of Misrule, presided over gaudy, and at times raucous, masquerade balls. In many locales a boy or a 'licens'd Fool' was designated to serve for the nonce as a satiric Bishop, a Mayor, or even a King. And no matter where the holiday was honoured, everyone relaxed for a night of revelry and reconciliation in which the immediate, though temporary, object was to forget about the social hierarchies and personal conflicts of ordinary existence and turn an everyday realm of affairs topsy-turvy.

Curiously, there are few if any explicit references to Twelfth Night within the play itself. But in the 'Uncivil Rule' of Sir Toby Belch and his boon companions, in the role of the Clown (Feste) who roams from one setting to another as Illyria's exponent of Folly, in the 'Madness' that seems to descend without warning upon even the gravest of personages, and in the epiphanies (revelations) that lead Olivia to declare the final scene 'most Wonderful', we have abundant indications that the title of the comedy is purposeful.

The same holds true for the work's subtitle. For if the words 'Twelfth Night' dispose us to anticipate a pageant about the triumph of 'good will', it would seem logical that a prerequisite to such a joyous outcome must be the subjection or banishment of 'bad will'. As it happens, the name 'Malvolio' means 'bad will', and at one point the detractors of Olivia's dyspeptic Steward describe him as an ill-tempered 'Puritan'. In that epithet Elizabethan audiences would have recognized not one but a legion of adversaries. Not only did England's Puritans oppose all 'Cakes and Ale'; many of them harboured an even stronger antipathy to the theatre, to pastimes such as bear-baiting, dancing, and card-playing, and to any activity they defined as idleness or frivolity.

What transpires with Malvolio amounts, in effect, to a combination of exorcism and ostracism, and one that the play's early seventeenth-century viewers would have applied to a full range of anti-festive Puritan attitudes. First Malvolio the unruly enemy of Misrule is 'tickled' into donning the very 'Mask' he claims to despise, that of a jovial merrymaker. Along the way Malvolio the scorner of Folly is gulled into displaying himself as an unwitting fool before the spectator (Lady Olivia) he most fervently wishes to impress with his judgement and sobriety. Then Malvolio the 'Madman' is made the central figure of a mumming in which a mock 'Curate' essays to free him of the demonic spirit that 'Sir Topas' pretends to regard as possessing the body and soul of a man long credited with solemnity. And finally, once he is exposed to public humiliation after his release from the lunatic's 'Dark Room', Malvolio the Victim is required to endure what he can only perceive as the vicious baiting of a 'whole Pack' of grinning mastiffs. Not surprisingly, he storms out of the chamber vowing vengeance.

The entertainer Steve Martin once quipped that 'comedy isn't pretty', and the comeuppance Malvolio is subjected to is so excruciating that many observers have preferred to respond to it, not as a 'Sport', but as a quasi-tragedy. At the very least the disciplining of the overbearing Steward would seem to mitigate the love and fellowship that Twelfth Night is normally expected to inculcate. Before we infer that the 'Malice' visited upon Malvolio spoils the party irrevocably, however, we should remember, first, that the Steward's own 'Humour of State' is what has incited 'the Whirligig of Time' to plague him with what the Greeks called Nemesis, and, second, that after being entreated 'to a Peace' he may in the fullness of 'Golden Time' forgive his tormentors and be restored to his proper place in the reconstituted household of his Lady and her new Lord. If so, Malvolio will have been induced to acquire some much-needed self-understanding, and any improvement in mental and emotional health that results will have justified the pain he suffered *en route* to that devoutly-to-be-wished consummation.

Something similar could be said of other characters in *Twelfth Night*. Early in the play Olivia tells Malvolio that he is 'sick of Self-love'. The Countess's diagnosis is accurate, of course, but what she fails to notice is that the physician is herself in need of attention. Olivia's prescription arrives almost immediately in the form of a Viola apparelled as 'Cesario'. As amusing as it may be for the theatre audience, the embarrassment the Lady experiences when she falls in love with this unresponsive 'Page' is as distressing for her as Malvolio's treatment is for the 'poor Fool' the Steward is shown to be by his ordeal.

Meanwhile Orsino, who believes himself to be the only conceivable match for Olivia, undergoes an agony of his own. When his rejection by the Countess is compounded by the apparent betrayal of his trusted emissary, the frenzied Duke is driven to a potentially savage retaliation. Fortunately, however, before he can execute his murderous impulse, the proceedings are interrupted by news that two other characters (Sir Toby and Sir Andrew) have just been administered a purgation that befits their own maladies. Then, just as suddenly, the play's confusions are astonishingly resolved by 'A Natural Perspective, that is and is not'. Once the mistaken identities are sorted out, it becomes evident that, like the 'Adversity' that proves 'Sweet' in *As You Like It*'s Forest of Arden, the 'blind Waves' that buffet the shores of Illyria have blessed Orsino's dukedom with a 'most happy Wrack'.

As You Like It culminates with an Epilogue in which Rosalind invites the audience to 'like as much of this Play as please you'. *Twelfth Night* moves to its close with Feste's musical reminder that 'Man's Estate' is a steady diet of 'the Wind and the Rain'. The Clown's words sound a more sombre note than do Rosalind's. But like the sentiments that arise from the earlier comedy, they keep us aware that whenever we need a respite from our travails, we can find solace in a company of thespians who'll 'strive to please [us] every Day'.

THE TEXT OF THE EVERYMAN SHAKESPEARE

Background

THE EARLY PRINTINGS OF SHAKESPEARE'S WORKS

Many of us enjoy our first encounter with Shakespeare when we're introduced to *Julius Caesar* or *Macbeth* at school. It may therefore surprise us that neither of these tragedies could ever have been read, let alone studied, by most of the playwright's contemporaries. They began as scripts for performance and, along with seventeen other titles that never saw print during Shakespeare's lifetime, they made their inaugural appearance as 'literary' works seven years after his death, in the 1623 collection we know today as the First Folio.

The Folio contained thirty-six titles in all. Of these, half had been issued previously in the small paperbacks we now refer to as quartos.* Like several of the plays first published in the Folio, the most trustworthy of the quarto printings appear to have been set either from Shakespeare's own manuscripts or from faithful copies of them. It's not impossible that the poet himself prepared some of these works for the press, and it's intriguing to imagine him reviewing proof-pages as the words he'd written for actors to speak and embody were being transposed into the type that readers would filter through their eyes, minds, and imaginations. But, alas, there's no indisputable evidence that Shakespeare had any direct involvement with the publication of these early editions of his plays.

What, then, about the scripts that achieved print for the first

---

* Quartos derived their name from the four-leaf units of which these small books were comprised: large sheets of paper that had been folded twice after printing to yield four leaves, or eight pages. Folios, volumes with twice the page-size of quartos, were put together from two-leaf units: sheets that had been folded once after printing to yield four pages.

time in the Folio? Had the dramatist taken any steps to give the permanency of book form to those texts before he died? We don't know. All we can say is that when a fatal illness seized him in 1616, Shakespeare was denied any opportunities he might otherwise have taken to ensure that his 'insubstantial Pageants' survived the mortal who was now slipping into the 'dark Backward and Abysm of Time'.

Fortunately, two of the playwright's colleagues felt an obligation, as they put it, 'to procure his Orphans Guardians'. Sometime after his death John Heminge (or Heminges) and Henry Condell made arrangements to preserve Shakespeare's theatrical compositions in a manner that would keep them vibrant for posterity. They dedicated their endeavour to two noblemen who had helped see England's foremost acting company through some of its most trying vicissitudes. They solicited several poetic tributes for the volume, among them a now-famous eulogy by fellow writer Ben Jonson. They commissioned an engraved portrait of Shakespeare to adorn the frontispiece. And they did their utmost to display the author's dramatic works in a style that would both dignify them and make them accessible to 'the great Variety of Readers'.

As they readied Shakespeare's plays for the compositors who would set them into stately Folio columns, Heminge and Condell (or editors and scribes designated to carry out their wishes) revised and augmented many of the entrances, exits, and other stage directions in Shakespeare's manuscripts. They divided most of the works into acts, and many into both acts and scenes.* For a number of plays they appended 'Names of the Actors', or casts of characters. Meanwhile they made every effort to guarantee that the Folio printers had reliable copy-texts for each of the titles: authoritative manuscripts for the plays that had not been published previously, and good quarto printings (annotated in some instances to insert staging details, mark script changes, and add supplementary material) for the ones that had been issued prior to the Folio. For several titles they supplied texts that were substantively different from, if not always demonstrably superior

---

* The early quartos, reflecting the unbroken sequence that probably typified Elizabethan and Jacobean performances of the plays, had been printed without the structural demarcations usual in Renaissance editions of classical drama.

to, the quarto versions that preceded them.

Like even the most accurate of the printings that preceded it, the Folio collection was flawed by minor blemishes. But it more than fulfilled the purpose of its generous-minded compilers: 'to keep the memory of so worthy a Friend and Fellow alive as was our Shakespeare'. In the process it provided a publishing model that remains instructive today.

MODERN EDITIONS OF THE PLAYS AND POEMS

When we compare the First Folio and its predecessors with the usual modern edition of Shakespeare's works, we're more apt to be impressed by the differences than by the similarities. Today's texts of Renaissance drama are normally produced in conformity with twentieth-century standards of punctuation and usage; as a consequence they look more neat, clean, and, to our eyes, 'right' than do the original printings. Thanks to an editorial tradition that extends back to the early eighteenth century, if not before, most of the rough spots in the early printings of Shakespeare have long been smoothed away. Textual scholars have ferreted out redundancies and eradicated inconsistencies. They've mended what they've perceived to be errors and oversights in the playscripts, and they've systematically attended to what they've construed as misreadings by the copyists and compositors who transmitted these playscripts to posterity. They've added '[Within]' brackets and other theatrical notations. They've revised stage directions they've judged incomplete or inadequate in the initial printings. They've regularized disparities in the speech headings. They've gone back to the playwright's sources and reinstated the 'proper' forms for many of the character and place names which a presumably hasty or inattentive author got 'wrong' as he conferred identities on his dramatis personae and stage locales. They've replaced obsolete words like *bankrout* with their modern heirs (in this case *bankrupt*). And in a multitude of other ways they've accommodated Shakespeare to the tastes, interests, and expectations of latter-day readers.

The results, on the whole, have been splendid. But interpreting the artistic designs of a complex writer is always problematical, and the task is especially challenging when that writer happens to have been a poet who felt unconstrained by many of the 'rules' that more conventional dramatists respected. The undertaking becomes further complicated when new rules, and new criteria of linguistic and social correctness, are imposed by subsequent generations of artists and critics.

To some degree in his own era, but even more in the neoclassical period (1660–1800) that came in its wake, Shakespeare's most ardent admirers thought it necessary to apologize for what Ben Jonson hinted at in his allusion to the 'small Latin, and less Greek' of an untutored prodigy. To be sure, the 'sweet Swan of Avon' sustained his popularity; in fact his reputation rose so steadily that by the end of the eighteenth century he'd eclipsed Jonson and his other peers and become the object of near-universal Bardolatry. But in the theatre most of his plays were being adapted in ways that were deemed advisable to tame their supposed wildness and bring them into conformity with the decorum of a society that took pride in its refinement. As one might expect, some of the attitudes that induced theatre proprietors to metamorphose an unpolished poet from the provinces into something closer to an urbane man of letters also influenced Shakespeare's editors. Persuaded that the dramatist's works were marred by crudities that needed expunging, they applied their ministrations to the canon with painstaking diligence.

Twentieth-century editors have moved away from many of the presuppositions that guided a succession of earlier improvers. But a glance at the textual apparatus accompanying virtually any modern publication of the plays and poems will show that emendations and editorial procedures deriving from such forebears as the sets published by Nicholas Rowe (1709), Alexander Pope (1723–25, 1728), Lewis Theobald (1733, 1740, 1757), Thomas Hanmer (1743–45, 1770–71), Samuel Johnson (1765), Edward Capell (1768), George Steevens (1773), and Edmond Malone (1790) retain a strong hold on today's renderings of the playwright's works. The consequence is a 'Shakespeare' who offers the tidiness we've come to expect in our libraries of treasured authors, but not necessarily the playwright a 1599 reader of the Second Quarto of *Romeo and Juliet* would still be able to recognize as a contemporary.

OLD LIGHT ON THE TOPIC

Over the last two decades we've learned from art curators that paintings by Old Masters such as Michelangelo and Rembrandt look a lot brighter when centuries of grime are removed from their surfaces – when hues that had become dulled with soot and other extraneous matter are allowed to radiate again with something approximating their pristine luminosity. We've learned from conductors like Christopher Hogwood that there are aesthetic rewards to be gained from a return to the scorings and instruments with which Renaissance and Baroque musical compositions were first presented. We've learned from twentieth-century experiments in the performance of Shakespeare's plays that an open, multi-level stage, analogous to that on which the scripts were originally enacted, does more justice to their dramaturgical techniques than does a proscenium auditorium devised for works that came later in the development of Western theatre. We've learned from archaeological excavations in London's Bankside area that the foundations of playhouses such as the Rose and the Globe look rather different from what many historians had expected. And we're now learning from a close scrutiny of Shakespeare's texts that they too look different, and function differently, when we accept them for what they are and resist the impulse to 'normalize' features that strike us initially as quirky, unkempt, or unsophisticated.

The Aims that Guide the Everyman Text

Like other modern editions of the dramatist's plays and poems, The Everyman Shakespeare owes an incalculable debt to the scholarship that has led to so many excellent renderings of the author's works. But in an attempt to draw fresh inspiration from the spirit that animated those remarkable achievements at the outset, the Everyman edition departs in a number of respects from the usual post-Folio approach to the presentation of Shakespeare's texts.

RESTORING SOME OF THE NUANCES OF RENAISSANCE PUNCTUATION

In its punctuation, Everyman attempts to give equal emphasis to sound and sense. In places where Renaissance practice calls for heavier punctuation than we'd normally employ – to mark the caesural pause in the middle of a line of verse, for instance – Everyman sometimes retains commas that other modern editions omit. Meanwhile, in places where current practice usually calls for the inclusion of commas – after vocatives and interjections such as 'O' and 'alas', say, or before 'Madam' or 'Sir' in phrases such as 'Ay Madam' or 'Yes Sir' – Everyman frequently follows the original printings and omits them.

Occasionally the absence of a comma has a significant bearing on what an expression means, or can mean. At one point in *Othello*, for example, Iago tells the Moor 'Marry patience' (IV.i.90). Inserting a comma after 'Marry', as most of today's editions do, limits Iago's utterance to one that says 'Come now, have patience.' Leaving the clause as it stands in the Folio, the way the Everyman text does, permits Iago's words to have the additional, agonizingly ironic sense 'Be wed to Patience'.

The early texts generally deploy exclamation points quite sparingly, and the Everyman text follows suit. Everyman also follows the early editions, more often than not, when they use question marks in places that seem unusual by current standards: at the conclusion of what we'd normally treat as exclamations, for example, or at the ends of interrogative clauses in sentences that we'd ordinarily denote as questions in their entirety.

The early texts make no orthographic distinction between simple plurals and either singular or plural possessives, and there are times when the context doesn't indicate whether a word spelled *Sisters*, say, should be rendered *Sisters*, *Sisters'*, or *Sister's* in today's usage. In such situations the Everyman edition prints the word in the form modern usage prescribes for plurals.

REVIVING SOME OF THE FLEXIBILITY OF RENAISSANCE SPELLING

Spelling had not become standardized by Shakespeare's time, and that meant that many words could take a variety of forms. Like

James Joyce and some of the other innovative prose and verse stylists of our own century, Shakespeare revelled in the freedom a largely unanchored language provided, and with that in mind Everyman retains original spelling forms (or adaptations of those forms that preserve their key distinctions from modern spellings) whenever there is any reason to suspect that they might have a bearing on how a word was intended to be pronounced or on what it meant, or could have meant, in the playwright's day. When there is any likelihood that multiple forms of the same word could be significant, moreover, the Everyman text mirrors the diversity to be found in the original printings.

In many cases this practice affects the personalities of Shakespeare's characters. One of the heroine's most familiar questions in *Romeo and Juliet* is 'What's in a Name?' For two and a half centuries readers – and as a consequence actors, directors, theatre audiences, and commentators – have been led to believe that Juliet was addressing this query to a Romeo named 'Montague'. In fact 'Montague' *was* the name Shakespeare found in his principal source for the play. For reasons that will become apparent to anyone who examines the tragedy in detail, however, the playwright changed his protagonist's surname to 'Mountague', a word that plays on both 'mount' and 'ague' (fever).* Setting aside an editorial practice that began with Lewis Theobald in the middle of the eighteenth century, Everyman resurrects the name the dramatist himself gave Juliet's lover.

Readers of *The Merchant of Venice* in the Everyman set will be amused to learn that the character modern editions usually identify as 'Lancelot' is in reality 'Launcelet', a name that calls attention to the clown's lusty 'little lance'. Like Costard in *Love's Labour's Lost*, another stage bumpkin who was probably played by the actor Will Kemp, Launcelet is an upright 'Member of the Commonwealth'; we eventually learn that he's left a pliant wench 'with Child'.

Readers of *Hamlet* will find that 'Fortinbras' (as the name of the Prince's Norwegian opposite is rendered in the First Folio and in

* For anyone who doubts that Shakespeare's alteration of Romeo's family name was part of a conscious artistic plan, it may be worth noting that 'Capulet', like 'Capilet' in *Twelfth Night* and *All's Well That Ends Well*, means 'small horse'.

most modern editions) appears in the earlier, authoritative 1604 Second Quarto of the play as 'Fortinbrasse'. In the opening scene of that text a surname that meant 'strong in arms' in French is introduced to the accompaniment of puns on *brazen*, in the phrase 'brazon Cannon', and on *metal*, in the phrase 'unimprooued mettle'. In the same play readers of the Everyman text will encounter 'Ostricke', the ostrich-like courtier who invites the Prince of Denmark to participate in the fateful fencing match that draws *Hamlet* to a close. Only in its final entrance direction for the obsequious fop does the Second Quarto call this character 'Osrick', the name he bears in all the Folio text's references to him and in most modern editions of Shakespeare's most popular tragedy.

Readers of the Everyman *Macbeth* will discover that the fabled 'Weird Sisters' appear only as the 'weyward' or 'weyard' Sisters. Shakespeare and his contemporaries knew that in his *Chronicles of England, Scotland, and Ireland* Raphael Holinshed had used the term 'weird sisters' to describe the witches who accost Macbeth and Banquo on the heath; but presumably because he wished to play on *wayward*, the playwright changed their defining epithet to *weyward*. Like Samuel Johnson, who thought punning vulgar and lamented Shakespeare's proclivity to seduction by this 'fatal Cleopatra', Lewis Theobald saw no reason to retain the playwright's weyward spelling of the witches' name. He thus restored the 'correct' form from Holinshed, and editors ever since have generally done likewise.

In many instances Renaissance English had a single spelling for what we now define as two separate words. For example, *humane* combined the senses of 'human' and 'humane' in modern English. In the First Folio printing of *Macbeth* the protagonist's wife expresses a concern that her husband is 'too full o'th' Milke of humane kindnesse'. As she phrases it, *humane kindnesse* can mean several things, among them 'humankind-ness', 'human kindness', and 'humane kindness'. It is thus a reminder that to be true to his or her own 'kind' a human being must be 'kind' in the sense we now attach to 'humane'. To disregard this logic, as the protagonist and his wife will soon prove, is to disregard a principle as basic to the cosmos as the laws of gravity.

In a way that parallels *humane*, *bad* could mean either 'bad' or 'bade', *borne* either 'born' or 'borne', *ere* either 'ere' (before) or 'e'er' (ever), *least* either 'least' or 'lest', *lye* either 'lie' or 'lye', *nere* either 'ne'er' or 'near' (though the usual spellings for the latter were *neare* or *neere*), *powre* either 'pour' or 'power', *then* either 'than' or 'then', and *tide* either 'tide' or 'tied'.

There were a number of word-forms that functioned in Renaissance English as interchangeable doublets. *Travail* could mean 'travel', for example, and *travel* could mean 'travail'. By the same token, *deer* could mean *dear* and vice versa, *dew* could mean *due*, *hart* could mean *heart*, and (as we've already noted) *mettle* could mean *metal*.

A particularly interesting instance of the equivocal or double meanings some word-forms had in Shakespeare's time is *loose*, which can often become either 'loose' or 'lose' when we render it in modern English. In *The Comedy of Errors* when Antipholus of Syracuse compares himself to 'a Drop / Of Water that in the Ocean seeks another Drop' and then says he will 'loose' himself in quest of his long-lost twin, he means both (a) that he will release himself into a vast unknown, and (b) that he will lose his own identity, if necessary, to be reunited with the brother for whom he searches. On the other hand, in *Hamlet* when Polonius says he'll 'loose' his daughter to the Prince, he little suspects that by so doing he will also lose his daughter.

In some cases the playwright employs word-forms that can be translated into words we wouldn't think of as related today: *sowre*, for instance, which can mean 'sour', 'sower', or 'sore', depending on the context. In other cases he uses forms that do have modern counterparts, but not counterparts with the same potential for multiple connotation. For example, *onely* usually means 'only' in the modern sense; but occasionally Shakespeare gives it a figurative, adverbial twist that would require a nonce word such as 'one-ly' to replicate in current English.

In a few cases Shakespeare employs word-forms that have only seeming equivalents in modern usage. For example, *abhominable*, which meant 'inhuman' (derived, however incorrectly, from *ab*, 'away from', and *homine*, 'man') to the poet and his contemporaries, is not the same word as our *abominable* (ill-omened, abhorrent). In his advice to the visiting players Hamlet complains about incompetent actors who imitate 'Humanity so abhominably' as to make the characters they depict seem unrecognizable as men. Modern readers who don't realize the distinction between Shakespeare's word and our own, and who see *abominable* on the page before them, don't register the full import of the Prince's satire.

Modern English treats as single words a number of word-forms that were normally spelled as two words in Shakespeare's time. What we render as *myself*, for example, and use primarily as a reflexive or intensifying pronoun, is almost invariably spelled *my self* in Shakespeare's works; so also with *her self*, *thy self*, *your self*, and *it self* (where *it* functions as *its* does today). Often there is no discernible difference between Shakespeare's usage and our own. At other times there is, however, as we are reminded when we come across a phrase such as 'our innocent self' in *Macbeth* and think how strained it would sound in modern parlance, or as we observe when we note how naturally the self is objectified in the balanced clauses of the Balcony Scene in *Romeo and Juliet*:

> Romeo, doffe thy name,
> And for thy name, which is no part of thee,
> Take all my selfe.

Yet another difference between Renaissance orthography and our own can be exemplified with words such as *today*, *tonight*, and *tomorrow*, which (unlike *yesterday*) were treated as two words in Shakespeare's time. In *Macbeth* when the Folio prints 'Duncan comes here to Night', the unattached *to* can function either as a preposition (with *Night* as its object, or in this case its destination) or as the first part of an infinitive (with *Night* operating figuratively as a verb). Consider the ambiguity a Renaissance reader would have detected in the original publication of one of the most celebrated soliloquies in all of Shakespeare:

> To morrow, and to morrow, and to morrow,
> Creeps in this petty pace from day to day,
> To the last Syllable of Recorded time:
> And all our yesterdayes, have lighted Fooles
> The way to dusty death.

Here, by implication, the route 'to morrow' is identical with 'the way to dusty death', a relationship we miss if we don't know that for Macbeth, and for the audiences who first heard these lines spoken, *to morrow* was not a single word but a potentially equivocal two-word phrase.

RECAPTURING THE ABILITY TO HEAR WITH OUR EYES
When we fail to recall that Shakespeare's scripts were designed initially to provide words for people to hear in the theatre, we sometimes overlook a fact that is fundamental to the artistic structure of a work like *Macbeth*: that the messages a sequence of sounds convey through the ear are, if anything, even more significant than the messages a sequence of letters, punctuation marks, and white spaces on a printed page transmit through the eye. A telling illustration of this point, and of the potential for ambiguous or multiple implication in any Shakespearean script, may be found in the dethronement scene of *Richard II*. When Henry Bullingbrook asks the King if he is ready to resign his crown, Richard replies 'I, no no I; for I must nothing be.' Here the punctuation in the 1608 Fourth Quarto (the earliest text to print this richly complex passage) permits each *I* to signify either 'ay' or 'I' (*I* being the usual spelling for 'ay' in Shakespeare's time). Understanding *I* to mean 'I' permits additional play on *no*, which can be heard (at least in its first occurrence) as 'know'. Meanwhile the second and third soundings of *I*, if not the first, can also be heard as 'eye'. In the context in which this line occurs, that sense echoes a thematically pertinent passage from Matthew 18:9: 'if thine eye offend thee, pluck it out'.

But these are not all the implications *I* can have here. It can also represent the Roman numeral for '1', which will soon be reduced, as Richard notes, to 'nothing' (o), along with the speaker's title, his worldly possessions, his manhood, and eventually his life. In Shakespeare's time, to become 'nothing' was, *inter alia*, to be emasculated, to be made a 'weaker vessel' (1 Peter 3:7) with 'no thing'. As the Fool in *King Lear* reminds another monarch who has abdicated his throne, a man in want of an 'I' is impotent, 'an O without a Figure' (I.iv.207). In addition to its other dimensions, then, Richard's reply is a statement that can be formulated mathematically, and in symbols that anticipate the binary system behind today's computer technology: 'i, o, o, i, for i must o be.'

Modern editions usually render Richard's line 'Ay, no; no, ay; for I must nothing be'. Presenting the line in that fashion makes good sense of what Richard is saying. But as we've seen, it doesn't make total sense of it, and it doesn't call attention to Richard's paradoxes in the same way that hearing or seeing three undifferentiated I's is likely to have done for Shakespeare's contemporaries. Their culture was more attuned than ours is to the oral and aural dimensions of language, and if we want to appreciate the special qualities of their dramatic art we need to train ourselves to 'hear' the word-forms we see on the page. We must learn to recognize that for many of what we tend to think of as fixed linkages between sound and meaning (the vowel 'I', say, and the word 'eye'), there were alternative linkages (such as the vowel 'I' and the words 'I' and 'Ay') that could be just as pertinent to what the playwright was communicating through the ears of his theatre patrons at a given moment. As the word *audience* itself may help us to remember, people in Shakespeare's time normally spoke of 'hearing' rather than 'seeing' a play.

In its text of *Richard II*, the Everyman edition reproduces the title character's line as it appears in the early printings of the tragedy. Ideally the orthographic oddity of the repeated I's will encourage today's readers to ponder Richard's utterance, and the play it epitomizes, as a characteristically Shakespearean enigma.

OTHER ASPECTS OF THE EVERYMAN TEXT

Now for a few words about other features of the Everyman text.

One of the first things readers will notice about this edition is its bountiful use of capitalized words. In this practice as in others, the Everyman exemplar is the First Folio, and especially the works in the Folio sections billed as 'Histories' and 'Tragedies'.* Everyman

---

* The quarto printings employ far fewer capital letters than does the Folio. Capitalization seems to have been regarded as a means of recognizing the status ascribed to certain words (*Noble*, for example, is almost always capitalized), titles (not only King, Queen, Duke, and Duchess, but Sir and Madam), genres (tragedies were regarded as more 'serious' than comedies in more than one sense), and forms of publication (quartos, being associated with ephemera such as 'plays', were not thought to be as 'grave' as the folios that bestowed immortality on 'works', writings that, in the words of Ben Jonson's eulogy to Shakespeare, were 'not of an age, but for all time').

makes no attempt to adhere to the Folio printings with literal exactitude. In some instances the Folio capitalizes words that the Everyman text of the same passage lowercases; in other instances Everyman capitalizes words not uppercased in the Folio. The objective is merely to suggest something of the flavour, and what appears to have been the rationale, of Renaissance capitalization, in the hope that today's audiences will be made continually aware that the works they're contemplating derive from an earlier epoch.

Readers will also notice that instead of cluttering the text with stage directions such as '[Aside]' or '[To Rosse]', the Everyman text employs unobtrusive dashes to indicate shifts in mode of address. In an effort to keep the page relatively clear of words not supplied by the original printings, Everyman also exercises restraint in its addition of editor-generated stage directions. Where the dialogue makes it obvious that a significant action occurs, the Everyman text inserts a square-bracketed phrase such as '[Fleance escapes]'. Where what the dialogue implies is subject to differing interpretations, however, the Everyman text provides a facing-page note to discuss the most plausible inferences.

Like other modern editions, the Everyman text combines into 'shared' verse lines (lines divided among two or more speakers) many of the part-lines to be found in the early publications of the plays. One exception to the usual modern procedure is that Everyman indents some lines that are not components of shared verses. At times, for example, the opening line of a scene stops short of the metrical norm, a pentameter (five-foot) or hexameter (six-foot) line comprised predominantly of iambic units (unstressed syllables followed by stressed ones). In such cases Everyman uses indentation as a reminder that scenes can begin as well as end in mid-line (an extension of the ancient convention that an epic commences *in media res*, 'in the midst of the action'). Everyman also uses indentation to reflect what appear to be pauses in the dialogue, either to allow other activity to transpire (as happens in *Macbeth*, II.iii.87, when a brief line 'What's the Business?' follows a Folio stage direction that reads '*Bell rings. Enter Lady*') or to permit a character to hesitate for a moment of reflection (as happens a few seconds later in the same scene when Macduff responds to a demand to 'Speak, speak' with the reply 'O gentle Lady, / 'Tis not for you to hear what I can speak').

Readers of the Everyman edition will note that many word-forms are printed with apostrophes to indicate contractions (*to't* for 'to it', for example, or *o'th'* for 'of the') or syllabic elisions (*look'd* for 'looked', for instance, or *nev'r* or *ne'er* for 'never'). In many cases these departures from ordinary spelling occur in verse contexts that call for the deletion of syllables which if voiced would result in minor violations of the metrical norm. Thus in *Twelfth Night*, II.iv.107, *loved* is syncopated to *lov'd* in Viola's statement 'My Father had a Daughter lov'd a Man'. On the other hand, in *A Midsummer Night's Dream*, II.i.26, *loved* is treated as a fully voiced two-syllable word in 'But she, perforce, withholds the loved Boy'. In situations such as these Everyman almost invariably retains the word-forms to be found in the early printings that have been adopted as control texts. At times this policy results in lines whose metre can be construed in different ways by different interpreters. In *A Midsummer Night's Dream*, III.ii.292, to cite one line for illustrative purposes, it could be argued that the first *Personage* should be syncopated to *Pers'nage* when Hermia says, 'And with her Personage, her tall Personage'. By the same token it could be maintained that words such as *even*, *Heaven*, and *whether* should be syncopated in pronunciation when, as is usual, they occur in positions that would normally demand a sound with the metrical value of a single syllable. The frequency with which syllabic elisions crop up in the original editions of Shakespeare's works would seem to suggest that the playwright and his colleagues placed a premium on metrical regularity. At the same time, the frequent absence of syncopated or contracted word-forms in settings where the metre would lead us to expect them (*I am* is only rarely rendered as *I'm*, for example, though it continually appears in positions that invite compression to one syllable) could be viewed as evidence that Shakespeare was anything but rigid in such matters, and may even have consciously opted for the subtle variations that derive from occasional unstressed syllabic additions to an otherwise steady march of iambic feet. Given the metrical ambiguity of the early texts, it is difficult if not impossible to determine how 'smooth' the verse-speaking was intended to be in the theatres for which Shakespeare wrote his scripts. Rather than impose a fixed order that might be incompatible with the poet's own aesthetic principles, then, the Everyman text merely preserves the metrical inconsistencies to be observed in the Quarto and Folio printings of Shakespeare's plays and poems.

Everyman also retains many of the other anomalies in the early texts. In some instances this practice affects the way characters are depicted. In *A Midsummer Night's Dream*, for example, the ruler of Athens is usually identified in speech headings and stage directions as 'Theseus', but sometimes he is referred to by his title as 'Duke'. In the same play Oberon's merry sprite goes by two different names: 'Puck' and 'Robin Goodfellow'.

Readers of the Everyman edition will sometimes discover that characters they've known, or known about, for years don't appear in the original printings. When they open the pages of the Everyman *Macbeth*, for example, they'll learn that Shakespeare's audiences were unaware of any woman with the title 'Lady Macbeth'. In the only authoritative text we have of the Scottish tragedy, the protagonist's spouse goes by such names as 'Macbeth's Lady', 'Macbeth's Wife', or simply 'Lady', but at no time is she listed or mentioned as 'Lady Macbeth'. The same is true of the character usually designated 'Lady Capulet' in modern editions of *Romeo and Juliet*. 'Capulet's Wife' makes appearances as 'Mother', 'Old Lady', 'Lady', or simply 'Wife'; but she's never termed 'Lady Capulet', and her husband never treats her with the dignity such a title would connote.

Rather than 'correct' the grammar in Shakespeare's works to eliminate what modern usage would categorize as solecisms (as when Mercutio says 'my Wits faints' in *Romeo and Juliet*), the Everyman text leaves it intact. Among other things, this principle applies to instances in which archaic forms preserve idioms that differ slightly from related modern expressions (as in the clause 'you are too blame', where 'too' frequently functions as an adverb and 'blame' is used, not as a verb, but as an adjective roughly equivalent to 'blameworthy').

Finally, and most importantly, the Everyman edition leaves unchanged any reading in the original text that is not manifestly erroneous. Unlike other modern renderings of Shakespeare's works, Everyman substitutes emendations only when obvious problems can be dealt with by obvious solutions.

The Everyman Text of Twelfth Night

Our only authority for the text of *Twelfth Night* is the version of the work that appeared in the 1623 First Folio. Some scholars believe that the Folio compositors set type from a scribal copy of the play's theatrical promptbook, but the more usual view at present is that the Folio text derives instead from a slightly edited transcript of Shakespeare's unpolished holograph (what textual bibliographers refer to as the dramatist's 'foul papers'). In either case it seems virtually certain that someone other than the author segmented the comedy into acts and scenes and inserted the Latin clauses *Finis, Actus Primus, Finis Actus secondus*, and *Finis Actus Quartus* that mark the ends of Acts I, II, and IV.*

Happily, notwithstanding a number of obvious misprints, there are comparatively few textual problems of consequence in the Folio *Twelfth Night*. For this reason Everyman adheres to the 1623 publication with considerable fidelity. One salient exception relates to the title of the work; the Folio employs the usual Renaissance spelling, *Twelfe* for what we now render as *Twelfth*, and even though Everyman retains *twelfe* when it occurs in the dialogue of the drama (see II.iii.92), it adopts the usual twentieth-century spelling for the name of the play.

Everyman also abides by the Folio's act and scene divisions. The only time this procedure seems questionable is when Viola and Fabian depart together after III.iv.296. Unless we assume that Sir Toby and Sir Andrew enter before Viola and Fabian have cleared the stage completely, we would ordinarily feel compelled to designate a new scene, III.v, to commence immediately following the *Exeunt* for Viola and Fabian.

Everyman preserves in unaltered form the vast majority of the Folio's speech headings and stage directions. Rather than normalize *Duke* to *Count* or to *Orsino*, then, or *Clown* to *Feste* or *Feste the Fool*, or *Toby* to *Sir Toby*, or *Andrew* to *Sir Andrew*,

---

* Like other modern editions, Everyman omits these clauses.

Everyman simply reproduces the designations of these characters as they appear in the 1623 printing of the play. In accordance with its customary policy, Everyman supplements the Folio's stage directions only sparingly, and it encloses in square brackets any material that has been supplied by the editor to augment the information provided by the Folio.

In a number of instances, many of them having to do with matters of punctuation, Everyman departs from the First Folio (F1) text. For each of the readings that follow the first listing, in boldface, is the one that appears in the Everyman edition; the second, in regular type, is the one that appears in the Folio. Unless the Folio word-form is itself pertinent to what has been emended, the second entry for each item is given in modern spelling.

I.i.	22	*Enter Valentine.* Placed after the second half of line 22 in the Folio.
	29	**Brine,** brine:
	34	**love** love,
I.ii.	13	**strong** sttong
I.iii.	54	ANDREW MA.
		Accost accost
	98	**will** wlll
	100	**does't** dost
	106	**Count** Connt
I.iv.	3	**advanc'd;** advanc'd,
	7	**Favours?** favours.
	15	**the** rhe
I.v.	24	**Points.** points
	101	**Guiltless** guitlesse
	159	**H'as** Ha's (compare V.i.177)
	178	**Veil** vaile
	231	**Olive** Olyffe
	254	**Face?** face:
II.i.	17	**Roderigo** Rodorigo
	20	**Heavens** Heanens
II.ii.	5	**, Sir.** (sir)
II.iii.	14	**drink.** drink,
	156	**What,** What
		Puritan? Puritan,

II.iv.	15	**Boy.** If boy, if
	22	**masterly;** masterly,
	82	**Lands;** lands,
	83	**her,** her:
	84	**her,** her
	95	**Heart,** heart:
	101	**much.** much,
II.v.	83	**Plot!** plot?
	96	**her** het
	126	**this. And** this, and
	155	**be,** be:
	162	**thee** thce
	167	**Fingers.** fingers
	168	**The** Tht
	170	**Politic** pollticke
III.i.	8	**King** Kings
	9	**Church** Chureh
	63	**come;** come,
	69	**Time,** time:
	129	**shewn;** shewn,
	160	**Clause:** clause,
	161	**Cause.** cause,
	162	**fetter:** fetter;
III.ii.	37	**with him;** with him
		places. places,
III.iii.	8	**Travel** rravell
	21	**Night:** night
	42	**Town;** Town,
III.iv.	6	**Fortunes.** fortunes,
	16	**merry** metry
	26	MARIA MAL.
	41	**Lady?** Lady.
	56	**to** too (so also in III.iv.65, 83, 104, 336, IV.i.3, IV.ii.121, V.i.212)
	59	**let** ler
	66	**Toby?** Toby,
	92	**Sanctity?** sanctity.
	110	**Heart.** heart
	127	**Sathan.** Sathan
	185	**You** Yon
		fit sit
		for't fot't
	228	**give?** give.

	236	**thee** the
	249	**Guard** gard
	286	**Promise,** promise
	314	**Souls.** souls,
	352	**reins** raines
	355	**Orsino.** Orsino
	377	**Persuasion?** persuasion.
	403	**himself;** himself,
	404	**true** ttue
	416	**Hare. His** Hare, his
	423	**Sword.** sword
IV.i.	66	**me.** me
IV.ii.	7	**in** in in
	41	**Clerestores** cleere stores
	123	**counterfeit?** counterfeit.
	126	**Brains.** brains
	129	**gone** goue
	141	**Goodman** good man
IV.iii.	4	**then?** then,
	8	**Counsel** councell
V.i.	70	**me:** me,
	118	**him.** him
	122	**nobly)? But** nobly) but
	125	**Favour,** favour:
	156	**Ripe,** ripe:
	157	**pass'd** past (so also in V.i.357, 373)
	169	**Overthrow?** overthrow:
	180	**Home** homc
	184	**incardinate** incardinatc
	209	**help,** help
	226	**Self?** self,
	253	**Attire,** attire:
	259	**Count.** count:
	265	**deceived:** deceived,
	275	**from** ftom
	329	**long,** long:
	379	**Lord** Lotd
	387	**yet;** yet,
	392	**Man:** Man:)
	394	**Queen).** Queen.

In the following passages Everyman adheres to the First Folio for readings that many, if not most, of today's editions emend. For each listing, the first entry, in boldface type, is the Everyman reading, derived from the Folio; the second, in regular type, is the reading to be found in other current editions.

I.i.
    10 **That** That,
    11 **Sea. Nought** sea, nought
    12 **ere** e'er (so also in V.i.117)
    25 **Heat** hence
    27 **vailed** veiled
    31 **lasting,** lasting
    36 **her.** her;
    38 **King.** king? (F1 king:)

I.ii.
    14 **Orion** Arion
    20 **I** Ay (so also in I.iii.79, II.iv.49, 103, II.v.130, 140, 142, III.iv.33, IV.ii.91)
       borne born (so also in I.iii.138, I.v.10, II.i.20, III.iv.45, V.i.375)
    21 **Travail** travel (compare II.v.58, V.i.165)
    22 **Duke** Duke,
  35–36 **Sight / And Company** company / And sight
    37 **World** world,
    38 **mellow** mellow,
    45 **will** well
    48 **Aid,** aid
    56 **Onely** Only (so also in III.ii.19, III.iii.35)

I.iii.
    7 **except,** except
    17 **Woer** wooer (compare I.iii.59)
    29 **indeed, almost** indeed all, most
    42 **Coystrill** coistrel
    45 *vulgo volto*
    54 **accost** Accost
    57 **Mary, accost** Mary Accost
    59 **woe** woo (so also in I.iv.42, 43)
    90 **to morrow** tomorrow (compare I.iii.104, I.v.329, II.iii.143, 144, III.iii.20, III.iv.226, 232, V.i.97, 290)
    91 *Pur-quoy Pourquoi*
    92 *purquoy Pourquoi*
    99 **cool my** curl by
    100 **we** me
    102 **Huswife** housewife
    115 **Kick-chawses** kickshawses
    128 **Carranto** coranto
    136 **dam'd** damned *or* dun- *or* flame-
       sit set

	140	**That** That's
I.iv.	16	**Gate** gait (so also in II.iii.172, III.i.90)
	29	**Nuntio's** nuncio's
	34	**shrill, and** shrill of
I.v.	38	**Quinapulus,** Quinapulus?
	57	**bad** bade (so also in I.v.59, II.iii.104, III.i.115, V.i.342)
	94	**Gard** guard
	95	**gag'd** gagg'd (so also in V.i.381)
	107	**indue** endue
	109	**Gentleman,** gentleman
	125	**for** for –
		comes. comes –
	132	**Sot.** sot?
	136	**Lechery, I** lechery? I
		Lechery: there's Lechery. There's
	157	**Lady, he's** Lady? He's
	171	**Pescod** peascod
	179	*Violenta Viola*
	183	**Will.** will?
	207	**shew** show (compare I.v.256, 334, II.iv.117, III.i.73, 129, III.ii.18, III.iv.163, 313, 370)
	216–17	**not Mad** mad
	220	**Sir,** Sir?
	224	**tell** MARIA Tell
		Mind, mind.
		I am VIOLA I am
	227	**Curtesy** courtesy (so also in IV.ii.38)
	296	**Hallow** Halloo
	325	**Counte's** County's
II.i.	8	**Love,** love
	9	**you,** you
	14	**Manners,** manners
	32	**salt Water** salt-water
II.ii.	13	**me, I'll** me! I'll
	21	**That** That sure
	26	**Man,** man; *or* man:
	32	**O** our
	33	**made, if** made of,
	40	**breath** breathe
II.iii.	2	*deliculo diliculo*
	10	**Lives** life
	16	**Harts** hearts (compare in III.iv.217)

26 **six Pence** sixpence (so also in line 34; compare *two*
    Pence in IV.i.32)
    Lemon leman
28 **impeticos** impetticoat
30 **Mermidons** Myrmidons
43 **true Love's** true-love's
46 **Lovers** lovers'
56 **am** am a
70 **Knight.** knight?
92 **O** O'
    Twelfe twelfth
123 **Tune** time
130 **stope** stoupe
140 **Knight,** knight.
146 **Malnolio** Malvolio
147 **an Ayword** a nayword
157 **Knight.** knight?
163 **Swarths** swathes
166 **grounds** ground
195 **true bred** true-bred
202 **Knight,** knight;

II.iv.
3 **antic** antique (F1 Anticke)
9 **it?** it.
49 **prethee** prithee (so also in IV.i.15, 53, 66, IV.ii.1,
    V.i.356)
52 **Fie . . . fie** Fly . . . fly
59 **strewn** strown
74 **Taffata** taffeta
88 **It** I
99 **suffer** suffers
114 **sate** sat

II.v.
2 **loose** lose (so also in III.iv.114)
12 **blew** blue
16 **Mettle** metal
22 **Close** Close,
39 TOBY FABIAN (so also in line 43)
65–66 **my some** my – some
107 **Lips** Lips,
109 **Numbers** number's
114 **Lucresse** Lucrece'
    Knife: knife,
115 **gore,** gore:
121 **him?** him!
122 **Stallion** staniel

	127	**portend,** portend?
	128	**me?** me!
	130	**O I O** ay (see I.ii.20)
	134	**out,** out?
	137	**Sequel** sequel;
	151	**become** born
		achieves achieve
	163	**remember, go** remember. Go
	166	**woorthy** worthy
	168	**Fortunate Unhappy** Fortunate-Unhappy
	169	**Champian** champaign *or* champain
	172	**Point Devise** point-devise
	188	**deero** dear *or* dear, O
	209	**vita** vitae
III.i.	6	**dooth** doth
	38	**Pilchers** pilchards
	39	**Husbands** husband's
	74	**Wise-men's** wise men,
	77	*vou guard vous garde*
	78	*vouz ousie vous aussi*
		vostre Serviture votre Serviteur
	80	**incounter** encounter
	91	*Gentlewoman* Viola
	99	**already** all ready
	107	**Complement** compliment
	117	**you,** you
		that, that
	120	**hear** here
	135	**Proud?** proud!
	137	**Wolf?** wolf!
	142	**hoe** ho
	149	**were,** were
	152	**beautiful?** beautiful
	153	**Lip,** lip!
	166	**has,** has;
III.ii.	1	**iot** jot (so also in III.iv.357)
	8	**see the** see thee the
	13	**me.** me?
	25	**baulk'd** balk'd
	57	**the** thy
		Cubiculo cubicle
	62	**deliver't.** deliver't?
	71	**mine** nine
	75	**Renegatho** renegado

	87	**him,** him:
III.iii.	8	**Jealousy,** jealousy
	15	**Thanks: and ever oft** thanks, and ever thanks; and oft
	19	**Reliques** relics
	20	**Lodging?** lodging
III.iv.	15	***Enter Malvolio.*** Delayed until after line 16 in most editions.
	21	**Sad Lady, Sad,** Lady?
	26	MARIA OLIVIA
		doest dost (so also in V.i.11)
	33	**sweet Heart** sweetheart
	38	**Request:** request?
	76	**langer** tang
	80	**foorth** forth
	97	**How** TOBY How
	127	**Sathan** Satan (so also in IV.ii.35)
	142	**least** lest (so also in III.iv.378)
	148	**thus** thus,
	158	**is't?** is't!
	165	**Note,** note; *or* note:
	218	**on't** out
	223	**Griefs** grief
	239	**Despight** despite
	267	**computent** competent
	291	**him,** him?
	305	**pacified,** pacified:
	322	**Oath** oath's
	325	**Vow,** vow;
	362	**do:** do
	363	**Purse.** purse?
	375	**now,** now?
	383	**Lying, Vainness** lying vainness
	393	**vild** vile
	424	**not.** not –
IV.i.	17	**Lady?** lady.
	37	**stroke** strook
IV.ii.	9	**Studient** student
	15	**Prage** Prague
	16	**Gorbodacke** Gorboduc
	30	**Man?** man!
	41	**Clerestores** clerestories
	56	**happily** haply
	77	**the Upshot** to the upshot

	97	**well:** well?
V.i.	92	**years** years'
	110	**ought** aught
	116	**have** hath
	120	**Thief,** thief
		Death death,
	130	**Spight** spite (so also in V.i.133)
	141	**me** me,
		beguil'd? beguild!
	145	**Whether** Whither
	165	**travail'd** travell'd
	189	**me,** me?
	196	**other gates** othergates
	198	**has** h'as
	203	**Panyn** pavin
	205	**him?** him!
	209	**help,** help?
	210	**a Knave,** a knave?
		Gull? gull!
	224	**thee?** thee!
	269	**Wrack** wreck
	314	**Shame:** shame;
	316	**madly us'd** madly-us'd
	336	**Hand,** hand; *or* hand:
	364	**confess** confess,
	371	**then** than
	374	**thee?** thee!
	376	**thrown** thrust
	384	**you?** you!
	411	**begon** begun

TWELFTH NIGHT,
or
WHAT YOU WILL

NAMES OF THE ACTORS

ORSINO, Duke (or Count) of Illyria
OLIVIA, a Countess

SEBASTIAN, Brother to Viola
VIOLA, Sister to Sebastian

SIR TOBY BELCH, Uncle to Olivia
MARIA, Olivia's Waiting Gentlewoman

MALVOLIO, Steward to Olivia
FESTE, a Clown
FABIAN, Servant to Olivia

SIR ANDREW AGUE-CHEEK

VALENTINE
CURIO } Gentlemen attending on Duke Orsino

ANTONIO, a Sea Captain, friend to Sebastian
SEA CAPTAIN, Friend to Viola

LORDS
PRIESTS
SAILORS
OFFICERS
MUSICIANS
ATTENDANTS

I.i.   The opening scene takes place at the Duke's palace in Illyria, a country (modern Croatia) on the east coast of the Adriatic Sea. Orsino and his lords are probably accompanied by musicians (playing flutes, recorders, and perhaps viols) who perform in response to their master's requests in lines 1–8.

2   **surfeiting**   becoming cloyed, over-full.

3   **so**   thus, as a result.

4   **a dying Fall**   a diminuendo, a cadence gradually becoming softer and perhaps lower on the musical scale (as if, like the 'Appetite', it had passed its point of peak intensity and was now 'surfeiting').

5   **sweet Sound**   the whisper of a scented breeze. Orsino uses *sweet* in reference to three senses: (a) smell, (b) hearing, and (c) taste.

9   **quick**   (a) alive, keen, (b) quickening, life-giving, and (c) rapid.
    fresh   both (a) hungry, uncloyed (compare lines 1–3), and (b) vigorous, unweary. But, like *quick*, *fresh* can also refer to fresh water, as distinguished from the saline water ('Brine', line 29) of 'the Sea' (line 11).

10   **notwithstanding thy Capacity**   despite the fact that your capacity would seem limited (at least by comparison with 'the Sea'). Modern editions normally omit the comma at the end of this phrase and place a comma rather than a full stop after 'Sea'. This edition retains the syntax of the First Folio printing. In line 11 *Receiveth* appears to mean *Receivest*. The form the verb takes is probably influenced by its position in the sentence, where it is swallowed up, as it were, by the implied 'as the Sea receiveth'.

11   **Nought**   nothing.

12   **Validity**   both (a) efficacy, strength, and (b) value, truthfulness.
    Pitch   a word combining such senses as (a) altitude (as with the high point of a falcon's flight), (b) height or key on the musical scale, (c) intensity, (d) worth, and (e) thrust (as an object that is pitched into the air before it falls into the 'Sea').
    ere   both (a) e'er (ever), and (b) ere (before, as in lines 1–8).

13   **Abatement**   here (a) a decline, (b) a lowering, (c) a 'dying Fall' (see note 4), and (d) a depreciation in value.

14   **So full of Shapes**   so abundantly endowed with images, so full of the capacity for inspiration.

ACT I

Scene 1

Enter Orsino, Duke of Illyria, Curio, and other Lords.

DUKE   If Music be the Food of Love, play on,
Give me Excess of it: that, surfeiting,
The Appetite may sicken, and so die.
That Strain again, it had a dying Fall:
O, it came o'er my Ear like the sweet Sound   5
That breathes upon a Bank of Violets,
Stealing, and giving Odour. Enough, no more,
'Tis not so Sweet now as it was before.
– O Spirit of Love, how quick and fresh art
   thou,
That notwithstanding thy Capacity,   10
Receiveth as the Sea. Nought enters there,
Of what Validity and Pitch so ere,
But falls into Abatement and Low Price
Even in a Minute. So full of Shapes is Fancy
That it alone is high Fantastical.   15
CURIO   Will you go hunt, my Lord?
DUKE   What, Curio?

---

14   **Fancy**   both (a) love, and (b) imagination (what the Renaissance often called 'invention'). The word derived from *fantasy*. Compare *A Midsummer Night's Dream*, V.i.1–27, 213–15.

15   **it . . . Fantastical**   it alone is capable of the heights of thought and creativity. This line explains lines 9–14; Orsino's point is that by comparison with 'Fancy', everything else, including the sweetest music, fades, declines, cloys, or falls into 'Low Price'.

16 **Hart** deer. In the next line Orsino plays on 'Heart' (and implicitly on the related homonyms, 'dear' and 'deer').

19 **purg'd** purified, cleansed.
Pestilence infection, disease.

21 **fell** fierce. *Fell* echoes *Fall*, *falls*, and *full* in lines 1–14.

20–22 **That . . . me** Orsino alludes to the story of Actaeon, a hunter who surprised the chaste goddess Diana while she was bathing; she caused stag's horns to spring from his head, whereupon his hounds, mistaking him for a 'Hart', chased him down and chewed him to death. Ovid told the story in Book III of the *Metamorphoses*, and it was used to illustrate both the destructive power of the passions (as here) and the frustrations of the cuckold (the husband who grew horns on his brow because his wife was unfaithful to him).

23 **might not be admitted** was unable to gain entrance.

25 **Element** sky.
till . . . Heat till seven hot summers have transpired.

27 **Cloistress** cloistered nun.
vailed both (a) veiled, shielded from view, and (b) vailed (humbled, bowed, with her eyelids lowered) in homage to the memory of the deceased.

29 **Eye-offending Brine** tears so salty that they sting and burn the eyes. Compare lines 9–11.
season both (a) flavour (with salt), and (b) preserve and ripen for a season. *Fresh* (line 30) echoes line 9.

32 **Frame** construction, composition.

33 **Debt of Love** This phrase could refer to the conjugal 'debt' a husband and his wife pledged themselves to when they vowed to become 'one flesh' (see Ephesians 5:28–33).

34 **Golden Shaft** the arrow by which Cupid incited love. The question implicit in lines 32–36 will be answered in 'Golden Time' (V.i.388).

37 **These sovereign Thrones** Orsino refers to the 'Liver, Brain, and Heart' (line 36) as the seats of the passions, the reason, and the affections, respectively.
supplied Here this word is more or less synonymous with 'fill'd' in the same line.

CURIO   The Hart.

DUKE   Why so I do, the Noblest that I have.
O when mine Eyes did see Olivia first,
Me thought she purg'd the Air of Pestilence;
That Instant was I turn'd into a Hart,   20
And my Desires, like fell and cruel Hounds,
E'er since pursue me.

                    Enter Valentine.

            – How now, what News from her?

VALENTINE   So please my Lord, I might not be
    admitted,
But from her Handmaid do return this Answer:
The Element it self, till seven years' Heat,   25
Shall not behold her Face at ample View,
But like a Cloistress she will vailed walk,
And water once a Day her Chamber round
With Eye-offending Brine, all this to season
A Brother's dead Love, which she would keep
    fresh   30
And lasting, in her sad Remembrance.

DUKE   O she that hath a Heart of that fine Frame
To pay this Debt of Love but to a Brother,
How will she love when the rich Golden Shaft
Hath kill'd the Flock of all Affections else   35
That live in her. When Liver, Brain, and Heart,
These sovereign Thrones, are all supplied, and
    fill'd
Her sweet Perfections with one self King.

37–38 **fill'd . . . King**   her perfect qualities fulfilled and ruled by one
        sovereign love ('all Affections' otherwise having been struck
        dead by the same love-shaft that made 'one self [sole] King').

8

40 **Bow'rs** wooded enclosures overhung with boughs.

I.ii This scene takes place on the coast of Illyria.

2 **And . . . Illyria?** And what am I doing in Illyria? Viola
probably stresses the words *what* and *I* to balance *Brother* in
the next line.

3 **Elysium** the Elysian Fields in the classical underworld. Viola
plays on the similarities between the words 'Illyria' and
'Elysium'. One of her implications is that it is only 'Perchance'
(by chance) that she, and not her brother, is in the one place
and not the other. As it happens, 'Chance' (seemingly random
accident or 'Fortune', and in Shakespearean comedy
frequently an agent of Providence) will play a major role in
relating Illyria to Elysium (Heaven) in the action that follows.
Viola's words anticipate I.v.72–80.

9 **those poor number** the pitiful few.

10 **driving** driven (by the wind and waves), and thus helpless.

11 **provident** resourceful, providing for himself with prudent
foresight. The Captain's adjective suggests that Providence
may have done its part to assist Viola's brother in his 'Peril'.

13 **liv'd** was at home (that is, was accustomed to floating).

14 **Orion** The Captain could be referring to the constellation
(named after a hunter the goddess Diana loved and killed
'perchance'), as it might be viewed by an observer looking
towards the sky just above a 'Dolphin's Back'. But he is
probably thinking of Arion, an ancient poet whose musical
skills with the lyre enabled him to charm a dolphin into
carrying him to shore after he leaped overboard to escape a
band of murderous sailors. That adventure occurred on a
voyage from Sicily to Greece, and Shakespeare could have
derived the story from Book II of Ovid's *Fasti*.

17 **unfoldeth to my Hope** gives me a reason to be hopeful. Here
unfoldeth means 'discloses' (literally, opens up).

18–19 **Authority . . . him** a basis for believing that the same good
fortune that saved me preserved him as well.

20 **I** both (a) I [do], and (b) Ay (yes).
borne both (a) carried, and (b) born.

21 **Travail** travel. But here as elsewhere, the older spelling
preserves a reminder that travel often meant travail (effort,
discomfort), as Viola already knows.

Away before me, to sweet Beds of Flow'rs;
Love-thoughts lie rich when canopied with
   Bow'rs.   *Exeunt.*   40

Scene 2

Enter Viola, a Captain, and Sailors.

VIOLA   What Country, Friends, is this?
CAPTAIN   This is Illyria, Lady.
VIOLA   And what should I do in Illyria?
  My Brother he is in Elysium.
  Perchance he is not drown'd: what think you,
    Sailors?
CAPTAIN   It is perchance that you your self were
  saved.   5
VIOLA   O my poor Brother, and so perchance may he
  be.
CAPTAIN   True, Madam, and to comfort you with
  Chance,
  Assure your self, after our Ship did split,
  When you, and those poor number sav'd with you,
  Hung on our driving Boat, I saw your Brother,   10
  Most provident in Peril, bind himself
  (Courage and Hope both teaching him the
    Practice)
  To a strong Mast that liv'd upon the Sea,
  Where, like Orion on the Dolphin's Back,
  I saw him hold acquaintance with the Waves,   15
  So long as I could see.
VIOLA   For saying so, there's Gold:
  Mine own Escape unfoldeth to my Hope,
  Whereto thy Speech serves for Authority
  The like of him. Know'st thou this Country?
CAPTAIN   I, Madam, well, for I was bred and borne   20
  Not three hours' Travail from this very place.

22 **Duke** Elsewhere in the play Orsino is called a Count. In this setting Shakespeare may have thought the titles largely interchangeable; see lines 31–32, and compare III.i.108.

26 **late** recently.

28 **Murmur** rumour, gossip, 'prattle' (line 29). *Fresh* (line 27) echoes I.i.9, 30.
Great Ones members of the nobility.

30 **What's she?** both (a) Who is she? and (b) What kind of person is she?

32 **since** ago.

34 **shortly** soon thereafter. Olivia's loss of a brother parallels Viola's situation. And the 'Eye-offending Brine' (I.i.29) with which Olivia waters her 'Chamber round' (both her eye and the chamber to which she has confined herself) provides a metaphorical link with the salty 'Waves' (I.ii.15) in which Viola's brother was last seen. *Dear* recalls I.i.16.

35 **abjur'd** renounced, denied herself.

35–36 **Sight/And Company** Many editions emend this phrase to 'company/And sight' to regularize the metre of the two lines. But the emendation does not improve the metre when the two lines are considered together or spoken on the stage; meanwhile, it yields a less logical word-order than does the phrase in the First Folio printing.

37 **delivered to the World** forced to deal with society. Viola's image suggests the trauma of a premature emergence from the womb.

38–39 **Till . . . is** till I had been able to use my own opportunities ('Occasion') and resources to 'mellow' (ripen, mature) myself and my situation and position ('Estate') first. Compare I.ii.29–31.

39 **compass** accomplish (literally, encompass or surround).

40 **Suit** overture, solicitation for the favour of her company.

42 **Fair** handsome, becoming. In this context the word means 'virtuous'.

45 **will believe** choose to have faith. Here as elsewhere, *will* alludes to 'What You Will', the subtitle of *Twelfth Night*. Most of today's editions obscure the thematic phrasing in the Folio by emending *will* to *well*.

VIOLA   Who governs here?
CAPTAIN   A noble Duke in Nature
  As in Name.
VIOLA   What is his name?
CAPTAIN   Orsino.
VIOLA   Orsino: I have heard my Father name him.
  He was a Bachelor then.
CAPTAIN   And so is now,   25
  Or was so very late: for but a Month
  Ago I went from hence, and then 'twas fresh
  In Murmur (as you know what Great Ones do,
  The Less will prattle of) that he did seek
  The Love of fair Olivia.
VIOLA   What's she?   30
CAPTAIN   A virtuous Maid, the Daughter of a Count
  That died some Twelvemonth since, then leaving
    her
  In the protection of his Son, her Brother,
  Who shortly also died; for whose dear Love,
  They say, she hath abjur'd the Sight   35
  And Company of Men.
VIOLA   O that I serv'd that Lady,
  And might not be delivered to the World
  Till I had made mine own Occasion mellow
  What my Estate is.
CAPTAIN   That were hard to compass,
  Because she will admit no kind of Suit,   40
  No, not the Duke's.
VIOLA   There is a Fair Behaviour in thee, Captain,
  And though that Nature with a beauteous Wall
  Doth oft close in Pollution, yet of thee
  I will believe thou hast a Mind that suits   45

45–46 **suits/With**   is in accord with, fits. *Suits* echoes line 40.

46   **Character** appearance, manner (as an actor adopts a persona).

47   **prethee** pray thee; this (rather than *prithee*) is the spelling in the First Folio text of the play.

49   **as haply shall become** as occasion shall make suitable. *Haply* can also mean 'happily': both (a) fitly, appropriately, and (b) felicitously, in a way that promotes contentment. Compare IV.ii.56.

52   **Pains** trouble, effort.

54   **allow me** earn me the credit for being (and the resulting compensation, as hinted in line 52).

55   **hap** chance to happen. Compare *haply* (perchance) in line 49.

56   **Onely** only, solely. *Shape* (conform) echoes I.i.14–15. *Wit* here means 'devising', design. But see the note to I.iii.86–87 for another sense that relates to Viola's interest in Orsino's marital status (line 25).

57   **Mute** an unspeaking servant (associated in Shakespeare's time with the same Mediterranean courts that employed eunuchs, *castrati*, as soprano-voiced male singers).

I.iii   This scene takes place at Olivia's house.

1   **What a plague** a mild oath, comparable to 'what the devil'.

4   **troth** faith, truth.

5   **a' Nights** at night. Here *a'* is an abbreviation of 'of'.
       Cousin kinswoman. Usually Sir Toby calls Olivia his niece. 'Cousin' was a term that could be applied to any relative, near or distant.

7   **except, before excepted** take exception, as she has done before. Sir Toby plays on the Latin legal phrase *exceptis excipiendis*, 'with the exceptions previously noted'. Sir Toby picks up on 'Exceptions' in line 6, and his reply indicates either (a) that he believes that he is excepted (exempted) from the rules that apply to other members of the household, or (b) that he has heard these complaints so many times 'before' that they are now as standard as the most routine legal jargon.

10   **Confine** restrict, constrain. Sir Toby puns on *confine my self* (dress myself) and *finer*, which can mean either (a) more elegantly, or (b) more tightly (from 'fine' in the sense of something refined to the smallest of particles).

12   **and they** if they.

With this thy fair and outward Character.
I prethee (and I'll pay thee bounteously)
Conceal me what I am, and be my Aid,
For such Disguise as haply shall become
The Form of my Intent. I'll serve this Duke;   50
Thou shalt present me as an Eunuch to him;
It may be worth thy Pains. For I can sing,
And speak to him in many sorts of Music,
That will allow me very worth his Service.
What else may hap, to Time I will commit;   55
Onely shape thou thy Silence to my Wit.
CAPTAIN   Be you his Eunuch, and your Mute I'll be;
   When my Tongue blabs, then let mine Eyes not
     see.
VIOLA   I thank thee: lead me on.   *Exeunt.*

Scene 3

Enter Sir Toby, and Maria.

TOBY   What a plague means my Niece to take the
   Death of her Brother thus? I am sure Care's an
   Enemy to Life.
MARIA   By my troth, Sir Toby, you must come in
   earlier a' Nights: your Cousin, my Lady, takes   5
   great Exceptions to your Ill Hours.
TOBY   Why let her except, before excepted.
MARIA   Ay, but you must confine your self within
   the modest Limits of Order.
TOBY   Confine? I'll confine my self no finer than   10
   I am. These Clothes are good enough to drink
   in, and so be these Boots too: and they be not,

13 **hang . . . Straps** Sir Toby varies the proverbial expression 'He may go hang himself in his own garters', a saying that will soon prove applicable to another character in *Twelfth Night*. For other allusions to the proverb, see *A Midsummer Night's Dream*, V.i.362–64, and *1 Henry IV*, II.ii.49–50.

14 **Quaffing** downing a vessel of drink in one gulp.

17 **Woer** Maria means 'wooer', of course, but it will soon be clear that Sir Andrew's wooing is a source of irritation, if not woe, for Olivia. Compare line 59, and see the note to I.iv.42.

18 **Ague-cheek** The name suggests a cadaverously pallid complexion, like that of someone with an ague (a malarial fever) that makes him shiver.

20 **tall** valiant. But Maria pretends to take it in the more usual sense as a reference to height.

22 **Ducats** gold coins worth between a fifth and a third of a pound.

24 **very** true, genuine.
Prodigal wastrel. Maria's point is that Sir Andrew's spending habits (particularly given the 'consulting fees' Sir Toby is charging to advance the gullible knight's suit for the hand of Olivia) will cause him to go through his entire estate in a single year. *Prodigal* alludes to the Parable of the Prodigal Son; see Luke 15:11–24.

25–26 **Viol de Gamboys** viola da gamba, the 'leg-viol' or bass viol. Playing this instrument was proverbially likened to engaging in erotic stroking.

27 **without Book** from memory, with total mastery. We will soon learn that Sir Andrew is 'without Book' in another sense: so ignorant as to be all but illiterate.

29 **Natural** Maria uses the word to mean imbecile or idiot. Here *almost* probably puns on 'all most' (see lines 27–28), and many editors so emend the phrase.

31 **allay** soften, modify.

32 **Gust** gusto, relish.

36 **Substractors** detractors, those who diminish the reputations of others.

42 **Coystrill** coistrel; knave; low character, groom. The word apparently derives from 'kestril', an inferior species of hawk.

let them hang themselves in their own Straps.

MARIA   That Quaffing and Drinking will undo you:
I heard my Lady talk of it yesterday, and of a   15
foolish Knight that you brought in one night
here, to be her Woer.

TOBY   Who, Sir Andrew Ague-cheek?

MARIA   Ay he.

TOBY   He's as tall a Man as any's in Illyria.   20

MARIA   What's that to th' Purpose?

TOBY   Why he has three thousand Ducats a Year.

MARIA   Ay, but he'll have but a Year in all these
Ducats: he's a very Fool, and a Prodigal.

TOBY   Fie, that you'll say so: he plays o'th' Viol   25
de Gamboys, and speaks three or four languages
word for word without Book, and hath all the
good Gifts of Nature.

MARIA   He hath indeed, almost Natural: for besides
that he's a Fool, he's a great Quarreller; and   30
but that he hath the Gift of a Coward to allay
the Gust he hath in Quarrelling, 'tis thought
among the Prudent he would quickly have the
Gift of a Grave.

TOBY   By this Hand, they are Scoundrels and   35
Substractors that say so of him. Who are they?

MARIA   They that add moreov'r he's Drunk nightly
in your company.

TOBY   With drinking Healths to my Niece: I'll drink
to her as long as there is a Passage in my   40
Throat, and Drink in Illyria. He's a Coward
and a Coystrill that will not drink to my Niece

43 **o'** on.

43–44 **Parish Top** a large 'whipping top' of the sort that many
       parishes (villages) kept on hand for the amusement of the idle.

45 **Castiliano vulgo** common Castilian (Spaniard). It is not clear
    what the phrase means in context. It may be that Sir Toby is
    calling for some cheap Spanish wine. Another possibility is
    that he is telling Maria that she is sounding too much like a
    sober-faced Spaniard. A third conjecture (the usual one) is
    that he is urging Maria to act respectful and serious around
    Ague-cheek, to avoid mocking him to his face. A fourth
    possibility is that *Castiliano* is meant to serve as a name for
    the Devil (here a Spanish Catholic), and that the expression is
    a variation on the proverb 'Speak of the Devil and who
    should appear'.

46 **Agueface** probably a jocular (and somewhat contemptuous)
    nickname.

49 **Shrew** Sir Andrew probably means this as a term of
    endearment. A shrew was a 'cursed' (beshrewed) woman, an
    unruly virago.

51 **Accost** greet with due courtesy (with a kiss). As a nautical term
    accost meant 'go alongside', and it was frequently used with
    erotic innuendo (as in lines 58–59).

53 **Chambermaid** lady in waiting, an unmarried gentlewoman.
    Acquaintance (line 55) echoes I.ii.15.

54 **Mistress accost** Most editions capitalize *accost*, on the
    assumption that Sir Andrew believes *Accost* to be the
    chambermaid's name. But the Folio rendering of the passage,
    preserved here, suggests that Sir Andrew is unsure of what
    accost means; inserting a comma before the word, or
    capitalizing it in accordance with line 56, would obscure Sir
    Andrew's uncertainty.

57 **Mary, accost** Most editions emend this phrase to 'Mary
    Accost' (in keeping with line 54); but the Folio rendering of it,
    reproduced here, suggests that Sir Andrew is instructing
    Maria to 'accost' (and thereby give him a hint about what
    accost signifies).

59 **woe** woo. Compare line 17, and see I.iv.42–43.

till his Brains turn o'th' Toe, like a Parish
Top.

Enter Sir Andrew.

What, Wench, *Castiliano vulgo:* for here comes   45
Sir Andrew Agueface.
ANDREW   Sir Toby Belch. How now, Sir Toby Belch?
TOBY   Sweet Sir Andrew.
ANDREW   – Bless you, fair Shrew.
MARIA   And you too, Sir.   50
TOBY   – Accost, Sir Andrew, accost.
ANDREW   What's that?
TOBY   My Niece's Chambermaid.
ANDREW   Good Mistress accost, I desire better
Acquaintance.   55
MARIA   My name is Mary, Sir.
ANDREW   Good Mistress Mary, accost.
TOBY   You mistake, Knight: 'accost' is front her,
boord her, woe her, assail her.
ANDREW   By my troth, I would not undertake her in   60
this company. Is that the meaning of 'accost'?
MARIA   Fare you well, Gentlemen.
TOBY   And thou let her part so, Sir Andrew, would
thou mightst never draw Sword again.

---

60   **undertake her**   The polite meaning of this phrase would be
'take in hand to get better acquainted with her'. But Sir
Andrew is clearly thinking of something not to be done in the
presence of others, as in (a) 'take up' her undergarments (a
sense reflected in IV.iii.160–61 of *The Taming of the Shrew*),
or (b) 'take her under'.

63   **And**   if; so also for line 65.

64   **draw Sword**   Sir Toby is probably referring to two different
ways of exhibiting one's manliness.

69   **Marry** truly. This adverb derives from an oath referring to the Virgin Mary. Shakespeare frequently employs it in contexts pertinent to the more usual modern sense of *marry*.

71   **Thought is free** There are no limits on what a person may think. Maria's reply is the proverbial response to 'Do you think me a fool?' (see lines 66–67).

72   **Butt'ry Bar** the ledge (bar) atop the half-door that served as entrance to the buttery, where butts (barrels) of ale and wine were kept in an inn. Maria's 'Metaphor' (line 73) carries the implication that Sir Andrew's hand is 'dry' (line 74) in the sense associated with sexual impotence. In productions of the play Maria frequently places Sir Andrew's hand on her own 'Butt'ry Bar' (bosom). Whether that is how the playwright intended to have lines 71–72 staged is uncertain; at the very least Maria takes Sir Andrew's hand into her own.

74   **dry** Here as in line 77 Maria's primary meaning for *dry* is 'ironic', a jest too subtle for the butt of it to understand. She picks up on another sense of the word (parched and withered) in 'barren' (line 80).

75–76 **I can keep my Hand dry** Sir Andrew is probably thinking of the proverb about one's having enough sense to come in out of the rain.

79   **I** both (a) I [am], and (b) Ay. Compare I.ii.20.

81   **thou . . . Canary** you need some sweet wine to lubricate your wits.

82   **put down** humiliated, with a hint at the sexual sense of the phrase (a rejection that amounts to enforced impotence).

85–86 **a . . . Man** Sir Andrew probably uses *Christian* to mean *Ordinary* (common). An 'ordinary' was a standard meal taken at a stock price at an inn, and often at a common table. Compare the use of *ordinary* in I.v.92.

86–87 **I am . . . Wit** Beef was thought to cause melancholy and stupidity. Although Sir Andrew cannot be expected to know it, *Wit* (like *Will*) can refer both to erotic desire and to the genitalia of either gender; see *Romeo and Juliet*, I.iii.42.

90   **to morrow** tomorrow. But here as elsewhere, *to morrow* can also mean 'to the morrow (morning)'. Compare line 104.

91   **Pur-quoy** *pourquoi*, French for 'why'. In line 92 Sir Andrew appears to take the word to refer to copulative 'doing'.

ANDREW   And you part so, Mistress, I would I might   65
never draw Sword again. Fair Lady, do you
think you have Fools in hand?

MARIA   Sir, I have not you by th' Hand.

ANDREW   Marry but you shall have, and here's my
Hand.   70

MARIA   Now Sir, Thought is free: I pray you bring
your Hand to th' Butt'ry Bar, and let it drink.

ANDREW   Wherefore, Sweetheart? What's your Metaphor?

MARIA   It's dry, Sir.

ANDREW   Why I think so: I am not such an Ass but I   75
can keep my Hand dry. But what's your Jest?

MARIA   A dry Jest, Sir.

ANDREW   Are you full of them?

MARIA   I, Sir, I have them at my Fingers' ends:
marry now I let go your Hand, I am barren.   *Exit*.   80

TOBY   O Knight, thou lack'st a cup of Canary: when
did I see thee so put down?

ANDREW   Never in your Life, I think, unless you see
Canary put me down. Me thinks sometimes I have
no more Wit than a Christian, or an Ordinary   85
Man has; but I am a great eater of Beef, and I
believe that does harm to my Wit.

TOBY   No question.

ANDREW   And I thought that, I'd forswear it. I'll
ride home to morrow, Sir Toby.   90

TOBY   *Pur-quoy*, my dear Knight?

ANDREW   What is *purquoy*? Do, or not do? I would I
had bestow'd that Time in the Tongues that I
have in Fencing, Dancing, and Bear-baiting: O
had I but followed the Arts.   95

---

93   **bestow'd**   applied, employed.
    the Tongues   the study of languages and literature. Compare Sir
      Toby's remarks in lines 25–28.

95   **follow'd the Arts**   given myself over to improving my mind.

96   **Then . . . Hair** Toby probably plays on 'Tongues' (line 93) to
      refer to 'tongs' for the curling of hair.

98–99 **it . . . Nature** following 'the Arts' (being expert in all the skills
      of a Renaissance man, including those that make me attractive
      to women) will not turn my hair straight and limp (symbolic
      of a 'cool' nature: bloodless, impotent, and cowardly). Most
      editions emend *cool my Nature* to *curl by Nature*.

100   **we** Sir Andrew probably means *me*, but he may be using *we* as
      a grammatically incorrect form for *us* (the royal plural). The
      sound of *we* is appropriate for a man of such wee intelligence
      and virility.

101   **like Flax on a Distaff** in straight strands, like wool or flax
      wound on a long thin staff for spinning.

102   **Huswife** both (a) an ordinary housewife doing domestic
      chores, and (b) a 'hussy' or slut. The clause 'take thee between
      her Legs and spin it off' works with either meaning: (a) hold
      the distaff between her legs while she unwinds the flax onto a
      spindle, or (b) take your 'Distaff', and thereby give you a
      venereal disease that will cause your hair to fall out. Compare
      the spinning imagery in lines 41–44.

107   **hard by** near by (but with an unintended reminder that
      Andrew is incapable of any kind of 'hardness'). *Count*, a title
      not used before for Orsino (see the note to I.ii.22), may have
      been introduced here to echo an English term (derived from
      the Latin word *cunnus*) for the genital 'Wit' of a 'Huswife';
      compare *Hamlet*, III.ii.118–30, for a similar wordplay on the
      'Country Matters' that lie 'between Maid's Legs'. The Folio
      spelling, *Connte*, is probably a misprint; but it could also be
      an authorial variant on the usual orthography and
      pronunciation. See the note to III.i.123.

110– **there's Life in't** there's still hope. But whether 'there's Life' in
11   the sapless Sir Andrew is another matter.

113   **strangest** Sir Andrew means 'most whimsical'; but *strange*
      could also mean 'alienated'.

115   **Kick-chawses** kickshaws (a plural from the French *quelque
      chose*, something); both (a) trifles, and (b) tidbits to
      accompany dishes of mutton (see line 121).

117   **under . . . Betters** excepting those of higher station.

118   **Old Man** Sir Andrew is probably referring to a more
      experienced and skilled elder such as Sir Toby. But *Old Man*
      could also mean wanton, unregenerate, 'corrupt through the
      deceivable lusts' (Ephesians 4:22, Geneva Bible).

TOBY   Then hadst thou had an excellent head of Hair.
ANDREW   Why, would that have mended my Hair?
TOBY   Past question: for thou seest it will not
cool my Nature.
ANDREW   But it becomes we well enough, does't not?   100
TOBY   Excellent, it hangs like Flax on a Distaff;
and I hope to see a Huswife take thee between
her Legs, and spin it off.
ANDREW   Faith I'll home to morrow, Sir Toby: your
Niece will not be seen, or if she be it's four   105
to one she'll none of me. The Count himself
here hard by woos her.
TOBY   She'll none o'th' Count: she'll not match
above her Degree, neither in Estate, Years, nor
Wit. I have heard her swear't. Tut there's   110
Life in't, Man.
ANDREW   I'll stay a Month longer. I am a Fellow
o'th' strangest Mind in the World: I delight
in Masks and Revels sometimes altogether.
TOBY   Art thou good at these Kick-chawses, Knight?   115
ANDREW   As any Man in Illyria, whatsoever he be,
under the Degree of my Betters, and yet I will
not compare with an Old Man.
TOBY   What is thy excellence in a Galliard, Knight?
ANDREW   Faith, I can cut a Caper.   120
TOBY   And I can cut the Mutton to't.

---

119   **Galliard**   a vigorous dance in triple time; its five steps included
a 'Caper' (line 120) or leap on the fourth.

121   **cut the Mutton to't**   Sir Toby plays on another kind of 'Caper':
a spicy berry (kickshaw) to be served as the sauce to a cut of
lamb. In all likelihood, Sir Toby is also alluding to a third
sense of *Caper* (sexual romp); *Mutton* was a euphemism for
'prostitute'. *Cut* anticipates II.iii.202–3.

122 **Back-trick**   the back-stepping movements in the galliard. But
        Sir Andrew's phrase can also refer to a 'trick' in the sense that
        relates to 'Mutton'.

124– **Wherefore . . . 'em?**   Why are these talents kept behind a drape
25   or veil rather than openly displayed? Sir Toby alludes to such
        biblical passages as Matthew 5:14–16, where Jesus says, 'Let
        your light so shine before men, that they may see your good
        works'. Curtains were used to shield paintings from light and
        dust; compare I.v.255–56.

126 **Mistress Mall's**   *Mall* was a diminutive of 'Mary'. Sir Toby may
        also be thinking of a 'Moll', a less respectable 'Mistress'.

128 **Carranto**   coranto; a quick-paced, 'running' dance. Toby is
        probably punning on 'car', chariot.

130 **Sink-a-pace**   cinquepace (from the French *cinque-pas*, five-
        pace), a dance similar to the galliard. Sir Toby puns on a
        'Sink' (sewer) for urinating (making water) and on 'apace'
        (swiftly).

133 **under the Star of**   under the influence of a star favourable to.

136 **dam'd**   Sir Andrew probably means 'damned' (cursed), but the
        Folio spelling also suggests 'damed' ('effeminate', or perhaps
        'made by a woman').
     Stock   stocking.

136– **sit about**   either (a) set about, or (b) sit and plan.
37

138 **borne**   both (a) born, and (b) carried and cradled. Compare
        I.ii.20.

139 **Taurus**   This zodiacal sign was said by some to govern one's
        'Legs and Thighs' (line 141) or shanks and feet; but most
        authorities connected it with the neck and throat. 'Sides and
        Heart' (line 140) were governed by Leo.

140 **That**   either (a) That's, or (b) Is that.

I.iv   This scene takes place at Orsino's palace.

1   **Duke**   In this scene Orsino is referred to as both a Duke and a
        Count (line 10). See the note to I.ii.22.

2   **Cesario**   the name Viola has adopted as part of her male
        disguise.
     like   likely.

ANDREW   And I think I have the Back-trick simply as
strong as any Man in Illyria.

TOBY   Wherefore are these things hid? Wherefore
have these Gifts a Curtain before 'em? Are   125
they like to take Dust, like Mistress Mall's
Picture? Why dost thou not go to Church in a
Galliard, and come home in a Carranto? My very
Walk should be a Jig: I would not so much as
make Water but in a Sink-a-pace. What doest   130
thou mean? Is it a World to hide Virtues in?
I did think by the excellent Constitution of
thy Leg, it was form'd under the Star of a
Galliard.

ANDREW   Ay, 'tis strong, and it does indifferent   135
well in a dam'd colour'd Stock. Shall we sit
about some Revels?

TOBY   What shall we do else? Were we not borne
under Taurus?

ANDREW   Taurus? That Sides and Heart.   140

TOBY   No Sir, it is Legs and Thighs: let me see
thee caper. Ha, higher: ha, ha, excellent.

Exeunt.

Scene 4

Enter Valentine, and Viola in Man's Attire.

VALENTINE   If the Duke continue these Favours
towards you, Cesario, you are like to be much
advanc'd; he hath known you but three Days,
and already you are no Stranger.

5   **Humour**   disposition, here referring to a person who is given to capriciousness. Viola seems to be referring to a temporary mood or whim.
    Negligence   neglect of duty (something that would cause the Duke to alter his attitude to me).

13   **Stand you awhile aloof**   Orsino addresses these words to his attendants; he wants them to stand to one side for a moment while he speaks privately to 'Cesario'.

14   **but all**   than everything.
    unclasp'd   opened up.

16   **Gate**   both (a) way, proceeding, means of entrance, and (b) gait, manner of walking. Compare *Hamlet*, I.ii.30–31.

18   **there thy fixed Foot shall grow**   your foot will be planted there. *Grow* can mean 'become larger and longer'. In line 17 *Access* is accented on the second syllable; so also with *Aspect* in line 29.

19   **Audience**   an opportunity to be heard.

20   **abandon'd to**   completely surrendered to.

22   **leap all Civil Bounds**   disregard all the constraints of civilized manners.

23   **make unprofited Return**   come back without accomplishing your mission.

26   **Surprise**   overwhelm. Here *Surprise* means 'surprise attack', as on a well-guarded fortress. *Unfold* (line 25) recalls I.ii.17.
    dear   both (a) loving, and (b) totally invested.

27   **act my Woes**   convey my sufferings through your own words and actions.

28   **attend**   pay attention to, respond to. Compare line 12.

29   **Nuntio**   nuncio, messenger.
    Grave Aspect   the solemn bearing of a dignified old man.

31   **yet . . . Years**   even overstate the number of carefree years you have lived.

33   **rubious**   ruby-red.
    Pipe   voice (literally, windpipe and vocal cords).

34   **shrill, and sound**   high-pitched and unbroken (like that of a boy whose voice has yet to change). See the note to I.ii.57.

VIOLA   You either fear his Humour or my Negligence,   5
    that you call in question the continuance of
    his Love. Is he Inconstant, Sir, in his Favours?
VALENTINE   No, believe me.
VIOLA   I thank you.

    Enter Duke, Curio, and Attendants.

    Here comes the Count.   10
DUKE   Who saw Cesario, ho?
VIOLA   On your Attendance, my Lord, here.
DUKE   – Stand you awhile aloof. – Cesario,
    Thou know'st no less but all: I have unclasp'd
    To thee the Book even of my secret Soul.   15
    Therefore, good Youth, address thy Gate unto
      her,
    Be not denied Access; stand at her Doors,
    And tell them, there thy fixed Foot shall grow
    Till thou have Audience.
VIOLA   Sure my noble Lord,
    If she be so abandon'd to her Sorrow   20
    As it is spoke, she never will admit me.
DUKE   Be clamorous, and leap all Civil Bounds,
    Rather than make unprofited Return.
VIOLA   Say I do speak with her, my Lord, what then?
DUKE   O then unfold the Passion of my Love,   25
    Surprise her with Discourse of my dear Faith.
    It shall become thee well to act my Woes:
    She will attend it better in thy Youth
    Than in a Nuntio's of more Grave Aspect.
VIOLA   I think not so, my Lord.
DUKE   Dear Lad, believe it;   30
    For they shall yet belie thy happy Years
    That say thou art a Man. Diana's Lip
    Is not more smooth, and rubious; thy small Pipe
    Is as the Maiden's Organ, shrill, and sound,

35 **semblative** like, resembling.
Woman's Part Orsino means 'the role played by a female in society'; but an Elizabethan audience would also have been reminded of the 'Woman's Part' (theatrical role) in a play such as *Twelfth Night*, and of the fact that 'Viola' was performed by a 'Cesario' (a young male actor) whose own genital 'part' was becoming less and less like that of a woman.

36 **Constellation** disposition (as determined by the position of the stars and planets at your birth).

40 **freely** both (a) unrestrictedly (free of hindrances), and (b) bounteously. Orsino little imagines what it will mean for 'Cesario' to 'Prosper well'.

42 **woe** woo. But here as in line 43 and in I.iii.17, 59, the Folio spelling will prove pertinent to the woe (distress) Viola's wooing causes herself and the 'Lady'. Compare *Measure for Measure*, II.ii.28, and *Love's Labour's Lost*, IV.iii.372, and *Romeo and Juliet*, III.iv.8, for other instances of the *woe/woo* pairing.
a barful Strife a conflict that bars (impedes) my efforts. *Bar* echoes I.iii.71–72.

I.v This scene takes place in Olivia's house.

4 **thy Absence** As we shall see, the Clown in this play (Feste) moves freely from one setting to another. This allows him to comment on the follies in all the major locales of the action.

5 **well hang'd** both (a) executed, (b) well supplied genitally, and (c) well connected copulatively (see the notes to *Measure for Measure*, II.i.250, IV.ii.40–41, and *Love's Labour's Lost*, IV.iii.56, V.ii.600). Compare I.iii.13. As the Clown speaks he may call attention to the Fool's alter ego, the bauble at the end of the stick that a professional jester carried. See the note to line 38.

6 **fear no Colours** fear nothing. The expression relates both to (a) the colours of deception or camouflage (line 8), and (b) military colours (the standards or banners of an army, line 12). Feste is also punning on hangman's 'collars' (nooses), and on 'cholers' (angers). Compare *Romeo and Juliet*, I.i.1–5. He may also be referring to female genital collars.

7 **Make that good** Justify that remark; make it apply.

9 **Lenten Answer** a reply as sparing as the fare one is permitted during the Lenten fast.

And all is semblative a Woman's Part.   35
I know thy Constellation is right apt
For this Affair. – Some four or five attend
    him,
All if you will: for I my self am best
When least in Company. – Prosper well in this,
And thou shalt live as freely as thy Lord,   40
To call his Fortunes thine.
VIOLA   I'll do my best
To woe your Lady.
                              – Yet a barful Strife:
Who e'er I woe, my self would be his Wife.
                                                    Exeunt.

Scene 5

Enter Maria, and Clown.

MARIA   Nay, either tell me where thou hast been, or
    I will not open my Lips so wide as a Bristle
    may enter, in way of thy Excuse: my Lady will
    hang thee for thy Absence.
CLOWN   Let her hang me: he that is well hang'd in   5
    this World needs to fear no Colours.
MARIA   Make that good.
CLOWN   He shall see none to fear.
MARIA   A good Lenten Answer. I can tell thee where
    that Saying was borne, of 'I fear no Colours.'   10
CLOWN   Where, good Mistress Mary?
MARIA   In the Wars, and that may you be bold to
    say in your Foolery.

---

10   **borne**   both (a) born, and (b) carried (as by an ensign bearing a
        battalion's colours). Compare I.iii.138.

14 **God . . . it** Feste echoes Matthew 25:29, 'For unto every man that hath, it shall be given, and he shall have abundance, and from him that hath not, even that he hath shall be taken away.'

16 **Talents** Feste alludes to the Parable of the Talents (Matthew 25:14–30). His implication is that since by definition Fools are endowed with folly, they exercise proper stewardship over what God has given them only when their behaviour is the opposite of conventional 'Wisdom'. *Talents* can also mean 'talons', as in *Love's Labour's Lost*, IV.ii.68–69, where Dull says, 'If a Talent be a Claw, look how he claws him with a Talent.' Feste probably puns on the sense of *Fools* (line 15) that relates to sexual prowess and licence; see the notes to III.i.35, 36. If so, *Talents* is phallic in implication.

18 **turn'd away** denied further patronage (employment). Maria also plays on 'turned off', a euphemism for hanging.

20 **Hanging** both (a) execution, and (b) set of sexual equipment. But Feste also refers to a sense of being 'turn'd away' (rejected in a bid for a 'turn' in bed, a sense employed in *Antony and Cleopatra*, II.v.57–58) that leaves a man 'Hanging' (extended but unengaged). He alludes to the proverbs 'Wedding and hanging go by destiny' and 'Better be half hanged than ill wed'.

21 **turning away** either (a) enjoying an unending succession of good turns (see the note to line 20), and thus 'bearing it out' (holding firm in a male's conjugal activities) as long as a man's turns can bear up under his weight, or (b) being turned away (see the note to line 18).

21 **let Summer bear it out** both (a) let the warm weather make it tolerable, and (b) let the corpse rot on the gibbet all summer. The Clown may be alluding to Will Summers, the jester to Henry VIII, or to *Summer's Last Will and Testament*, a play by Thomas Nashe produced in 1592 and published in 1600.

22 **Resolute** obdurate, set against amending your behaviour. Often *Resolute* means 'prepared to die in an act of valour against great odds', as in *Hamlet*, III.i.80–85.

25–26 **That . . . fall** Maria puns on *Points*, taking Feste to mean the tagged laces that support a man's 'Gaskins' (wide, loose breeches) by attaching them to his doublet (jacket).

27 **Apt** both (a) pertinent, and (b) showing commendable skill at the kind of 'Fooling' (repartee) the jester considers to be his stock in trade.

CLOWN   Well, God give them Wisdom that have it;
and those that are Fools, let them use their   15
Talents.

MARIA   Yet you will be hang'd for being so long
absent; or to be turn'd away, is not that as
good as a Hanging to you?

CLOWN   Many a good Hanging prevents a bad   20
Marriage; and for turning away, let Summer bear it out.

MARIA   You are Resolute then?

CLOWN   Not so neither, but I am resolv'd on two
Points.

MARIA   That if one break, the other will hold: or   25
if both break, your Gaskins fall.

CLOWN   Apt, in good faith, very apt. Well, go thy
way: if Sir Toby would leave Drinking, thou
wert as witty a piece of Eve's Flesh as any in
Illyria.   30

MARIA   Peace, you Rogue: no more o' that. Here
comes my Lady: make your Excuse wisely, you
were best.   [*Exit.*]

Enter Lady Olivia, with Malvolio [and Attendants].

CLOWN   – Wit, and't be thy Will, put me into good

28–30 **if . . . Illyria** Feste tells Maria that she would make a superb
      wife for Sir Toby if he would only sober up. By *witty* Feste
      probably means both (a) mentally sharp, and (b) erotically
      appealing and lively; see the note to I.iii.86–87.

32–33 **make . . . best** You would be well advised to have a good
      explanation for your truancy. *Excuse* (explanation) echoes
      line 3.

34   **Wit** Feste invokes inspiration from his 'Wit' (both his
      intelligence and his sense of humour), addressing it as if it
      were a deity. See the notes to I.iii.86–87 (on *Wit*) and line 16
      (on *Fooling*, line 35). Like *Wit*, *Will* can refer both to exotic
      desire and to the genitalia.

38 **Quinapalus** an 'authority' invented by Feste to give mock dignity to his ad hoc proverb. He may be addressing the bauble that hangs from the end of his stick.

40 **Take the Fool away** Olivia's reply makes it clear that Maria is right: Feste's mistress is so displeased with him that she is ready to dismiss him from her service. He will need to have his wits about him if he is to survive this crisis.

43 **Go to** a term of dismissal or reproof, which can be either serious or jocular, depending on the context; comparable to 'come, come', or 'Get out of here!'
Dry Fool Olivia probably means 'barren', dried up, and thus ready to be discarded ('turn'd away', line 18). But see the note on *Dry* at I.iii.74. Lines 43–47 echo I.iii.71–82.

44 **Dishonest** wanton, licentious.

50 **Botcher** clothes-mender. But *Botcher* can also refer to a man who meddles with 'Women's Matters'; see the wordplay on *Cobbler* in *Julius Caesar*, I.i.19–31, and compare *All's Well That Ends Well*, IV.iii.210–14.

54 **Syllogism** logical demonstration. Feste's clauses about various forms of patching parody the form of a deductive proof. It is a 'simple' (simple-minded) syllogism, in keeping with the 'patch'd' (particoloured) attire of the court fool, and its implicit point is that nothing (including human nature) is as 'simple' (all of a kind) as some would prefer. Compare *All's Well That Ends Well*, IV.iii.83–87, where we hear that 'The Web of our Life is of a Mingled Yarn, Good and Ill together'.

55–56 **no true Cuckold but Calamity** The implication of this clause would seem to be that the only true victim of cuckoldry (here, the suffering brought on by Fortune's reversals, her proverbial infidelity to those who put their faith in her) is the person who allows it to be a 'Calamity' and is defeated by it. In lines 72–78 Feste 'proves' that an apparent 'Calamity' may be a blessing when viewed from a higher perspective.

56 **so Beauty's a Flower** This clause appears to represent the other side of the coin: the person who stakes all on 'Beauty' (here a symbol of Fortune's favour) will soon discover that it fades and dies like a flower. The point of the sentence would seem to be that the only 'Remedy' (line 55) is to rise above both good and bad Fortune. See II.iv.38–39.

57 **bad** bade. The Folio spelling is the usual form in Shakespeare for the past tense of *bid*.

Fooling. Those Wits that think they have thee   35
do very oft prove Fools; and I that am sure I
lack thee, may pass for a Wise Man. For what
says Quinapalus, 'Better a witty Fool than a
foolish Wit.' – God bless thee, Lady.

OLIVIA   Take the Fool away.   40

CLOWN   – Do you not hear, Fellows, take away the
Lady.

OLIVIA   Go to, y'are a Dry Fool: I'll no more of
you. Besides, you grow Dishonest.

CLOWN   Two Faults, Madonna, that Drink and Good   45
Counsel will amend. For give the Dry Fool
Drink, then is the Fool not Dry. Bid the
Dishonest Man mend himself, if he mend he is
no longer Dishonest; if he cannot, let the
Botcher mend him. Any thing that's mended is   50
but patch'd; Virtue that transgresses is but
patch'd with Sin, and Sin that amends is but
patch'd with Virtue. If that this simple
Syllogism will serve, so; if it will not, what
Remedy? As there is no true Cuckold but   55
Calamity, so Beauty's a Flower. – The Lady
bad take away the Fool: therefore I say
again take her away.

OLIVIA   Sir, I bad them take away you.

CLOWN   Misprision in the highest Degree. Lady,   60
Cucullus non facit monachum: that's as much
to say as I wear not Motley in my Brain.

---

60   **Misprision** a mistake (literally, a mis-apprising).

61   **Cucullus non facit monachum** a Latin proverb, 'the cowl does
not make the monk'. Feste goes on to note that it is an error
to judge things by outward appearances: his 'Motley'
(patched costume), for example, or his 'simple' syllogisms.

63 **Madonna** an Italian term meaning 'my Lady'.
   leave permission.

66 **Dexteriously** dexterously (with all the adroitness of those who
   use their right hands adeptly).

68 **catechize you** instruct you by means of a series of questions
   and brief responses (here ones that will lead you to the
   answers fundamental to Christian doctrine).

70 **want** lack.

71 **bide** both (a) await, and (b) abide, tolerate.

80 **mend** both (a) improve, and (b) 'patch' the follies of others.
   Compare lines 43–55. The Clown's proof that Olivia's
   brother is 'in Heaven' echoes Viola's fear that her brother is
   'in Elysium' (I.ii.3).

82–83 **Infirmity . . . Fool** Having implied that the kind of 'mending'
   (improving) the Fool does simply makes him more foolish,
   Malvolio now suggests that the Fool's way of getting 'better'
   (line 83) is to become progressively more 'ill' (decayed
   through 'Infirmity') in wisdom.

84–85 **God . . . Folly** Feste's invocation is both a prayer and a curse.
   It will soon be fulfilled.

86 **Fox** Feste's primary meaning is 'man of cunning' or 'wise
   man'. But Shakespeare may also be alluding to a traditional
   Twelfth Night custom whereby a fox was released in a great
   hall, captured, and then incinerated in the fireplace; the ritual
   symbolized the casting of Satan into Hell-fire, and it signalled
   the triumph of the 'Good Will' (Luke 2:14) associated with
   the Christmas season.

87 **pass** either (a) exchange, as with currency, or (b) pledge.
   Compare lines 36–37.

92 **with** either (a) by, or (b) along with. *Put down* echoes
   I.iii.81–82.
   an ordinary Fool Malvolio probably means a 'tavern fool' (a
   jester who performs in an 'ordinary'). But he may mean a real
   fool (a 'natural'). Compare I.iii.84–87, where *Ordinary* hints
   at the same set of implications.

94 **out of his Gard** both (a) caught off guard (a term from
   fencing), and (b) naked, without the trim (*gard* or *guard*) that
   should adorn his livery, a sense that recalls lines 47–53,
   61–62, 80–83.

Good Madonna, give me leave to prove you a
Fool.

OLIVIA   Can you do it?   65

CLOWN   Dexteriously, good Madonna.

OLIVIA   Make your Proof.

CLOWN   I must catechize you for it, Madonna. Good
my Mouse of Virtue, answer me.

OLIVIA   Well Sir, for want of other Idleness, I'll   70
bide your Proof.

CLOWN   Good Madonna, why mourn'st thou?

OLIVIA   Good Fool, for my Brother's Death.

CLOWN   I think his Soul is in Hell, Madonna.

OLIVIA   I know his Soul is in Heaven, Fool.   75

CLOWN   The more Fool, Madonna, to mourn for your
Brother's Soul, being in Heaven. – Take away
the Fool, Gentlemen.

OLIVIA   – What think you of this Fool, Malvolio,
doth he not mend?   80

MALVOLIO   Yes, and shall do, till the Pangs of Death
shake him. Infirmity, that decays the Wise,
doth ever make the better Fool.

CLOWN   God send you, Sir, a speedy Infirmity, for
the better increasing your Folly. Sir Toby   85
will be sworn that I am no Fox, but he will
not pass his Word for two Pence that you are
no Fool.

OLIVIA   How say you to that, Malvolio?

MALVOLIO   I marvel your Ladyship takes delight in   90
such a barren Rascal: I saw him put down the
other Day with an ordinary Fool, that has no
more Brain than a Stone. Look you now, he's
out of his Gard already. Unless you laugh and

95　**minister Occasion**　provide him a chance to do his thing.
　　gag'd　either (a) gaged (engaged, bound, like a man who has
　　　been issued a challenge), and (b) gagged (stifled, rendered
　　　speechless).

96　**crow**　laugh uproariously.

98　**Zanies**　assistants, sub-fools.

100　**distemper'd**　ill; imbalanced, ungoverned; not 'of Free
　　　Disposition' (line 101). *Appetite* recalls I.i.1–3.

101　**of Free Disposition**　not dominated by any humours. *Free*
　　　echoes I.iv.40.

102　**Bird-bolts**　blunt arrows for shooting birds.

103–4 **There . . . Fool**　What a licensed fool is permitted to say is not
　　　to be thought of as slandering (railing unfairly at) anyone.

105　**a . . . Man**　a man with a reputation for sound judgement.

107　**Mercury . . . Leasing**　may the sly god give you the power to lie.
　　　Indue (endue) here means both 'clothe' and 'endow'. *Leasing*
　　　is used in this passage as a euphemism for 'stealing'; Mercury
　　　is the patron deity of thieves and other deceivers. *Leasing* may
　　　also function here as an aphetic form of *releasing*: setting
　　　'Free' a 'Disposition' that is now 'distemper'd'.

112　**fair**　both (a) attractive, and (b) light-complexioned.

113　**attended**　accompanied with subordinates. Compare I.iv.28, 37.

114　**People**　servants.

117　**Madman**　the kind of raving associated with lunatics.

118　**Suit**　amorous solicitation for an audience.

119–
20
　　What you will　Say whatever you wish. Olivia's phrase states
　　　the subtitle of *Twelfth Night*; see the note to I.ii.45.

121　**old**　wearisome, stale.

123–
24
　　Thou . . . Fool　Feste pretends that Olivia's remarks are
　　　directed not at him but at Sir Toby. Feste's implication is that
　　　Olivia has reproached Sir Toby 'for us' (on Feste's behalf),
　　　and as if Toby were not her uncle but a prodigal son whose
　　　'Fooling' (licentious behaviour) must now come to a stop.
　　　Feste's remarks are probably intended as an allusion to the
　　　proverb 'A wise man commonly hath a fool to his heir.'

126　**Pia mater**　brain (actually the membrane enclosing it); a Latin
　　　phrase that literally means 'mild mother'.

minister Occasion to him, he is gag'd. I   95
protest I take these Wise Men, that crow so at
these set kind of Fools, no better than the
Fools' Zanies.

OLIVIA   O you are sick of Self-love, Malvolio, and
taste with a distemper'd Appetite. To be   100
Generous, Guiltless, and of Free Disposition
is to take those things for Bird-bolts that
you deem Cannon-bullets. There is no Slander
in an allow'd Fool, though he do nothing but
rail; nor no Railing in a known Discreet Man,   105
though he do nothing but reprove.

CLOWN   Now Mercury indue thee with Leasing, for
thou speak'st well of Fools.

Enter Maria.

MARIA   Madam, there is at the Gate a young Gentleman,
much desires to speak with you.   110

OLIVIA   From the Count Orsino, is it?

MARIA   I know not, Madam, 'tis a fair young Man,
and well attended.

OLIVIA   Who of my People hold him in delay?

MALVOLIO   Sir Toby, Madam, your Kinsman.   115

OLIVIA   Fetch him off, I pray you; he speaks nothing
but Madman: fie on him.   [*Exit Maria.*]
– Go you, Malvolio. If it be a Suit from the
Count, I am sick, or not at home. What you
will, to dismiss it.   *Exit Malvolio.*   120
– Now you see, Sir, how your Fooling grows old,
and people dislike it.

CLOWN   Thou hast spoke for us, Madonna, as if thy
eldest Son should be a Fool: whose Skull Jove
cram with Brains, for here he comes.   125

Enter Sir Toby.

127 **What** what kind of person.

131– **A plague . . . Herring** Sir Toby has probably just belched or
32 hiccuped, and is blaming his condition on pickled herring
rather than on his having drunk too much. *Plague* echoes
I.iii.1–2.

132 **Sot** fool. Sir Toby greets Feste.

135 **Lethargy** drunken stupor. Toby's mis-hearing illustrates
Olivia's point.

136 **one** either (a) a visitor, or (b) an embodiment of lechery. The
second reading would play on the virile sense *one* has in other
Shakespearean contexts; compare III.iii.35, and see the notes
to *Julius Caesar*, I.ii.154, III.i.66, 69–71, and *Macbeth*, I.v.73,
I.vii.25–27, 72–74.

138 **marry** truly, indeed. See the note to I.iii.69. Olivia's phrase
(rendered 'I marry' in the Folio) will prove relevant to the 'he'
in question.

139 **Divel** the preferred spelling for Devil in the Folio text of this
play.
and if.

140 **give me Faith** a pious expression to ward off the Devil.
it's all one it's all the same, it makes no difference.

143 **one Draught above Heat** one drink more beyond the point
where one feels a sensation of warmth that goes beyond the
body's normal temperature.

145 **Crowner** coroner (the officer who presides over inquests to
determine the cause of a person's death). See the note to
V.i.321–24.

146 **sit o'** sit on, hold an inquest on.

148– **the Fool . . . Madman** Feste's statement has the flavour both of
49 a proverb and a prophecy. It implies that things have now
degenerated to the point where the only people left to 'look
to' (care for) madmen are fools. Later (in IV.ii) 'the Fool'
(Feste) 'shall look to' a different 'Madman'.

152– **he takes . . . you** he says that he understands that to be the case
53 and has come for that very reason. The implication of lines
151–56 is that the messenger at the door has come to attend
to Olivia's sickness and wake her from a lethargy. There is a
sense in which both the 'diagnosis' and the implied 'cure' are
apt. At this point Olivia is unhealthily preoccupied with her

One of thy Kin has a most weak *Pia mater*.

OLIVIA   By mine Honour, half Drunk. – What is he at
the Gate, Cousin?

TOBY   A Gentleman.

OLIVIA   A Gentleman? What Gentleman?   130

TOBY   'Tis a Gentleman here. A plague o' these
pickle Herring. – How now, Sot.

CLOWN   Good Sir Toby.

OLIVIA   Cousin, Cousin, how have you come so early
by this Lethargy?   135

TOBY   Lechery, I defy Lechery: there's one at the
Gate.

OLIVIA   Ay marry, what is he?

TOBY   Let him be the Divel and he will, I care not;
give me Faith, say I. Well, it's all one.   *Exit.*   140

OLIVIA   What's a Drunken Man like, Fool?

CLOWN   Like a Drown'd Man, a Fool, and a Madman:
one Draught above Heat makes him a Fool, the
second mads him, and a third drowns him.

OLIVIA   Go thou and seek the Crowner, and let him   145
sit o' my Coz. For he's in the Third Degree
of Drink; he's Drown'd. Go look after him.

CLOWN   He is but Mad yet, Madonna, and the Fool
shall look to the Madman.   [*Exit.*]

Enter Malvolio.

MALVOLIO   Madam, yond young Fellow swears he   150
will speak with you. I told him you were sick;
he takes on him to understand so much, and
therefore comes to speak with you. I told him
you were asleep; he seems to have a fore-
knowledge of that too, and therefore comes to   155

---

role as a mourner for her deceased brother; like Malvolio, she
is 'sick' with a kind of 'Self-love' (line 99) or indulgence and
needs to be restored to the world of the living.

156– **What . . . Denial**   This sentence, punctuated here as it appears
57   in the Folio, seems to mean 'Whatever is said to him, he is
         prepared with an argument to counter it.' Most editions
         replace the comma after *Lady* with a question mark.

159   **H'as**   he has.

160   **Sheriff's Post**   a decorated post placed outside a sheriff's office
         as a symbol of authority.

161   **Supporter**   prop, supporting leg. Compare I.iv.16–19.

165   **Manner**   type. But in line 166 Malvolio gives the word a sense
         that relates to manners.

167   **will you or no**   This phrase is one of the play's many reminders
         that *Twelfth Night* is largely about 'What You Will' (the
         subtitle it bears in the First Folio printing). Compare lines
         119–20.

170   **Squash**   an unripe peapod ('Pescod,' line 171).

171   **Pescod**   peascod, peapod.
         Codling   an immature or unripe apple. *Codling* can also mean
         'small cod', with *Cod* referring to the part of a male anatomy
         that is housed in a codpiece (the baggy flap that covers the
         crotch in a man's breeches).

172   **in Standing Water**   water at the turning of the tide. Compare
         Antony and Cleopatra, I.iv.44–47, III.ii.48–50.

173   **well-favoured**   of a handsome face (favour).

174   **shrewishly**   saucily, with a sharp tongue, like someone who is
         beshrewed, cursed. Compare I.iii.49.

179   **Embassy**   both (a) message, and (b) messenger (ambassador).

S.D.   **Violenta**   Viola. The Folio entrance direction may be a scribal
         or compositorial error; but it may also be an authorial
         insignia for a manner that fits the way Viola is described in
         lines 150–67, 214–16, 226–36. The name *Violenta* occurs in
         All's Well That Ends Well, and on a page the Folio
         compositor who set this part of *Twelfth Night* may have
         worked upon shortly before he produced this stage direction.

speak with you. What is to be said to him,
Lady, he's fortified against any Denial.

OLIVIA   Tell him, he shall not speak with me.

MALVOLIO   H'as been told so; and he says he'll
stand at your Door like a Sheriff's Post, and   160
be the Supporter to a Bench, but he'll speak
with you.

OLIVIA   What kind o' Man is he?

MALVOLIO   Why, of Mankind.

OLIVIA   What Manner of Man?   165

MALVOLIO   Of very Ill Manner: he'll speak with you,
will you or no.

OLIVIA   Of what Personage and Years is he?

MALVOLIO   Not yet Old enough for a Man, nor Young
enough for a Boy: as a Squash is before 'tis a   170
Pescod, or a Codling when 'tis almost an
Apple: 'tis with him in Standing Water, between
Boy and Man. He is very well-favour'd, and he
speaks very shrewishly. One would think his
Mother's Milk were scarce out of him.   175

OLIVIA   Let him approach. Call in my Gentlewoman.

MALVOLIO   – Gentlewoman, my Lady calls.   *Exit*.

Enter Maria.

OLIVIA   – Give me my Veil. Come throw it o'er my
Face:
We'll once more hear Orsino's Embassy.

Enter Violenta.

VIOLA   The honourable Lady of the House, which is   180
she?

OLIVIA   Speak to me, I shall answer for her: your
Will.

VIOLA   Most radiant, exquisite, and unmatchable
Beauty – I pray you tell me if this be the   185
Lady of the House, for I never saw her. I would

187 **loath** unwilling, reluctant.
cast away discard, as if it were trash.

189 **con** memorize and master. *Pains* recalls I.ii.52 and anticipates
lines 211, 307.

190 **sustain** be subjected to.
comptible sensitive, vulnerable.

191 **sinister Usage** discourteous (literally, 'left-handed') treatment.

194 **out of my Part** not written into my script. *Part* recalls I.iv.35.

195 **modest** reasonable, appropriate. *Modest* can also refer to the
proficiency with which an actor performs his role.

198 **Comedian** actor.

200 **I am . . . play** What Viola means privately is (a) 'I am not the
person I appear to be', and (b) 'my heart is not in my effort to
win you for the man I myself secretly love'. On the
Elizabethan stage, the line would have had yet another level of
complexity: the speaker *would* have been a 'Comedian' (line
198), a young man impersonating Viola, but more nearly
resembling a 'real' 'Cesario'. See the note to I.iv.35.

202 **usurp my self** pretend to be someone I am not.

204–5 **what . . . reserve** Viola's point is that a woman's duty is to
'bestow' herself on a man and bear fruit for the future. She
may be thinking of such teachings as the Parable of the
Talents (Matthew 25:14–30); see lines 14–16, and compare
Sonnets 1–14.

205–6 **from my Commission** beyond what I have been instructed and
authorized to say.

207 **shew** show.

213 **feigned** counterfeited; merely pretended. Lines 211–13 echo *As
You Like It*, III.iii.18–19, where Touchstone says that 'the
truest Poetry is the most faining'.

214 **saucy** impudent, discourteous.

215 **allow'd your Approach** permitted you to enter.

216 **wonder at you** marvel at the kind of person who would behave
with such effrontery.

be loath to cast away my Speech: for, besides
that it is excellently well penn'd, I have
taken great Pains to con it. Good Beauties,
let me sustain no Scorn; I am very comptible,   190
even to the least sinister Usage.

OLIVIA   Whence came you, Sir?

VIOLA   I can say little more than I have studied,
and that Question's out of my Part. Good Gentle
One, give me modest Assurance, if you be the   195
Lady of the House, that I may proceed in my
Speech.

OLIVIA   Are you a Comedian?

VIOLA   No, my profound Heart: and yet (by the very
Fangs of Malice, I swear) I am not that I play.   200
Are you the Lady of the House?

OLIVIA   If I do not usurp my self, I am.

VIOLA   Most certain, if you are she, you do usurp
your self: for what is yours to bestow is
not yours to reserve. But this is from my   205
Commission: I will on with my Speech in your
Praise, and then shew you the Heart of my
Message.

OLIVIA   Come to what is important in't: I forgive
you the Praise.   210

VIOLA   Alas, I took great Pains to study it, and
'tis Poetical.

OLIVIA   It is the more like to be feigned, I pray
you keep it in. I heard you were saucy at my
Gates, and allow'd your Approach rather to   215
wonder at you than to hear you. If you be not

216– **If . . . gone** [assuming that you have no real business with me,]
17 if you are not too insane to leave on your own power [before I
  have you ejected], be on your way.

217 **if . . . Reason** both (a) if you are in full control of your mind,
  and (b) if you have a legitimate reason to be here (a suit or
  message I haven't already refused to entertain in the past).

218– **'Tis . . . Dialogue** The present phase of the Moon is not
19 favourable to my taking part in so lunatic and frivolous a
  conversation.

220 **Will you** if you will. Compare line 167.

222 **Swabber** a sailor who keeps the ship's decks scrubbed clean.
  hull remain anchored. Viola dismisses Maria as a 'Handmaid'
  (I.i.24).

223 **Some . . . Giant** Viola is either excusing her insult to the
  diminutive Maria or asking the Lady to mollify (pacify) her.
  In medieval romances ladies were sometimes guarded by
  giants.

227 **Curtesy** courtesy (spelled *curtesie* in the Folio) plays on *cur*;
  compare *The Merchant of Venice*, I.iii.129–30.
  Fearful defiant, threatening.

228 **Speak your Office** Say what your duty bids you to say.

230 **Taxation of Homage** demand that you surrender and pay a
  tribute (tax).

231 **Olive** an 'Overture' (signal) of peace. Viola puns on 'Olivia'.
  She will soon discover that she does indeed 'hold the Olive' in
  her 'Hand'.

236 **my Entertainment** the way I have been received.

237 **as secret as Maidenhead** as private as a maiden's 'maidenhead',
  and as securely protected as her virginity.

239 **Profanation** irreverence, a violation of the sacredness of holy
  writ.

241 **this Divinity** Olivia's ostensible meaning is 'this divine
  discourse'. But subsequent events suggest that the phrase
  carries another, private meaning.

242 **your Text** Olivia picks up on 'Divinity' and plays on 'Text' as
  the biblical passage that will be the basis for the sermon to be
  delivered (another sense of 'Text').

Mad, be gone; if you have Reason, be brief.
'Tis not that time of Moon with me to make one
in so skipping a Dialogue.

MARIA   Will you hoist Sail, Sir, here lies your   220
Way.

VIOLA   No, good Swabber, I am to hull here a little
longer. – Some Mollification for your Giant,
sweet Lady; tell me your Mind, I am a
Messenger.   225

OLIVIA   Sure you have some Hideous Matter to
deliver, when the Curtesy of it is so Fearful.
Speak your Office.

VIOLA   It alone concerns your Ear. I bring no
Overture of War, no Taxation of Homage; I   230
hold the Olive in my Hand. My Words are as
full of Peace as Matter.

OLIVIA   Yet you began rudely. What are you? What
would you?

VIOLA   The Rudeness that hath appear'd in me have   235
I learn'd from my Entertainment. What I am,
and what I would, are as secret as Maidenhead:
to your Ears, Divinity; to any others',
Profanation.

OLIVIA   – Give us the Place alone: we will hear   240
this Divinity.   [*Exeunt all but Olivia and Viola.*]
– Now Sir, what is your Text?

VIOLA   Most sweet Lady.

OLIVIA   A comfortable Doctrine, and much may be
said of it. Where lies your Text?   245

VIOLA   In Orsino's Bosom.

OLIVIA   In his Bosom? In what Chapter of his Bosom?

---

244   **A comfortable Doctrine**   a divine teaching that comforts
(edifies) the faithful.

248 **by the Method** in accordance with liturgical and expository procedure.

250 **Heresy** false doctrine.

253 **Commission** authorization, charge. See lines 205–6.

255 **we** Olivia means 'I'; as a Countess, she is entitled to use the royal plural (based on the idea that a ruler embodied his or her people).
draw the Curtain remove the veil. Compare I.iii.124–25.

256– **such . . . Present** Olivia refers to her face as if it were a portrait
57 painted just a moment earlier.

259 **in Grain** indelible. Olivia means that the colours will hold fast (as opposed to 'water-colours', which can be washed off or smeared). Her implication is that she wears no cosmetics ('God did all').

261 **blent** blended, composed.

262 **cunning** skilled; literally, knowing.

265 **Copy** offspring. Viola makes explicit what she had implied in lines 203–5.

267 **divers Schedules** a number of lists. Olivia deliberately mis-takes *Copy* to refer to a piece of paper or a full transcript; she will provide not one but many. *Copy* (from the Latin word *copia*) almost meant 'copious abundance'.

268– **Particle and Utensil** particular and detail.
69

269 **labell'd** attached as a codicil (an addendum to a last will and testament).

270 **indifferent red** of an ordinary [not different] red hue.

276– **such . . . recompens'd** so intense is his love that at best it could
77 be reciprocated on equal terms [and never exceeded].

277 **though** even if.

278 **The Nonpareil of Beauty** the unparalleled example of beauty.

279 **fertile** abounding. See the note to line 267.

281 **Mind** resolve, disposition. Up to this point Olivia has declined to treat Orsino's ambassador with enough respect to address him in verse. From this point on, she speaks iambic pentameter and thereby signals that she regards the 'young Man' as a person of some dignity. *Mind* echoes line 224.

VIOLA   To answer by the Method, in the First of his
Heart.

OLIVIA   O, I have read it: it is Heresy. Have you   250
no more to say?

VIOLA   Good Madam, let me see your Face.

OLIVIA   Have you any Commission from your Lord to
negotiate with my Face? You are now out of
your Text: but we will draw the Curtain and   255
shew you the Picture. Look you, Sir, such a
one I was this Present: is't not well done?

VIOLA   Excellently done, if God did all.

OLIVIA   'Tis in Grain, Sir, 'twill endure Wind and
Weather.   260

VIOLA   'Tis Beauty truly blent, whose Red and White
Nature's own sweet and cunning Hand laid on.
Lady, you are the cruell'st She alive
If you will lead these Graces to the Grave
And leave the World no Copy.   265

OLIVIA   O Sir, I will not be so hard-hearted: I
will give out divers Schedules of my Beauty.
It shall be inventoried, and every Particle
and Utensil labell'd to my Will. As, Item, two
Lips indifferent red; Item, two grey Eyes,   270
with Lids to them; Item, one Neck, one Chin,
and so forth. Were you sent hither to praise
me?

VIOLA   I see you what you are, you are too Proud:
But if you were the Divel, you are Fair.   275
My Lord and Master loves you: O such Love
Could be but recompens'd, though you were
crown'd
The Nonpareil of Beauty.

OLIVIA   How does he love me?

VIOLA   With Adorations, fertile Tears,
With Groans that thunder Love, with Sighs of
Fire.   280

OLIVIA   Your Lord does know my Mind, I cannot love
him;

283 **fresh** unspoiled; pure and vital. Compare I.i.9, 30, I.ii.27.

284 **In Voices well divulg'd** well spoken of (of good reputation).
Free liberal, generous, noble. Compare line 101.

285 **Dimension . . . Nature** stature and appearance.

286 **A Gracious Person** a person endowed with many graces (gifts
and attractive features). *Person* often means 'body', and that
sense is applicable here.

288 **Flame** passion.

289 **deadly Life** a life little more desirable than death.

290 **Sense** reason. Orsino's difficulty, of course, is that he doesn't
appeal to Olivia's 'Sense' in the sense that relates to sexual
desire; before long, however, Orsino's messenger will find that
Olivia's erotic sensibility is capable of being ignited.

291 **what would you?** what would you do?

292 **a Willow Cabin** a shelter put together out of willow boughs
(willow being the symbol of pining love).

294 **loyal Cantons** true songs (cantos).
contemned Love love treated with contempt.

296 **Hallow** both (a) hallow (bless, as in the clause 'Hallowed be
thy name', Matthew 6:9), and (b) halloo, holler.
reverberate reverberating, echoing.

297 **the babbling Gossip of the Air** a personification of Echo.

299 **Between . . . Earth** anywhere on earth or in the air.

302 **yet . . . well** but my current social position is satisfactory, given
my inability to enjoy the 'Fortunes' normal to one of my
birth.
State estate, condition. Viola's phrasing echoes, and gives
prophetic implications to, what she has said in I.iii.36–39.

307 **spend this for me** At this point Olivia offers 'Cesario' a tip.
Perchance (line 305) echoes I.ii.4–6.

308 **Feed Post** messenger who accepts fees for his services.

310 **Love . . . love** May the God of Love punish you by making you
fall in love with a man whose heart will be as hard as flint.
Ironically, the 'curse' in lines 310–12 is being fulfilled even as
'Cesario' speaks.

Yet I suppose him Virtuous, know him Noble,
Of great Estate, of fresh and stainless Youth;
In Voices well divulg'd, Free, Learn'd, and
    Valiant;
And in Dimension, and the Shape of Nature,   285
A Gracious Person. But yet I cannot love him:
He might have took his Answer long ago.

VIOLA   If I did love you in my Master's Flame,
With such a Suff'ring, such a deadly Life,
In your Denial I would find no Sense,   290
I would not understand it.

OLIVIA   Why, what would you?

VIOLA   Make me a Willow Cabin at your Gate,
And call upon my Soul within the House;
Write loyal Cantons of contemned Love,
And sing them loud even in the dead of Night;   295
Hallow your Name to the reverberate Hills,
And make the babbling Gossip of the Air
Cry out 'Olivia'. O, you should not rest
Between the Elements of Air and Earth,
But you should pity me.

OLIVIA   You might do much: 300
What is your Parentage?

VIOLA   Above my Fortunes, yet my State is well:
I am a Gentleman.

OLIVIA   Get you to your Lord;
I cannot love him; let him send no more,
Unless, perchance, you come to me again,   305
To tell me how he takes it. Fare you well;
I thank you for your Pains; spend this for me.

VIOLA   I am no Feed Post, Lady; keep your Purse;
My Master, not my self, lacks Recompense.
Love make his Heart of Flint that you shall
    love,   310
And let your Fervour like my Master's be,

312 **Plac'd in Contempt** scorned contemptuously.

313 **'What ... Parentage?'** This short line is indented in this edition
to indicate a pause between Viola's exit and the beginning of
Olivia's reflections on what the 'Youth' said.

317 **Do ... Blazon** do proclaim you five times over to be a
gentleman. *Blazon*, a term from heraldry, refers either to one's
coat of arms or to a description of one's armorial insignia. As
a verb, *blazon* means 'proclaim'. Here its sound, echoing
blazing, is an indication of the passion that is now heating
Olivia's feverish blood (see line 319).
soft, soft stay, wait a moment. These two extrametrical words
retard the verse and thus accomplish dramatically precisely
what their sense calls for.

319 **catch the Plague** become 'infected' with Love's infatuation.
Plague echoes lines 131–32.

320 **Perfections** here pronounced as a four-syllable word.

324 **peevish** both (a) silly, and (b) petulant.

325 **Counte's** Here the metre calls for the two-syllable word
supplied by the Folio. Like *County*, the title of Paris in *Romeo
and Juliet*, *Counte* is an English version of the Italian word
conte. See the note to I.iii.107.

327 **Desire** request.
flatter with provide encouragement to.

328 **hold him up** maintain him. Olivia wants Orsino's passion to be
'put down' (I.iii.82) for good. The erotic suggestiveness of
hold him up is reinforced by *Reasons*, which sometimes plays
on *raisings* in Shakespeare (see *All's Well That Ends Well*,
I.iii.29–40), *hie*, a homonym for *high* (see *Romeo and Juliet*,
II.iv.69–79, and *Macbeth*, I.v.22, 27), and *come*, which can
refer to orgasm (see *Measure for Measure*, II.iv.31,
IV.i.45–51, 74–75).

329 **to morrow** tomorrow. But here as in I.iii.90, 104, other senses
of 'to morrow' may also be pertinent; compare *Macbeth*,
V.v.19–23, and see I.v.60–63 and II.iii.59–60 of the same
play.

330 **Hie** make haste.

Plac'd in Contempt. Farewell, fair Cruelty.   *Exit*.
OLIVIA   'What is your Parentage?'
  'Above my Fortunes, yet my State is well:
  I am a Gentleman.' I'll be sworn thou art: 315
  Thy Tongue, thy Face, thy Limbs, Actions, and
      Spirit
  Do give thee five-fold Blazon. – Not too fast:
      soft, soft,
  Unless the Master were the Man. How now?
  Even so quickly may one catch the Plague?
  Me thinks I feel this Youth's Perfections   320
  With an invisible and subtle Stealth
  To creep in at mine Eyes. Well, let it be.
  – What ho, Malvolio.

                Enter Malvolio.

MALVOLIO   Here Madam, at your Service.
OLIVIA   Run after that same peevish Messenger,
  The Counte's Man: he left this Ring behind him,   325
  Would I or not. Tell him I'll none of it.
  Desire him not to flatter with his Lord,
  Nor hold him up with Hopes; I am not for him.
  If that the Youth will come this way to morrow,
  I'll give him Reasons for't. Hie thee, Malvolio.   330
MALVOLIO   Madam, I will.   *Exit*.

332 **I ... what** I am behaving in a way that 'my Mind' cannot explain or justify. Olivia's words echo a number of New Testament passages, among them Romans 7:20, where the Apostle Paul says that 'I do that I would not'. Compare Galatians 5:17, where Paul notes that 'the flesh lusteth against the Spirit, and the Spirit against the flesh: and these are contrary the one to the other: so that ye cannot do the things that ye would.' Compare III.i.145–46.

333 **Flatterer** deceiver, one who curries favour by hiding or misinterpreting the truth. Compare line 327.

334 **Fate ... Force** Olivia is surrendering her mind and will to a power outside her own control. This is the first of several speeches in which characters in Illyria put their destinies in the hands of 'Fate', 'Time', or some other providential force beyond themselves. Compare II.ii.41–42, III.iv.404–5, IV.i.62–65, IV.iii.1–21, 34–35.

    owe own. Here the word has the implication of 'rule'. For Elizabethans it was axiomatic that a person owed everything to God, and 'owned' possessions only in the sense in which a steward was entrusted with certain goods or talents to use in keeping with his Lord's will; see the notes to lines 16, 204–5, and compare Luke 12:42–48.

335 **decreed** predetermined by Fate or Destiny.

OLIVIA – I do I know not what, and fear to find
  Mine Eye too great a Flatterer for my Mind.
  – Fate, shew thy Force. Our selves we do not
    owe,
  What is decreed must be: and be this so.   *Exit.*   335

II.i   This scene takes place on the coast of Illyria.

1   **stay** wait.

3   **By your patience** if you will allow me to appeal to your
        tolerance and forbearance.
        My Stars the stars and planets that govern my fortunes.

4   **The Malignancy of my Fate** both (a) the malevolent influence
        that besets my destiny, and (b) the disease that afflicts me.

5   **distemper** both (a) destabilize, and (b) infect. Like *Malignancy*,
        distemper is a word with both psychological and medical
        implications. Both words figure in the vocabulary of astrology
        as well. See I.v.99–100.

6   **leave** permission, consent.

7   **were** would be.
        Recompense reward. Compare I.v.276–78, 309.

9   **whither** to where.

10   **sooth** truly.
        determinate Voyage itinerary and proposed destination.

11   **mere Extravagancy** pure aimlessness. But line 45 suggests that
        Sebastian is simply trying to discourage Antonio from
        following him.

12   **Modesty** tact, gentle manners.

13   **extort from me** force out of me.
        I am willing I would prefer. Compare I.iii.45, I.v.119–20, 167,
        220.

14–15   **Therefore . . . self** For that reason I feel that out of courtesy I
        owe it to you to tell you voluntarily what you are too polite to
        ask. *Manners* recalls I.v.165–66 and anticipates lines 42–45.

16   **which I call'd** which I said was.

18   **Messaline** apparently a city of Shakespeare's invention. It may
        derive from the Latin name for Marseilles.

20   **borne in an Hour** twins. Here as in I.v.10, *borne* can mean
        both (a) born, and (b) borne, carried.

21   **would** I wish.

23   **Breach** probably a reference to the breaking waves. But *Breach*
        could also allude to the 'split' of the 'Ship' bearing Sebastian
        and his sister (I.ii.8), and to the separation of the twins that
        resulted.

ACT II

Scene 1

Enter Antonio and Sebastian.

ANTONIO   Will you stay no longer? Nor will you not
that I go with you?

SEBASTIAN   By your patience, no. My Stars shine
darkly over me. The Malignancy of my Fate
might perhaps distemper yours: therefore I   5
shall crave of you your leave that I may bear
my Evils alone. It were a bad Recompense for
your Love, to lay any of them on you.

ANTONIO   Let me know of you, whither you are bound.

SEBASTIAN   No, sooth, Sir: my determinate Voyage   10
is mere Extravagancy. But I perceive in you so
excellent a touch of Modesty that you will not
extort from me what I am willing to keep in.
Therefore it charges me in Manners, the rather
to express my self. You must know of me then,   15
Antonio, my name is Sebastian, which I call'd
Roderigo. My Father was that Sebastian of
Messaline, whom I know you have heard of. He
left behind him my self and a Sister, both
borne in an Hour. If the Heavens had been   20
pleas'd, would we had so ended. But you, Sir,
alter'd that, for some Hour before you took me
from the Breach of the Sea was my Sister
drown'd.

ANTONIO   Alas the Day.   25

SEBASTIAN   A Lady, Sir, though it was said she
much resembled me, was yet of many accounted
beautiful. But though I could not with such

29 **estimable Wonder** admiration worthy of the esteem of others. Sebastian is still being modest, declining to overpraise his sister in order to avoid appearing to praise himself for the identical qualities. *Wonder* echoes I.v.214–16.

30 **publish her** proclaim her to the world.

30–31 **she . . . Fair** Sebastian is praising his sister not only for her intelligence but also for her virtues. Since her mind ruled her senses and passions, she exhibited the kind of self-control that made her 'Fair' within (beautiful in her thoughts and motives) as well as without. Here *Envy* means both 'malice' and 'rivalry'.

34 **more** Sebastian refers to his tears. Compare I.i.25–31, where Valentine describes the 'Eye-offending Brine' with which Olivia would 'keep fresh' the 'Remembrance' of her brother. The phrase *salt Water* in line 32 links the sea to the salty tears it has occasioned. See the note to I.ii.34, and compare I.iii.128–30, I.v.172–73.

35 **Entertainment** treatment (inadequate hospitality). Compare I.v.235–36.

36 **your Trouble** the pains I have put you to in my distress.

37 **murther . . . Love** make my love for you prove to be the death of me.

40 **recover'd** rescued, restored to life.

43 **Manners of my Mother** a womanly disposition to cry. For other references to the shame men experience when they feel reduced to 'weaker vessels' (1 Peter 3:7), see *Hamlet*, IV.vii.181–87, *Macbeth*, IV.ii.27–29, and *The Merchant of Venice*, II.iii.13–14.

47 **Gentleness** benevolence, kind favour.

49 **see thee there** escort you there, see that you arrive there safely.

50 **But come what may** Antonio is saying that he has just changed his mind: whatever the risks he runs, he will follow Sebastian to 'Orsino's Court'.

II.ii This scene takes place on a street or road not far from Olivia's house.

estimable Wonder over-far believe that, yet
thus far I will boldly publish her, she bore   30
a Mind that Envy could not but call Fair. She
is drown'd already, Sir, with salt Water, though
I seem to drown her Remembrance again
with more.

ANTONIO   Pardon me, Sir, your bad Entertainment.   35

SEBASTIAN   O good Antonio, forgive me your Trouble.

ANTONIO   If you will not murther me for my Love,
let me be your Servant.

SEBASTIAN   If you will not undo what you have done
(that is, kill him whom you have recover'd),   40
desire it not. Fare ye well at once; my Bosom
is full of Kindness, and I am yet so near the
Manners of my Mother that upon the least
Occasion more mine Eyes will tell Tales of
me. I am bound to the Count Orsino's Court;   45
farewell.   *Exit.*

ANTONIO   The Gentleness of all the Gods go with
thee.
I have many Enemies in Orsino's Court,
Else would I very shortly see thee there:
But come what may, I do adore thee so   50
That Danger shall seem Sport, and I will go.
                                                   Exit.

Scene 2

Enter Viola and Malvolio at several Doors.

MALVOLIO   Were not you ev'n now with the Countess
Olivia?

VIOLA   Even now, Sir; on a moderate pace I have
since arriv'd but hither.

MALVOLIO   She returns this Ring to you, Sir. You   5
might have sav'd me my Pains, to have taken it

8–9   **put . . . him** assure your Lord that his suit is 'desperate' (hopeless), because my Lady will have nothing to do with him. Compare I.v.327–28. *Pains* (line 6) echoes I.v.189, 211, 307.

10   **hardy** bold, foolhardy. See the note to lines 10–11.

10–11 **in his Affairs** representing him in this matter. Like *hardy* (which hints at tumescence, as in I.iii.107), *come* is suggestive here in ways that Malvolio scarcely imagines; see the note to I.v.328.

11–12 **your Lord's taking of this** how your Lord receives (a) this message, and (b) her refusal to accept the ring you have brought her from him.

13   **She . . . me** Viola knows, of course, that she has not brought a ring to Olivia; it is therefore of interest that she plays along with Olivia's fiction without letting Malvolio in on the secret.

14   **you peevishly threw it to her** Malvolio is extrapolating from what Olivia told him in I.v.324–25.

15   **her Will** her wish. What Malvolio doesn't realize is that Olivia's 'Will' (her erotic infatuation) is involved in this transaction in an even deeper sense. See the notes to I.iii.86–87, and compare Sonnets 135, 136. *Will* recalls II.i.13.

16   **there it lies** As he speaks, Malvolio tosses the ring to the ground.

16–17 **in your Eye** where you can see it (and pick it up if you so desire).

19   **charm'd** captivated, placed under a spell.

21   **her Eyes had lost her Tongue** she was so preoccupied with staring at me that she had forgotten how to speak.

23   **the Cunning of her Passion** the cleverness or devising to which her emotions prompt her. See the note to III.i.123.

away your self. She adds, moreover, that you
should put your Lord into a desperate Assurance,
she will none of him. And one thing more, that
you be never so hardy to come again in his   10
Affairs, unless it be to report your Lord's
taking of this: receive it so.

VIOLA   She took the Ring of me, I'll none of it.

MALVOLIO   Come Sir, you peevishly threw it to her:
and her Will is, it should be so return'd. If   15
it be worth stooping for, there it lies, in
your Eye; if not, be it his that finds it.   *Exit.*

VIOLA   — I left no Ring with her: what means this
        Lady?
Fortune forbid my Outside have not charm'd her.
She made good View of me, indeed so much   20
That me thought her Eyes had lost her Tongue,
For she did speak in Starts distractedly.
She loves me sure, the Cunning of her Passion
Invites me in this churlish Messenger.
None of my Lord's Ring? Why he sent her none;   25
I am the Man, if it be so, as 'tis,

---

26   **I am the Man**   Viola means 'I am the man she loves'. But *Man*
        also means 'servant', and she is Orsino's man in that sense.
        Viola's phrasing reminds us that the young man portraying
        Olivia in the Elizabethan theatre (which permitted no
        actresses on public stages) would himself have been a 'Man'
        (servant) in the livery of the Lord Chamberlain, official patron
        of Shakespeare's acting company. See the note to I.iv.35.
        Most editions place a semicolon or a full stop after 'Man'. But
        an equally good case could be made for such punctuation
        after ''tis'. Given that ambiguity, Everyman simply retains the
        punctuation in the Folio text.

27   **were better**   would be better off to.

29   **pregnant Enemy**   Viola refers to Satan, who is 'pregnant' (filled to capacity) with wicked schemes. See the note to lines 10–11. The phrase *does much* echoes I.v.300.

30   **the proper False**   men whose falseness (deceptiveness) is disguised by their 'proper' (benign, handsome, seemingly appropriate) appearance.

31   **In Women's . . . Forms**   to seal (imprint) their images (the designs on their signet rings) in the wax that comprises women's soft hearts.

32   **Frailty**   weakness. See the note to II.i.43, and compare *Hamlet*, I.ii.146, and *Measure for Measure*, II.iv.126–40.

34   **fadge**   turn out, come off.

35   **fond**   infatuated (foolishly doting). Viola calls herself a *Monster* because of the ambiguity of her gender. Like a hermaphrodite, she is neither wholly male nor wholly female at present; she is sexually undefined, appearing to be a man on the 'Outside' (line 19), but knowing herself to be a woman on the inside. See the notes to I.iv.35, I.v.200.

40   **thriftless**   unprofitable, unavailing, literally, 'unthriving'.
      breath   breathe.

42   **Knot**   To a theatre audience *Knot* would be indistinguishable from *not*, and that sense applies to the 'not' Olivia has decreed in answer to Orsino's suit.

II.iii   This scene takes place in Olivia's household.

2   **betimes**   early.

2–3   **deliculo surgere**   Sir Toby refers to the Latin maxim, '*Diliculo surgere saluberrimum est*' (to arise at dawn is healthful). English schoolboys learned it at grammar school.

4   **I know not**   Not having 'followed the Arts', Sir Andrew is incapable of following Sir Toby's witty sophistry. The only response he can manage is a tautology (defining a thing in terms of itself) whose sole virtue is to be in accord with common sense. Here as in line 19, *troth* means 'faith'.

7   **Can**   tankard, a drinking vessel for ale.

9–10   **Does . . . Elements?**   Are not our lives (our bodies and everything in the world that influences them) constituted by the four elements? Sir Toby states the most basic principle of Elizabethan science: the view that all matter is comprised of the elements of Earth, Water, Air, and Fire.

Poor Lady, she were better love a Dream.
— Disguise, I see thou art a Wickedness,
Wherein the pregnant Enemy does much.
— How easy is it for the proper False   30
In Women's waxen Hearts to set their Forms.
Alas, O Frailty is the Cause, not we,
For such as we are made, if such we be.
How will this fadge? My Master loves her
      dearly,
And I, poor Monster, fond as much on him;   35
And she, mistaken, seems to dote on me.
What will become of this? As I am Man,
My State is desperate for my Maister's Love;
As I am Woman (now alas the Day),
What thriftless Sighs shall poor Olivia
      breath?   40
— O Time, thou must untangle this, not I:
It is too hard a Knot for me t' untie.   [*Exit.*]

Scene 3

Enter Sir Toby, and Sir Andrew.

TOBY   Approach, Sir Andrew: not to be a-Bed after
   Midnight is to be up betimes, and '*deliculo
   surgere*', thou know'st.
ANDREW   Nay by my troth I know not: but I know, to
   be up Late, is to be up Late.   5
TOBY   A false Conclusion: I hate it as an unfill'd
   Can. To be up after Midnight, and to go to Bed
   then, is early: so that to go to Bed after
   Midnight is to go to Bed betimes. Does not our
   Lives consist of the four Elements?   10
ANDREW   Faith, so they say, but I think it rather
   consists of Eating and Drinking.

13   **Scholar** Sir Toby means 'expert in eating and drinking'.
        Compare I.iii.25–29, 84–99.

14   **stoup** a large vessel.

16   **Harts** both (a) noble stags, and (b) hearts. Compare *Hamlet*,
        III.ii.296–300, V.ii.371, and *A Midsummer Night's Dream*,
        IV.ii.25–26.

17   **Picture of 'We Three'** Feste alludes to a picture (often to be
        seen on the signboards of Elizabethan inns) showing two fools
        or assheads and bearing the caption 'We Three'. It carried the
        implication that the viewer of the picture constituted the third
        member of the group. The idea was also conveyed through a
        'perspective' painting that showed two fools when looked at
        straight on and added an ass when viewed from a side angle.
        See the note to V.i.221.

18   **a Catch** a round to be sung by three or more unaccompanied
        voices ('Brother John' is a familiar example).

20   **Breast** both (a) chest, and (b) 'Breath' (line 21), singing voice,
        resonance.

21   **Leg** both (a) strong and nimble limb, and (b) dancing
        technique. Compare I.iii.119–42.

23   **gracious Fooling** Sir Andrew probably means gifted (inspired)
        wit.

24–25   **Pigrogromitus . . . Queubus** Assuming that Sir Andrew has
        accurately recalled what he heard, this nonsense is probably
        the Fool's parody of learned scholastic discourse. The
        'Equinoctial' was the equator of the celestial spheres; it may
        be, then, that 'Queubus' is an alphabetical sequel to 'Phoebus'
        (the Sun). *Queubus* may also play on *Cubus*, the Earth in
        Platonic cosmology, and on *quivis*, Latin for 'anyone you
        please' (a variation on 'what you will'). *Vapians* may refer to
        those who take it easy. And *Pigrogromitus* has been glossed as
        a coinage meaning 'lazy scab'. Another reading of the passage
        takes *Vapians* to refer to foul vapours, *Equinoctial* to refer to
        the anus, and *Queubus* to refer to a 'buss' (kiss) on the *queue*
        (French for 'tail').

26   **Lemon** Sir Andrew may mean 'Leman', mistress, but it is not
        inconceivable that he refers to the citrus fruit (as Berowne
        does, with bawdy innuendo, in *Love's Labour's Lost*,
        V.ii.636), perhaps because Feste was using a lemon as a prop
        in his 'Fooling'.

TOBY   Th'art a Scholar: let us therefore eat and
drink. – Marian, I say, a stoup of Wine.

Enter Clown.

ANDREW   Here comes the Fool i'faith.   15
CLOWN   How now, my Harts. Did you never see the
Picture of 'We Three'?
TOBY   Welcome, Ass, now let's have a Catch.
ANDREW   By my troth, the Fool has an excellent
Breast. I had rather than forty Shillings I   20
had such a Leg, and so sweet a Breath to sing,
as the Fool has. – In sooth, thou wast in very
gracious Fooling last night, when thou spok'st
of Pigrogromitus, of the Vapians passing the
Equinoctial of Queubus: 'twas very good,   25
i'faith. I sent thee six Pence for thy Lemon;
hadst it?
CLOWN   I did impeticos thy Gratilllity: for
Malvolio's Nose is no Whip-stock. My Lady has

---

28   **I did . . . Gratillity**   probably Fool-talk for 'I did "empetticoat"
[pocket up] your tiny gratuity'. Feste may mean that he spent
Sir Andrew's gratuity on a 'petticoat', a wench; compare 2
Henry IV, II.ii.89–90, where Falstaff's page says that he
thought his master 'had made two Holes in the Alewive's
Petticoat and so peeped through', and III.ii.164–66, where
Falstaff asks a would-be soldier, 'Wilt thou make as many
Holes in an Enemy's Battaile as thou hast done in a Woman's
Petticoat?'

29   **Whip-stock**   whip-handle. The Fool implies that Malvolio's
nose (which he is always inserting into everyone else's
business) is harmless (not attached to a real whip). See the
note to V.i.382.

30–31 **the Mermidons . . . Houses** 'Bottle-ale Houses' are taverns that
serve cheap ale. It has been speculated that the Fool alludes to
one or more that bore images of the Myrmidons (the
henchmen of Achilles) on their signs. He may also be playing
on *mermaidens*, with the implication that Lady Olivia's
steward is more of a decorative mermaid than a virile,
daunting Myrmidon. Malvolio may have a large 'Nose', Feste
implies, but he lacks a real man's 'Whipstock'. Compare the
'Nose' imagery in *Antony and Cleopatra*, I.ii.54–56, and the
'Whip' references in *Love's Labour's Lost*, III.i.181–210,
V.i.70–71.

36 **Testril** Sir Andrew's name for a tester, a sixpence coin.

38–39 **a Song of Good Life** The Fool probably means a drinking song
about 'the good life' (the pleasures of the flesh); Sir Andrew
seems to fear that Feste is offering to inflict on them a song
about virtue.

47 **Wise Man's Son** It was proverbial that wise men's sons were
often fools. Here the Clown's implication is that even a 'Son'
who is not 'Wise' looks forward to the 'coming' (line 43,
echoing II.ii.10–11) that signifies 'Lovers Meeting' (line 46).

52 **still** always. Here *to come* means 'yet to come'; see the note to
line 47.

53 **In Delay . . . Plenty** This moral is related to the advice Viola
gives Olivia in I.v.263–65. But *Plenty* can refer to pleasure as
well as to fruit (offspring), and the primary burden of this
love-song is that because 'Youth's a stuff will not endure', we
should seize 'Present Mirth' while it is offered to us.

54 **sweet and twenty** either (a) twenty times as sweetly as sweet,
or (b) sweetly twenty times over.

56 **mellifluous** flowing with honey.

57 **contagious** Sir Toby means 'catching' (seductive), with puns on
(a) a musical 'catch', and (b) 'catching' an infection (thus
implying foul 'Breath'). In line 66 Feste plays on two other
senses: (c) grab and fetch like a dog, and (d) grip like a latch
(another kind of 'dog'). *Catch* (line 62) echoes line 18.

60 **the Welkin** the heavens.

a white Hand, and the Mermidons are no Bottle-   30
ale Houses.

ANDREW   Excellent: why this is the best Fooling,
when all is done. Now a Song.

TOBY   Come on, there is six Pence for you. Let's
have a Song.   35

ANDREW   There's a Testril of me too: if one Knight
give a —

CLOWN   Would you have a Love-song, or a Song of
Good Life?

TOBY   A Love-song, a Love-song.   40

ANDREW   Ay, ay. I care not for Good Life.

CLOWN *sings*

> *O Mistress mine, where are you roaming?*
> *O stay and hear: your true Love's coming,*
>   *That can sing both high and low.*
> *Trip no further, pretty Sweeting:*   45
> *Journeys end in Lovers Meeting,*
>   *Every Wise Man's Son doth know.*

ANDREW   Excellent good, i'faith.

TOBY   Good, good.

CLOWN

> What is Love, 'tis not hereafter,   50
> Present Mirth hath present Laughter;
>   What's to come is still unsure.
> In Delay there lies no Plenty,
> Then come kiss me sweet and twenty:
>   Youth's a stuff will not endure.   55

ANDREW   A mellifluous Voice, as I am true Knight.

TOBY   A contagious Breath.

ANDREW   Very sweet and contagious i'faith.

TOBY   To hear by the Nose, it is Dulcet in
Contagion. But shall we make the Welkin dance   60

62-63 **draw three Souls out of one Weaver** Sir Toby alludes to the view that music had the power to put one into an ecstasy (literally, a state of being 'beside oneself', with one's soul seemingly transported out of one's body). Weavers were noted for their love of psalms set to music. *Three* recalls lines 16–17 and anticipates lines 83–84.

64 **And** if.

71 **constrain'd** compelled.

73-74 **constrain'd . . . Knave** driven someone to call me Knave, probably both (a) in a catch, and (b) in a quarrel. *Knave* was often contrasted with *Knight* and could mean either (a) valet, or (b) villain.

75 **Hold thy peace** remain silent. But in line 76 Feste puns on *piece* ('piece of Flesh,' as in *Romeo and Juliet*, I.i.31–32), with implications similar to those of another court jester in *King Lear*, I.iv.198.

76 **hold** both (a) grasp, and (b) withhold, constrain. See the note to line 75.

78 **Caterwauling** the groaning and howling of a cat at mating time. Maria's image suggests that these merry 'dogs' sound more like frustrated felines. The Folio spelling, *catterwalling*, suggests a tom cat atop a wall as he awaits his encounter with a female in heat.

82 **Catayan** Cathayan (Chinese). The word often carried the implication of a person not to be trusted. But Sir Toby may also be suggesting that 'my Lady's' scolding is another form of caterwauling.
    Politicians Sir Toby probably means clever intriguers, with the implication that 'we can outwit both my Lady and her Steward'.

83 **Peg-a-Ramsey** This phrase implies that Malvolio is no more to be feared than a spoilsport scarecrow. The name *Peg-a-Ramsey* derives from a ribald ballad, and here it appears to allude to a nosy, guard-like matron; see the notes to lines 29, 30–31. But it could also refer to a wanton female, and thus imply that, for all his strictness of manner, Malvolio is harbouring a lustful imagination. In this speech, as elsewhere, the italicized passages (reproduced as they appear in the Folio) probably indicate snatches of popular ballads that are to be sung by their speakers.

84 **consanguinious** her kinsman, 'of her Blood' (line 85).

indeed? Shall we rouse the Night-owl in a
Catch, that will draw three Souls out of one
Weaver? Shall we do that?

ANDREW   And you love me, let's do't. I am a Dog
at a Catch.   65

CLOWN   By'r Lady, Sir, and some Dogs will catch
well.

ANDREW   Most certain: let our Catch be 'Thou
Knave'.

CLOWN   'Hold thy peace, thou Knave', Knight. I   70
shall be constrain'd in't to call thee Knave,
Knight.

ANDREW   'Tis not the first time I have constrain'd
one to call me Knave. Begin, Fool: it begins,
'Hold thy peace'.   75

CLOWN   I shall never begin if I hold my peace.

ANDREW   Good i'faith: come begin.   *Catch sung.*

Enter Maria.

MARIA   What a Caterwauling do you keep here? If my
Lady have not call'd up her Steward Malvolio,
and bid him turn you out of Doors, never trust   80
me.

TOBY   My Lady's a Catayan, we are Politicians,
Malvolio's a Peg-a-Ramsey, and *Three Merry
Men be We*. Am not I consanguinious? Am I not
of her Blood: tilly-vally. Lady, *There dwelt a*   85
Man in Babylon, Lady, Lady.

---

85   **tilly-vally**   a term of dismissal, equivalent to 'fiddle-faddle.'

85–86 **There . . . Babylon**   Sir Toby quotes the first line of a ballad
        about the Elders' lust for 'Constant Susanna' in the
        Apocrypha.

87   **Beshrew**   curse.

91   **more natural**   Sir Andrew probably means 'with less artifice and
       fewer allusions'. But *Natural* also meant 'fool or idiot', as in
       I.iii.29.

92   **Twelfe**   This is the normal spelling of 'twelfe' in the Folio text,
       which renders the title *Twelfe Night*.

95   **Wit**   common sense. Compare I.v.34.

96   **Tinkers**   itinerant menders of pots and pans. Tinkers were
       noted for drunkenness.

98   **Coziers'**   cobblers' (shoe-menders').

99   **Mitigation or Remorse of Voice**   moderation of your voices out
       of deference to others at this late hour.

101   **keep Time**   maintain proper rhythm. Malvolio meant 'be
       mindful of the time of night'.

101–2 **Sneck up**   Go hang yourself. Compare I.v.1–21.

103   **be round**   speak plainly and openly (having done with all
       beating around the bush).

104   **harbours you**   shelters and protects you; gives you residence.
       Here as in I.v.57, 59, *bad* is the Elizabethan form for *bade*.

105   **nothing allied**   in no way akin or in sympathy with.

111– **Farewell . . . gone**   Here and in the lines that follow, Sir Toby
  12   and Feste quote (and probably sing) snatches from a ballad,
       'Corydon's Farewell to Phyllis'.

CLOWN Beshrew me, the Knight's in admirable
Fooling.
ANDREW Ay, he does well enough if he be dispos'd,
and so do I too: he does it with a better grace,   90
but I do it more natural.
TOBY *O the Twelfe Day of December.*
MARIA For the love o' God, peace.

Enter Malvolio.

MALVOLIO My Masters, are you Mad? Or what are you?
Have you no Wit, Manners, nor Honesty, but to   95
gabble like Tinkers at this time of Night? Do
ye make an Alehouse of my Lady's House, that
ye squeak out your Coziers' Catches without
any Mitigation or Remorse of Voice? Is there
no Respect of Place, Persons, nor Time in you?   100
TOBY We did keep Time, Sir, in our Catches. Sneck
up.
MALVOLIO Sir Toby, I must be round with you. My Lady
bad me tell you that though she harbours you
as her Kinsman, she's nothing allied to your   105
Disorders. If you can separate your self and
your Misdemeanours, you are welcome to the
House; if not, and it would please you to
take leave of her, she is very willing to bid
you farewell.   110
TOBY *Farewell, dear Heart, since I must needs be
gone.*
MARIA Nay good Sir Toby.
CLOWN *His Eyes do shew his Days are almost done.*
MALVOLIO Is't even so?   115
TOBY *But I will never die.*
CLOWN *Sir Toby, there you lie.*
MALVOLIO This is much Credit to you.
TOBY *Shall I bid him go?*

123 **Out o' Tune, Sir, ye lie** Sir Toby tells Malvolio, who is only a 'Steward' (chief household servant), that he is the one who is showing 'no Respect of Place, Persons, nor Time' (line 100). By failing to recognize his own position in society, and the higher station of the persons he is addressing so archly, Malvolio has committed a serious breach of etiquette and social harmony. Many editors emend the Folio's *tune* to *time*; but the two words, and concepts, were so closely associated in Shakespeare's time as to be virtually interchangeable. Compare *Hamlet*, III.i.162, where Ophelia describes the Prince's 'Reason' as 'Like sweet Bells jangled out of Time, and Harsh' in the Second Quarto, and 'out of tune' in the First Folio printing. Also see *King Lear*, IV.iii.40–43, and *Richard II*, V.v.40–47.

125– **Cakes and Ale** a combination traditionally symbolic of
26 merrymaking (particularly on holidays and other festive occasions). Puritans opposed such revelry.

127 **Saint Anne** mother of the Virgin Mary.
Ginger This spice was frequently added to ale.

129– **rub . . . Crumbs** polish the gold chain you wear as a symbol of
30 your position, perhaps with crumbs from the cakes you would take away from others.

130 **stope** stoup. Compare line 14. Sir Toby's pronunciation may be a sign of his inebriation; it may also be intended as a play on *stop*, in defiance of Malvolio's attempts to impede the carousing.

133 **give Means** supply the wine (requested in line 130).
Uncivil Rule this 'rule' (misrule) of uncivilised behaviour. 'Uncivil Rule', a temporary suspension of normal decorum, was one of the traditions of Twelfth Night, when it was customary to mock authority and turn the normal social hierarchy upside down in irreverent pageants. *Contempt* (line 132) recalls I.v.310–12.

135 **Go shake your Ears** a dismissive remark implying that the overbearing Malvolio is an ass.

137– **to challenge . . . him** to challenge him to a duel and then fail to
38 show up for the encounter. This is 'Indignation' (line 141) indeed. It is characteristic of Sir Andrew that he believes he'd make another man look foolish by the cowardly, disreputable device he describes.

145 **out of Quiet** disquieted, in a state of agitation.

CLOWN *What and if you do?*   120

TOBY *Shall I bid him go, and spare not?*

CLOWN *O no, no, no, no, you dare not.*

TOBY – Out o' Tune, Sir, ye lie. Art any more than
a Steward? Dost thou think because thou art
Virtuous, there shall be no more Cakes and   125
Ale?

CLOWN Yes by Saint Anne, and Ginger shall be hot
i'th' Mouth too.

TOBY Th'art i'th' right. – Go Sir, rub your
Chain with Crumbs. – A stope of Wine, Maria.   130

MALVOLIO – Mistress Mary, if you priz'd my Lady's
Favour at any thing more than Contempt, you
would not give Means for this Uncivil Rule;
she shall know of it, by this Hand.   *Exit.*

MARIA Go shake your Ears.   135

ANDREW 'Twere as good a Deed as to drink when a
Man's a-hungry, to challenge him the Field,
and then to break Promise with him, and make a
Fool of him.

TOBY Do't, Knight, I'll write thee a Challenge: 140
or I'll deliver thy Indignation to him by word
of Mouth.

MARIA Sweet Sir Toby, be patient for to night.
Since the Youth of the Count's was to day with
my Lady, she is much out of Quiet. For   145

146 **let me alone with him** leave it to me to deal with him. *Malnolio*
may be a misprint; but it may also be a parody of Malvolio's
name that satirizes his nay-saying and his nose (see lines
28–31). Compare I.iii.46, II.iii.30, and see the note to line
130.

147 **gull** trick, fool.
Ay-word byword (a name proverbially associated with 'gull' or
its equivalent). Here *ay* may mean 'aye' (forever). Many
editions emend to 'a nayword'. Either would continue the
wordplay on *no* if the Folio's *Malnolio* is correct in line 146.
To a theatre audience 'an Ay-word' would sound much the
same as 'a Nay-word'.

148 **a common Recreation** a laughingstock for everyone.

151 **Possess us** make us possessors of your secret; let us in on your
plan.

153 **Puritan** Maria means a straitlaced moralist, such as those
reformers who agitated to simplify the rituals of the Church
of England and to enforce tight controls on merrymaking and
other pleasures.

156 **exquisite** choice, fastidious.

161 **Time-pleaser** time-server, obsequious sycophant (an apt
description in light of line 100). Like 'affection'd [affected]
Ass', this term captures Malvolio's zeal to please, to 'con
State' (memorize terms and practise mannerisms that will
make him appear to be a courtier rather than a mere steward).
Cons recalls I.v.188–89.

163 **by great Swarths** in large swaths (quantities). The phrase
without Book echoes I.iii.27.

163– **The . . . himself** holding himself in the highest esteem.
64

165– **his grounds of Faith** the basis of his self-concept, his conceit.
66

167 **that Vice** Maria's diagnosis recalls Olivia's earlier observation
that Malvolio is 'sick of Self-love' (I.v.99).

170 **in his way** along his normal passage. *Way* recalls I.v.220–21.
obscure veiled in shadow, ambiguous.

Monsieur Malnolio, let me alone with him: if
I do not gull him into an Ay-word, and make
him a common Recreation, do not think I have
Wit enough to lie straight in my Bed. I know
I can do it.   150

TOBY   Possess us, possess us, tell us something of
him.

MARIA   Marry Sir, sometimes he is a kind of Puritan.

ANDREW   O, if I thought that, I'd beat him like a
Dog.   155

TOBY   What, for being a Puritan? Thy exquisite
Reason, dear Knight.

ANDREW   I have no exquisite Reason for't, but I
have Reason good enough.

MARIA   The div'l a Puritan that he is, or any   160
thing constantly but a Time-pleaser, an
affection'd Ass, that cons State without
Book, and utters it by great Swarths. The
best persuaded of himself: so cramm'd, as he
thinks, with Excellencies that it is his   165
grounds of Faith that all that look on him
love him. And on that Vice in him will my
Revenge find notable Cause to work.

TOBY   What wilt thou do?

MARIA   I will drop in his way some obscure Epistles   170
of Love, wherein by the Colour of his Beard,

172 **Gate** gait. But here as in I.iv.16, *Gate* can also allude to a
gateway. It relates to Malvolio's vanity that he has unimpeded
access to his Lady and unrestricted means of denying entrance
to those her gatekeeper regards as unfit for her company. See
the note to line 83. *Gate* echoes I.v.109, 136–37, 214–15,
291–92.

173 **Expressure** expression. The context suggests that the word
refers specifically to indentations (furrows and wrinkles).

175 **feelingly personated** movingly and precisely described.

176– **on ... Hands** when we are looking at a piece of writing that
77 neither of us can remember, we can barely tell whose
handwriting it is.

181 **they** the contents.

183 **Purpose** 'Device' (line 178), stratagem. *Purpose* could also
refer to a thought or riddle to be 'smelled out' in a festive
guessing game.
a ... Colour Maria's expression is proverbial, and in this
context it suggests that her 'Purpose' will have the same effect
on Malvolio that the Trojan Horse had on those who were
beguiled to take it inside the gates of Troy. *Colour* echoes line
171 and anticipates II.v.211–13.

185 **Ass ... not** Maria is punning on the phrase 'as I doubt not'.
Meanwhile, she is calling Sir Andrew an ass as well.

186 **admirable** both (a) to be wondered at, and (b) to be praised.

187 **Physic** medicine, medical treatment. Maria continues the idea
that Malvolio needs to be cured of an illness.

190 **his Construction of it** both (a) how he construes (interprets) it,
and (b) how he builds on it in his imagination. See the note to
III.i.123.

193 **Penthisilea** Penthesilia, Queen of the Amazons, a tribe of
warlike women eventually conquered by Theseus.

194 **Before me** a mild oath meaning 'on my soul'.

195 **Beagle** a dog, normally used for hunting hares, but often kept
as a pet.

196 **what o' that?** but so what?

197 **ador'd** One meaning of *dored* is 'made a fool of', and without
realizing it Sir Andrew is reminding his listeners that 'many do
call me Fool' (II.v.88).

the Shape of his Leg, the Manner of his Gate,
the Expressure of his Eye, Forehead, and
Complexion, he shall find himself most
feelingly personated. I can write very like   175
my Lady your Niece; on a forgotten matter we
can hardly make distinction of our Hands.

TOBY   Excellent, I smell a Device.

ANDREW   I have't in my Nose too.

TOBY   He shall think by the Letters that thou wilt   180
drop that they come from my Niece, and that
she's in love with him.

MARIA   My Purpose is indeed a Horse of that Colour.

ANDREW   And your Horse now would make him an Ass.

MARIA   Ass, I doubt not.   185

ANDREW   O 'twill be admirable.

MARIA   Sport Royal, I warrant you: I know my Physic
will work with him. I will plant you two, and
let the Fool make a third, where he shall find
the Letter: observe his Construction of it.   190
For this night to Bed, and dream on the Event.
Farewell.

TOBY   Good night, Penthisilea.   *Exit* [*Maria*].

ANDREW   Before me she's a good Wench.

TOBY   She's a Beagle true bred, and one that adores   195
me: what o' that?

ANDREW   I was ador'd once too.

TOBY   Let's to Bed, Knight. Thou hadst need send
for more Money.

200–1 **If . . . out** If I fail to win your niece, I am out of a great deal of money. The expression 'a foul way out' literally refers to losing one's way and getting stuck in the mire.

203   **Cut** Sir Toby probably refers to the name of a horse or dog with a docked (cut) tail; both were considered inferior. But *Cut* was also a term for (a) a gelding (a castrated horse), and (b) the female genitalia (comparable to 'Fault', referring to a woman's lack of a hanging 'tail'). Compare the use of *cut* as a verb in I.iii.120–21, and see II.v.94–98. The phrase *i'th'End* reinforces the genital sense. Another pertinent meaning of *Cut* is 'cut in the head', an expression that meant 'drunk'. By the final scene of the play an inebriated Sir Toby will suffer a literal laceration, a 'bloody Coxcomb' (V.i.178).

206   **burn some Sack** heat up some Spanish wine and spice it with brown sugar.

II.iv   This scene takes place at Orsino's palace.

3   **antic** quaint. Here *antic* may also mean 'antique' (old-fashioned). Compare *Hamlet*, I.v.163, V.ii.353.

4   **Passion** emotional distress. Compare I.iv.25, II.ii.23–24.

5   **light Airs** frivolous tunes.
   recollected Terms Just what this phrase means is subject to debate. One possibility is that *recollected* means 're-collected' (recycled with newfangled variations). Another possibility is that it refers to terms that are artificial, ready-made, and clichéd.

6   **brisk and giddy-paced Times** Orsino is contrasting the dizzying pace of the present with a more settled and dignified era in the past. Compare line 33.

7   **but** only.

8–9   **He . . . it?** Most editions emend the Folio's question mark to a full stop. But Curio's reply may be interrogative rather than declarative.

13   **about** somewhere around.

18   **Unstaid . . . else** unstable and mercurial in every other thought or emotion. What Orsino describes in lines 18–20 is lovers' inability to concentrate for more than a moment on anything other than thoughts of the objects of their affections.

ANDREW   If I cannot recover your Niece, I am a foul   200
   way out.
TOBY   Send for Money, Knight, if thou hast her not
   i'th' End, call me Cut.
ANDREW   If I do not, never trust me, take it how
   you will.   205
TOBY   Come, come, I'll go burn some Sack. 'Tis too
   late to go to Bed now. Come Knight, come
   Knight.   *Exeunt.*

Scene 4

Enter Duke, Viola, Curio, and Others.

DUKE   Give me some Music. — Now good morrow,
   Friends.
   — Now good Cesario. — But that piece of Song,
   That old and antic Song we heard last night,
   Me thought it did relieve my Passion much,
   More than light Airs, and recollected Terms   5
   Of these most brisk and giddy-paced Times.
   Come, but one Verse.
CURIO   He is not here, so please your Lordship,
   that should sing it?
DUKE   Who was it?   10
CURIO   Feste the Jester, my Lord, a Fool that the
   Lady Olivia's Father took much delight in. He
   is about the House.
DUKE   Seek him out, and play the Tune the while.
                    [*Exit Curio.*] *Music plays.*
   — Come hither, Boy. If ever thou shalt love,   15
   In the sweet Pangs of it remember me:
   For such as I am, all true Lovers are,
   Unstaid and skittish in all Motions else
   Save in the constant Image of the Creature
   That is belov'd. How dost thou like this Tune?   20

21   **It . . . Seat** it echoes (vibrates in harmony with) the throne (heart).

24   **stay'd . . . Favour** lingered upon and thus been captivated by some face.

25   **by your Favour** This phrase normally meant something equivalent to 'by your grace' or 'if you'll pardon me'. Here Viola says it with a private implication: 'by your face'. Her other answers during this exchange are similarly double in their meanings.

26   **Complexion** both (a) appearance, and (b) disposition. The word originally referred to one's 'complex' (mixture) of humours (substances derived from the four elements that comprised all matter). See the note to II.iii.9–10.

27   **Years** age.

29   **still** always.

30   **so wears she to him** either (a) so she fits herself to him, or (b) so she serves him as a garment that he finds well fitting.

31   **So sways she level** so she holds her own as a levelling influence, balancing the forces in his heart and serving as a counterweight (as on a pair of scales) to his own 'Fancies' (line 33). *Sways* anticipates II.v.116.

33   **Fancies** affections, loves.
      giddy and unfirm unstable and inconstant. See line 6.

34   **longing** desiring what they lack.

37   **hold the Bent** maintain the intensity (as with a bow pulled back to shoot an arrow).

39   **display'd** opened up in full bloom. *Flow'r* recalls I.v.55–56.

41   **die** wither and 'fall' (line 39). But Viola may also be using *die* in the erotic sense that refers to orgasm, a kind of 'Perfection' (completion) that causes women to 'fall' (yield, line 39) and 'grow' in another sense: become pregnant. Compare V.i.134–35, and see *Antony and Cleopatra*, I.ii.127–41.

44   **Spinsters** spinners, women who spin flax or wool. Compare I.iii.96–103.

45   **free** probably both (a) free of attachments, and (b) free of cares. Compare I.v.99–103.
      Bones bone bobbins.

VIOLA   It gives a very Echo to the Seat
  Where Love is thron'd.
DUKE   Thou dost speak masterly;
  My Life upon't, young though thou art, thine Eye
  Hath stay'd upon some Favour that it loves.
  Hath it not, Boy?
VIOLA   A little, by your Favour.   25
DUKE   What kind of Woman is't?
VIOLA   Of your Complexion.
DUKE   She is not worth thee then. What Years
    i'faith?
VIOLA   About your Years, my Lord.
DUKE   Too old, by Heaven: let still the Woman take
  An elder than her self: so wears she to him,   30
  So sways she level in her Husband's Heart.
  For Boy, however we do praise our selves,
  Our Fancies are more giddy and unfirm,
  More longing, wavering, sooner lost and worn,
  Than Women's are.
VIOLA   I think it well, my Lord.   35
DUKE   Then let thy Love be younger than thy self,
  Or thy Affection cannot hold the Bent:
  For Women are as Roses, whose fair Flow'r,
  Being once display'd, doth fall that very Hour.
VIOLA   And so they are: alas, that they are so,   40
  To die, even when they to Perfection grow.

Enter Curio and Clown.

DUKE   O Fellow, come, the Song we had last night.
  – Mark it, Cesario, it is old and plain;
  The Spinsters and the Knitters in the Sun,
  And the free Maids that weave their Thread
    with Bones,   45

46   **Do use** are accustomed.

      chaunt chant. This and other *au* spellings occur frequently in texts that appear to derive from Shakespeare's own manuscripts.

      silly sooth either (a) innocent, in truth (in which case *sooth* would normally be preceded by a parenthetical comma today), or (b) simple truth.

47   **dallies** plays caressingly.

48   **the Old Age** the good old days of yore.

49   **I** either (a) I, or (b) Ay. Compare I.iii.79.

50   **Come away** come take me away.

51   **in sad Cypress** either (a) in a cypress coffin, or (b) draped in boughs of cypress. Compare III.i.129–31.

52   **Fie away** begone.

54   **stuck all with Yew** adorned with yew branches.

56   **My part of Death.** both (a) my role in dying, and (b) my portion of Death *Part* recalls I.v.194.

60   **greet** do homage to; mourn. In line 59 *strewn* is pronounced 'strown' to rhyme with *thrown*.

66   **Pains** efforts, labours. In the next line Feste mis-takes the Duke to mean discomforts, sufferings. As the Duke speaks this line, he hands Feste a tip. *Pains* recalls I.ii.52, I.v.188–89, 211–12, 307, II.ii.6.

69   **Pleasure will be paid** Feste alludes to a proverb indicating that pleasure will be recompensed with pain, and exhorting one to eschew a life of pleasure (indulgence of the flesh) in favour of a life of discipline and responsibility.

72   **the Melancholy God** Feste probably refers to Saturn, the god most associated with sullen, melancholic personalities.

73   **Doublet** a man's close-fitting jacket.

73–74 **changeable Taffata** a taffeta (silk) material woven in threads of varying colours so that its hue alters as it catches the light at different angles.

74   **Opal** a gemstone of many colours, and one whose hues change with the light. See the note to IV.ii.68.

Do use to chaunt it. It is silly sooth,
And dallies with the Innocence of Love,
Like the Old Age.

CLOWN   Are you ready, Sir?

DUKE   I prethee sing.   *Music.*

THE SONG

CLOWN   *Come away, come away, Death,*   50
          And in sad Cypress let me be laid.
      Fie away, fie away, Breath,
          I am slain by a fair cruel Maid.
      My Shroud of White, stuck all with Yew,
          O prepare it.   55
      My part of Death no one so true
          Did share it.

      Not a Flower, not a Flower sweet
          On my black Coffin, let there be strewn;
      Not a Friend, not a Friend greet   60
      My poor Corpse, where my Bones shall be
          thrown.
      A thousand thousand Sighs to save,
          Lay me O where
      Sad true Lover never find my Grave,
          To weep there.   65

DUKE   There's for thy Pains.

CLOWN   No Pains, Sir, I take Pleasure in Singing, Sir.

DUKE   I'll pay thy Pleasure then.

CLOWN   Truly Sir, and Pleasure will be paid one time
or another.   70

DUKE   Give me now leave, to leave thee.

CLOWN   Now the Melancholy God protect thee,
and the Tailor make thy Doublet of changeable
Taffata, for thy Mind is a very Opal. I would

75 **Constancy** Feste is being ironic; the images he uses in lines
72–78 are all indicative of man's inconstancy (fickleness).

75–77 **put to Sea ... every where** set adrift on the sea (another
symbol of inconstancy), so that their business and destination
would be as indefinable and variable as the boundless,
shapeless waters. Compare II.i.9–11.

77–78 **makes ... Nothing** probably both (a) travels to no purpose,
and (b) brings back nothing from the voyage. Lines 74–78
hint at the kind of 'Pleasure' that requires men of firm
'Constancy' and a full 'Intent' of 'Business' as they seek 'a
good Voyage of Nothing'. *Constancy* plays on *stand* (see
Julius Caesar, III.i.61–74). *Business* frequently carries genital
implications, as in *Romeo and Juliet*, II.iii.56–58, where
Romeo says 'my Business was great, and in such a Case as
mine a Man may strain Curtesy'. And *Nothing* can function
as a term for the 'Fault' (the crack or genital flaw) of a female
vessel with 'no thing'); see the notes to II.v.130, 135, and
compare III.iv.219. Lines 74–78 recall II.i.10–11.

80 **sovereign Cruelty** This is another version of Viola's earlier
description of Olivia as 'the cruell'st She alive' (I.v.263).
Compare I.v.312.

83 **The Parts ... her** Olivia's position and possessions.

84 **I hold ... Fortune** either (a) I consider to be subject to unstable
Fortune's sway, and thus no more to be valued or relied upon
than Fortune herself, or (b) I value as slightly as Fortune does
(and Fortune could take them away as readily as she has
bestowed them). *Giddily* echoes lines 6, 17–20, 33–35.

86 **pranks** adorns. Compare *The Winter's Tale*, IV.iv.10.

88 **It ... answer'd** My message of love to her cannot be answered
that way. Modern editions normally emend *It* to *I* here;
Viola's reply shows that that is her sense of what Orsino
means, whatever he says.
Sooth indeed. Compare line 46. *Pang* (line 90) echoes line 16
and recalls I.v.81–82.

96 **Retention** (a) capacity, (b) continence, and (c) constancy. It
should not escape our notice that, by contradicting what he
said in lines 29–35, Orsino is illustrating the very
changeableness he describes there and is now attributing to
women rather than to men.

have men of such Constancy put to Sea, that their   75
Business might be every thing, and their Intent
every where, for that's it that always makes a
good Voyage of Nothing. Farewell.   *Exit.*

DUKE   Let all the rest give place.
                    [*Exeunt all but the Duke and Viola.*]
                              – Once more, Cesario,
Get thee to yond same sovereign Cruelty: 80
Tell her my Love, more Noble than the World,
Prizes not Quantity of dirty Lands;
The Parts that Fortune hath bestow'd upon her,
Tell her, I hold as giddily as Fortune:
But 'tis that Miracle and Queen of Gems   85
That Nature pranks her in attracts my Soul.

VIOLA   But if she cannot love you, Sir.

DUKE   It cannot be so answer'd.

VIOLA   Sooth, but you must.
Say that some Lady, as perhaps there is,
Hath for your Love as great a Pang of Heart   90
As you have for Olivia; you cannot love her;
You tell her so. Must she not then be answer'd?

DUKE   There is no Woman's Sides
Can bide the Beating of so strong a Passion
As Love doth give my Heart, no Woman's Heart   95
So big to hold so much: they lack Retention.
Alas, their Love may be call'd Appetite,
No motion of the Liver, but the Palate,
That suffer Surfeit, Cloyment, and Revolt;

---

99   **Surfeit, Cloyment, and Revolt**   overindulgence, satiety, and
        revulsion. Here *Revolt* may refer to nausea as well as to the
        appetite's refusal to accept any more of a given food.

100 **all as Hungry as the Sea** Orsino is distinguishing between the 'Appetite' governed by the 'Palate' (the sense of taste) and the deeper hunger governed by the 'Liver' (seat of the consuming passions). *Appetite* recalls I.v.100. And lines 93–101 echo what Orsino has said in I.i.1–15.

103 **I** both (a) I, and (b) Ay. Compare line 49.

105 **owe** both (a) own (possess or be possessed by), and (b) bestow. See the second note to I.v.334.

108 **As** both (a) in the same way as, and (b) as much as.

110 **told** revealed (probably with a submerged pun on 'tolled').

112 **Damask Cheek** Viola compares her complexion to that of a damask rose (mingled red, or pink, and white); she says that her 'Concealment' was like the unseen working of a canker-worm, eating the heart out of the rosebud before it could bear fruit in a bloom.

113 **a green and yellow Melancholy** both (a) a pallid, sickly complexion, and (b) a psychological 'complexion' (condition) to match it. *Green* alludes to the 'green sickness', a form of anaemia that was thought to afflict lovesick maidens; compare *Romeo and Juliet*, III.v.157, and *Antony and Cleopatra*, III.ii.4–6.

114 **sate** sat. Here the context suggests ironic word play on another sense of *sate*, 'became satiated'.
Patience on a Monument an allegorical personification of Patience sculpted on a tomb. Here the concept of 'Patience' hovers between the Christian virtue (enduring pain and loss without complaint and 'Smiling at Grief') and the unnecessary suffering of one whose failure to turn 'Thought' into action makes her susceptible to the 'Worm i'th' Bud' (line 111) and prompts the advice Viola gave in I.v.263–65 and the counsel Feste proffered in his song of II.iii.50–55.

117 **Our ... Will** our 'Vows' are more than our actual 'Love' (line 118).
still always.

120– **I ... not** If Orsino were really registering what 'Cesario' says
21 in this enigmatic sentence, he would realize that the 'Boy' answers his question without appearing to do so. Viola's reference to 'all the Brothers' suggests that she is now losing hope that Sebastian will turn up alive. Line 119 echoes II.i.37–38.

But mine is all as Hungry as the Sea,   100
And can digest as much. Make no Compare
Between that Love a Woman can bear me
And that I owe Olivia.
VIOLA   I, but I know —
DUKE   What dost thou know?
VIOLA   Too well what Love Women to Men may owe.   105
In faith they are as true of Heart as we.
My Father had a Daughter lov'd a Man
As it might be, perhaps, were I a Woman,
I should your Lordship.
DUKE   And what's her History?
VIOLA   A Blank, my Lord: she never told her Love,   110
But let Concealment like a Worm i'th' Bud
Feed on her Damask Cheek: she pin'd in Thought,
And with a green and yellow Melancholy
She sate like Patience on a Monument,
Smiling at Grief. Was not this Love indeed?   115
We Men may say more, swear more, but indeed
Our Shews are more than Will: for still we prove
Much in our Vows, but little in our Love.
DUKE   But died thy Sister of her Love, my Boy?
VIOLA   I am all the Daughters of my Father's House,   120
And all the Brothers too: and yet I know not.
Sir, shall I to this Lady?
DUKE   Ay, that's the Theme,
To her in Haste; give her this Jewel; say
My Love can give no place, bide no Denay.   *Exeunt.*

124   **give no place**   surrender no territory, concede no ground.
        bide no Denay   accept no denial.

II.v This scene takes place in the garden of Olivia's house.

2 **loose** both (a) forgo, release, and (b) lose, be deprived of.
Scruple a third of a dram; a tiny measure.

4 **Melancholy** Melancholy was a humour thought to be caused by an excess of black bile (a substance derived from the element Earth). When Fabian says 'boil'd to death with Melancholy', then, he is probably punning on 'boil' and 'bile'.

5 **niggardly** both stingy and straitlaced.

6 **Sheep-biter** a dog that bites or pesters sheep, and thus by extension a person who is bitingly critical. Compare *Measure for Measure*, V.i.347.

9 **Bear-baiting** The Puritans were especially opposed to this sport, which took place in theatre-like arenas in the same suburban locales that featured public playhouses. Compare I.iii.92–95.

12 **fool** bait (bite). In fact the 'Sport' (line 3) to follow will have some of the same features as a baiting, with Malvolio figuratively tied to a stake and set upon by attacking dogs.
blew blue. But at times Shakespeare employs this spelling in contexts that support wordplay on the past tense of *blow*; compare lines 47–48, where Fabian says 'look how Imagination blows him', and lines 74–75; also see *Hamlet*, V.i.267.

14 **And** if.
it . . . Lives may our lives be in peril.

16 **Mettle of India** Sir Toby is probably punning on *Mettle* (virtue) and *Metal*; the two words were not firmly distinguished in Shakespeare's time. Sir Toby is probably thinking not only of India but also of the Indies (both East and West); all three locales were associated with gold and other forms of wealth. Sir Toby's 'little Villain' (here a term of endearment) is an exotic gem.

22 **contemplative Idiot** the most ludicrous kind of fool, the kind who believes himself to be wiser than anyone else.
Close remain secretive; hide and be quiet.

23 **Jesting** The Folio spelling, *ieasting*, hints at the possibility of wordplay on *yeasting* (compare *Romeo and Juliet*, I.iii.45, II.iii.72–73). Like dough that has been laced with yeast, Malvolio will become increasingly 'Great' (line 151) as the scene proceeds.

Scene 5

Enter Sir Toby, Sir Andrew, and Fabian.

TOBY   Come thy ways, Signior Fabian.

FABIAN   Nay I'll come: if I loose a Scruple of this
Sport, let me be boil'd to death with
Melancholy.

TOBY   Wouldst thou not be glad to have the niggardly   5
rascally Sheep-biter come by some notable
Shame?

FABIAN   I would exult, Man: you know he brought me
out o' Favour with my Lady, about a Bear-baiting
here.   10

TOBY   To anger him we'll have the Bear again, and
we will fool him black and blew. – Shall we
not, Sir Andrew?

ANDREW   And we do not, it is pity of our Lives.

Enter Maria.

TOBY   Here comes the little Villain. – How now, my   15
Mettle of India?

MARIA   Get ye all three into the Box-tree:
Malvolio's coming down this Walk, he has been
yonder i'th' Sun practising Behaviour to his
own Shadow this half Hour. Observe him for the   20
love of Mockery: for I know this Letter will
make a contemplative Idiot of him. Close in
the name of Jesting.   [*The Men hide themselves.*]
– Lie thou there: [*She drops the Letter on the Walk.*]
for here comes the Trout, that must be caught   25
with Tickling.   [*She too withdraws.*]

---

26   **Tickling**   both (a) caressing under the gills (a traditional means
of catching trout), and (b) titillating, arousing. See *Troilus and
Cressida*, II.ii.9, III.i.124–26, V.ii.45–46, for references to
erotic tickling.

28 **affect me** love me. In line 30 *fancy* also means 'fall in love'.

30 **Complexion** both (a) skin colour, and (b) disposition, as in II.iv.26.

34 **overweening** inappropriately ambitious. This adjective links Malvolio to many figures in Greek and Roman literature whose prideful self-love (*hubris* in Greek) makes them susceptible to what the Greeks called atê (a temporary blindness to danger that makes them foolishly imprudent). *Hubris* and *atê* bring on the corrective ministrations of *Atê* (the Goddess of Retribution) to punish a person's breach of ordained boundaries. See the note to *Julius Caesar*, II.ii.49.

36 **jets** literally, juts. Here the word refers not only to Malvolio's strutting manner (his social ambitions), but also to his sexual ambitions.

36–37 **advanc'd Plumes** uplifted feathers. 'Plumes' were traditionally associated with ostentatious display. Compare *Richard II*, IV.i.107–10.

38 **Slight** a contraction for 'by God's light'. But here, as in III.ii.13, Sir Andrew's epithet calls attention to his own slenderness of frame and wit.

44 **Example** a model. The instance Malvolio cites is not one that has been successfully linked to any historical 'Lady of the Strachey'.

45 **Yeoman of the Wardrobe** the servant in charge of a noble household's linens and clothing.

46 **Jezebel** the proud, 'painted' wife of Ahab, a king of Israel (2 Kings 9). See the notes to II.iii.30–31, 83.

48 **blows** swells, puffs up. Compare lines 12, 23.

50 **State** throne and other trappings of majesty. *State* echoes II.iii.162–63.

53 **branch'd** embroidered with branch or floral patterns.

55 **Brimstone** sulphur, the fuel of Hell-fire.

57 **Humour of State** condescending manner and grand caprices of those with noble or royal bearings.

Enter Malvolio.

MALVOLIO 'Tis but Fortune, all is Fortune. Maria
   once told me she did affect me, and I have
   heard her self come thus near, that should she
   fancy, it should be one of my Complexion.   30
   Besides she uses me with a more exalted
   Respect than any one else that follows her.
   What should I think on't?

TOBY Here's an overweening Rogue.

FABIAN Oh peace: Contemplation makes a rare   35
   Turkey-cock of him, how he jets under his
   advanc'd Plumes.

ANDREW 'Slight, I could so beat the Rogue.

TOBY Peace, I say.

MALVOLIO To be Count Malvolio.   40

TOBY Ah Rogue.

ANDREW Pistol him, pistol him.

TOBY Peace, peace.

MALVOLIO There is Example for't: the Lady of the
   Strachy married the Yeoman of the Wardrobe.   45

ANDREW Fie on him, Jezebel.

FABIAN O peace, now he's deeply in: look how
   Imagination blows him.

MALVOLIO Having been three Months married to her,
   sitting in my State.   50

TOBY O for a Stone-bow to hit him in the Eye.

MALVOLIO Calling my Officers about me, in my
   branch'd Velvet Gown: having come from a
   Day-bed, where I have left Olivia sleeping.

TOBY Fire and Brimstone.   55

FABIAN O peace, peace.

MALVOLIO And then to have the Humour of State;

58   **demure . . . Regard** a solemn survey of everyone in attendance. *Travail* can mean either (a) effort, or (b) travel (here referring to the eye's movements).

61   **Bolts and shackles** fetters to clamp the legs of a prisoner. Sir Toby is appalled at the presumption of Malvolio's referring to him as a 'Kinsman'.

65–66   **my . . . Jewel** Malvolio probably pauses between *my* and *some*, changing his mind about the kind of 'Jewel' (in addition to the one at the end of his gold chain) he will fondle; but *some* could also be an abbreviated form of *somewhat*.

68   **Shall . . . live?** Shall this puffed-up knave escape execution for this offence?

70   **Cars** chariots or carts pulled by horses.

72   **familiar** friendly, as befits a kinsman. But of course Malvolio is also being 'familiar' (inappropriately close) in the way that breeds contempt.
    austere Regard grave, carefully reserved expression. Compare line 58.

73   **Control** both (a) self-control (with Malvolio restraining his natural tendency to be friendly to a kinsman), and (b) discipline (with Malvolio assuming his responsibility to correct a kinsman's faults). For the second sense of *control*, see *Titus Andronicus*, II.iii.60.

74   **take . . . Lips** give you a punch in the mouth. *Blow* echoes line 48.

77   **Prerogative** privilege, advantage.

80   **You . . . Drunkenness** One of the beauties of this eavesdropping scene is that it places Malvolio's tormentors in a position where they must endure some pointed barbs as well. *Amend* echoes I.v.45–55, 79–85.

81   **Scab** a term of abuse (more or less equivalent to 'Scurvy Knave').

82   **Sinews** strength (musculature and connective tissue).

89   **Employment** business. Malvolio will soon find himself employed (commissioned, sent on an errand) on what he regards as a means of rising above his present employment to a station where he can employ those who now treat him with disrespect.

91   **Woodcock** a bird too stupid to avoid a 'Gin' (trap).

and after a demure travail of Regard, telling
them I know my Place, as I would they should do
theirs; to ask for my Kinsman Toby.   60
TOBY   Bolts and Shackles.
FABIAN   Oh peace, peace, peace, now, now.
MALVOLIO   Seven of my People with an obedient Start,
make out for him: I frown the while, and
perchance wind up my Watch, or play with my   65
some rich Jewel. Toby approaches; curtsies
there to me.
TOBY   Shall this Fellow live?
FABIAN   Though our Silence be drawn from us with
Cars, yet peace.   70
MALVOLIO   I extend my Hand to him thus: quenching
my familiar Smile with an austere Regard of
Control.
TOBY   And does not Toby take you a Blow o'the Lips
then?   75
MALVOLIO   Saying 'Cousin Toby, my Fortunes having
cast me on your Niece, give me this Prerogative
of Speech.'
TOBY   What, what?
MALVOLIO   'You must amend your Drunkenness.'   80
TOBY   Out, Scab.
FABIAN   Nay patience, or we break the Sinews of our
Plot!
MALVOLIO   'Besides, you waste the Treasure of your
Time with a Foolish Knight.'   85
ANDREW   That's me, I warrant you.
MALVOLIO   'One Sir Andrew.'
ANDREW   I knew 'twas I, for many do call me Fool.
MALVOLIO   [*Noticing the Letter*] What Employment
have we here?   90
FABIAN   Now is the Woodcock near the Gin.

92–93 **and . . . him**   and may the spirit that presides over the humours prompt him to read aloud [so we can hear]. *Humour* echoes line 57.

95   **her very . . . T's**   Without realizing it, Malvolio spells out a term for the female genitalia (see the note to II.iii.203) and then compounds his unconscious naughtiness with an inadvertent reference to the Lady's 'P's' (pees) in the clause that follows. To be sure that no one has missed this revealing item, Shakespeare has Sir Andrew repeat the phrase.

96–97 **in . . . question**   without doubt. In fact Malvolio is treating 'question' with 'contempt', not pausing to ask whether there is any reason to be sceptical about what he is reading. *Contempt* recalls I.v.294, 311–12, II.iii.131–33.

98   **why that?**   The answer, though lost on the foolish Sir Andrew, is that Malvolio's Puritan mind is preoccupied with forbidden matters. See the note to II.iii.83.

100–1 **By . . . Wax**   Malvolio asks 'permission' to break the seal. Compare *King Lear*, IV.vi.256–58, and *Hamlet*, V.ii.15–18.

101   **Soft**   Malvolio notes that the wax is still fresh. But *soft* may also mean 'hush, wait, be attentive', as in I.v.317.

102   **Lucrece**   Olivia's seal-ring leaves the image ('Impressure' or impression) of a heroine proverbial for chastity who stabbed herself rather than live with the shame of having been raped.

104   **Liver and all**   beginning with his liver (love-passion, as noted in II.iv.100) and proceeding to the rest of his mind and body.

109–   **The Numbers alter'd**   the number of metrical feet changed
10   [from line 2 to line 4]. After he speaks this clause, Malvolio appears to refocus on 'But who?' (line 106). If so, to his delight, he discovers that both metre and rhyme are 'alter'd' back to a regular pattern when he substitutes 'Malvolio' for that phrase to yield 'Jove knows I love / Malvolio'.

112   **Brock**   badger, a beast proverbial for its bad smell. *Marry* (an oath that originally referred to the Virgin Mary) here means 'truly'; but it also serves as a reminder that Malvolio's lust to marry above his station is about to 'hang' him. Compare I.v.138, II.iii.153. *Hang* recalls I.v.1–21. *Adore* (line 113) recalls II.iii.195–97.

TOBY   Oh peace, and the Spirit of Humours intimate
reading aloud to him.

MALVOLIO   By my Life, this is my Lady's Hand: these
be her very C's, her U's, and her T's, and thus   95
makes she her great P's. It is in contempt of
question her Hand.

ANDREW   Her C's, her U's, and her T's: why that?

MALVOLIO   'To the Unknown Belov'd, this, and
my Good Wishes.' Her very Phrases. – By your   100
leave, Wax. Soft, and the Impressure her
Lucrece, with which she uses to seal: 'tis my
Lady. To whom should this be?

FABIAN   This wins him, Liver and all.

MALVOLIO   'Jove knows I love,   105
                   But who?
                 Lips do not move;
                   No Man must know.'
'No Man must know.' What follows? The Numbers
alter'd: 'No Man must know.' If this should be   110
thee, 'Malvolio'?

TOBY   Marry hang thee, Brock.

MALVOLIO   'I may command where I adore,
           But Silence, like a Lucresse Knife:
           With bloodless Stroke my Heart doth gore,   115
           M.O.A.I. doth sway my Life.'

FABIAN   A fustian Riddle.

TOBY   Excellent Wench, say I.

MALVOLIO   'M.O.A.I. doth sway my Life.' Nay but
first let me see, let me see, let me see.   120

---

116   **M.O.A.I. . . . Life**   This 'Riddle' has been explained as a
reference to the four elements (*Mare*, water, *Orbis*, earth, *Aer*,
air, and *Ignis*, fire) that rule (*sway*) a person's disposition (see
the note to II.iii.9–10). Here as elsewhere, *sway* can mean
'cause to sway or totter'; compare IV.i.54.

117   **fustian**   pretentious and nonsensical.

121   **dress'd**   (a) prepared, (b) addressed (served, with play on the address of a letter), and (c) attired.

122   **the Stallion checks at it**   Sir Toby is probably comparing Malvolio to Pegasus, the winged horse who was the classical symbol of poetic inspiration: Malvolio is demonstrating some inspired flights of fancy as he interprets the letter. Here *checks at it* (a falconer's term) means 'turns aside to pursue it'. Modern editions normally emend *Stallion* to *staniel* (a kind of hawk). Compare *Hamlet*, II.ii.625, where *Stallion* means 'male prostitute'.

125   **any formal Capacity**   any normal intelligence. Here *formal* keeps us aware of Malvolio's 'Capacity' to impart form, to bring his own 'Construction' (II.iii.190) to material whose import would not be 'evident' to a more objective observer.

126   **Obstruction**   obstacle to my optimistic reading of this clause. *End* echoes II.iii.202–3.

127   **portend**   point to (literally, stretch toward).

130   **I**   Here and elsewhere below (lines 140–42), the Folio prints *I* where the usual modern edition would print 'ay'. To preserve the letter puns, this edition retains the Folio spellings. *I, eye,* and *O* frequently have genital implications in Shakespeare. Like the number *1*, *I* can stand for the male member (see *The Two Gentlemen of Verona*, II.v.25–38, and compare I.i.96–128 in the same play); meanwhile *eye* and *O* can both signify the 'cut' in a 'weaker vessel' with 'no thing' (see the notes to I.v.136, II.i.43, II.iii.203, and II.v.95, and compare *Hamlet*, III.ii.118–30). Malvolio's construction of the letter makes it clear that he is fantasizing about an 'Alphabetical Position' (line 127) that will 'make up' (connect) his erect letter 'I' with Lady Olivia's open, oohing 'O'.

131– **Sowter . . . Fox**   Sowter (cobbler, here a hunting dog's name)
32   will bark at the trail despite this (the fact that the 'Scent' is 'Cold', too faint to be pursued with success), though it is as worthless as a fox is cunning.

135   **Faults**   Fabian refers to cold scents (line 130), breaks in the scent. But Malvolio is pursuing a trail he hopes will lead him to Olivia's 'fault'. See the note to II.iii.203.

136   **Consonancy**   consistency, coherence.

137   **that . . . Probation**   that will yield to 'proving'. Compare lines 146–47.

FABIAN   What Dish a' Poison has she dress'd him?

TOBY   And with what Wing the Stallion checks at it?

MALVOLIO   'I may command where I adore.' Why she
   may command me: I serve her, she is my Lady.
   Why this is evident to any formal Capacity.   125
   There is no Obstruction in this. And the End:
   what should that Alphabetical Position portend,
   if I could make that resemble something in me?
   Softly, *M.O.A.I.*

TOBY   O I, make up that: he is now at a Cold Scent.   130

FABIAN   Sowter will cry upon't for all this, though
   it be as rank as a Fox.

MALVOLIO   *M*, Malvolio, *M*, why that begins my Name.

FABIAN   Did not I say he would work it out, the Cur
   is excellent at Faults.   135

MALVOLIO   *M*. But then there is no Consonancy in
   the Sequel that suffers under Probation. *A* should
   follow, but *O* does.

FABIAN   And O shall end, I hope.

TOBY   I, or I'll cudgel him, and make him cry 'O'.   140

MALVOLIO   And then *I* comes behind.

FABIAN   I, and you had any Eye behind you, you
   might see more Detraction at your Heels than
   Fortunes before you.

MALVOLIO   *M.O.A.I.* This Simulation is not as the   145
   former: and yet to crush this a little, it would
   bow to me, for every one of these Letters are in
   my Name. Soft, here follows Prose.

---

139   **And O shall end**   a reference to the hangman's noose. But *O*
   can also mean 'Oh', a groan of agony, as in line 140.
   Compare I.v.3–21.

142   **and**   if.

145   **Simulation**   riddle, puzzle to be solved.

149 **revolve** turn over in your mind. Actors often revolve physically here to illustrate Malvolio's obedience.

151 **become Great** grow 'Great' simply by virtue of who they are. Later in the play this phrase is rendered *are borne Great*, and most of today's editions emend it here to *are born great*.

154 **Blood** both (a) noble bloodline, and (b) spirited passion, courage.

155 **inure** accustom.

156 **cast thy humble Slough** discard your servant's livery the way a snake leaves behind the skin it has sloughed off.
Fresh in a new skin. Compare I.v.283.

157 **opposite** argumentative, quarrelsome.

158 **tang Arguments of State** ring with matters of political import. *State* recalls lines 50, 57.

159 **the Trick of Singularity** the affectations and eccentricities of a VIP.

161– **Yellow Stockings** Yellow stockings seem to have been
62 fashionable among lively bachelors; they were also associated with jealous husbands and cuckolds (who may have felt the need to appear as sprightly as the rivals they feared).

162 **cross-Garter'd** garters crossed above and below the knees.

163 **go to** get to it. Often *go to* is an expression of disapproval or dismissal; here it seems to be an exhortation to do as one is told.

164 **made** transformed into one of Fortune's darlings. Compare *A Midsummer Night's Dream*, IV.ii.17–18.

164– **see . . . still** continue to think of you merely as a steward
65 without the ambition to seize the fortune now proffered you.

165 **Fellow** peer, equal. In line 166 *woorthy* is the Folio spelling for *worthy*.

167– **alter Services with thee** become your servant rather than your
68 mistress. This phrase is usually construed to mean 'exchange services (places) with you'; but *would alter Services with you* could also be heard, and interpreted, as 'would do altar services with you'. Compare *Measure for Measure*, III.i.504–5, where 'Angelo will not be alter'd' carries similar ambiguities.

'If this fall into thy Hand, revolve. In my
Stars I am above thee, but be not afraid of   150
Greatness. Some become Great, some achieves
Greatness, and some have Greatness thrust
upon 'em. Thy Fates open their Hands, let
thy Blood and Spirit embrace them. And to
inure thy self to what thou art like to be,   155
cast thy humble Slough and appear Fresh. Be
opposite with a Kinsman, surly with Servants;
let thy Tongue tang Arguments of State; put
thy self into the Trick of Singularity. She
thus advises thee that sighs for thee.   160
Remember who commended thy Yellow
Stockings, and wish'd to see thee ever cross-
Garter'd. I say remember, go to, thou art
made if thou desir'st to be so: if not, let me
see thee a Steward still, the Fellow of   165
Servants, and not woorthy to touch Fortune's
Fingers. Farewell. She that would alter
Services with thee,   The Fortunate Unhappy.'
　Daylight and Champian discovers not more: this
is open. I will be Proud, I will read Politic   170
Authors, I will baffle Sir Toby, I will wash
off Gross Acquaintance, I will be Point Devise,

---

169 **Champian discovers not more**   champaign (a flat landscape)
　　discloses no more.

170– **Politic Authors**   probably both (a) writers who explain
　71　statecraft, and (b) writers who are in vogue at Court. *Politic*
　　echoes II.iii.82–84.

171 **baffle**   treat contemptuously (as if revoking his knighthood).
　　See V.i.374.

172– **Point Devise, the very Man**   precisely like the man the letter
　73　specifies. *Man* recalls II.ii.26.

174 **jade** trick, deceive. *Imagination* means 'mere imaginings'. The verb *excites* (spurs) provides an ironic and amusing indication of how little dispassionate 'Reason' is prompting Malvolio. See the note on *Reasons* at I.v.328.

181 **Strange, Stout** aloof, proud.

183 **Jove ... praised** Malvolio's 'piety' (giving all the credit to Jove and to those astrological influences by which the ways of Providence are manifested) echoes that of the Calvinist Puritans of Shakespeare's day. It may be that 'Jove' in the 1623 Folio text replaces references to 'God' in the original script of the play; after 1606 an anti-profanity law forbade references to the Deity in secular works.

185 **entertain'st** Here *entertain* means 'receive hospitably'. Compare II.i.35.

187 **still** unceasingly, always.

188 **deero** This word, usually emended to *dear*, may be a First Folio misprint for *deere*, as the Second Folio renders it. But it could also be interpreted to mean either (a) dear O, or (b) dearo (a term of endearment playing on *deer*).

190 **thou** It is not clear whether this refers to Jove or to Olivia. To Malvolio, of course, it makes little difference: ultimately the command comes from the Deity, who has bestowed such bountiful grace upon this humble servant.

192– **the Sophy** The Shah of Persia. In 1599 Sir Anthony Sherley had
93   returned from Persia much honoured and enriched by the Shah. *Part* (line 191) recalls II.iv.56.

194 **Device** trick. Compare line 172, and see II.iii.178.

199 **Gull-catcher** trickster. 'Gull' was the name for a gullible fool. See II.iii.147.

200 **set ... Neck** vaunt your triumph over me. Here as elsewhere, the witless Sir Andrew apes his mentor by requesting the same treatment from Maria.

202 **play my Freedom at Tray-trip** wager my liberty at dice. In tray-trip, the winning number was three (tray or trey).

205 **Dream** hallucinations, reverie. Sir Toby refers both to Malvolio's dream-world state and to the fact that he believes that his wildest dreams have just come true. Compare II.ii.27, II.iii.191.

the very Man. I do not now fool my self, to let
Imagination jade me; for every Reason excites
to this, that my Lady loves me. She did commend   175
my Yellow Stockings of late, she did praise my
Leg being cross-Garter'd, and in this she
manifests her self to my Love, and with a kind
of Injunction drives me to these Habits of her
liking. I thank my Stars, I am happy. I will be   180
Strange, Stout, in Yellow Stockings, and cross-
Garter'd, even with the swiftness of putting on.
Jove and my Stars be praised. Here is yet a
Postscript: 'Thou canst not choose but know
who I am. If thou entertain'st my Love, let   185
it appear in thy Smiling, thy Smiles become
thee well. Therefore in my Presence still smile,
deero my Sweet, I prethee.' – Jove, I thank
thee, I will smile, I will do every thing
that thou wilt have me.   *Exit.*   190

FABIAN   I will not give my Part of this Sport for
a Pension of thousands to be paid from the
Sophy.

TOBY   I could marry this Wench for this Device.

ANDREW   So could I too.   195

TOBY   And ask no other Dowry with her but such
another Jest.

Enter Maria.

ANDREW   Nor I neither.

FABIAN   Here comes my noble Gull-catcher.

TOBY   Wilt thou set thy Foot o' my Neck?   200

ANDREW   Or o' mine either?

TOBY   Shall I play my Freedom at Tray-trip, and
become thy Bondslave?

ANDREW   I'faith, or I either?

TOBY   Why, thou hast put him in such a Dream that   205
when the Image of it leaves him he must run
Mad.

209   **Aqua-vitae**   brandy or another kind of strong liquor.

213– **a Colour ... detests**   Maria's remarks make it clear that
14   Malvolio's 'Imagination' (line 174) has jaded him so
      completely that he even 'crushes' his own memories to make
      them fit what the letter tells him (lines 173–80). See the notes
      to lines 125, 174.

215– **unsuitable to her Disposition**   incompatible with her
16   melancholic state. Compare I.v.101.

217– **turn him into a notable Contempt**   transform him from a
18   much-favoured steward into a man she can regard only with
      contempt. *Contempt* echoes lines 96–97.

220   **Tartar**   Tartarus, the classical equivalent of Hell. *Wit* recalls
      I.iii.86–87; compare I.ii.56, I.iii.108–10, I.v.27–39,
      II.iii.146–50.

222   **make one**   come along. The pitiful Sir Andrew is so desperate to
      'make one' (be one of the boys) that he would probably
      follow Sir Toby into damnation itself to win a dram of
      acceptance. See the notes on *one* at line 130 and at I.v.136.

MARIA   Nay but say true, does't work upon him?

TOBY   Like Aqua-vita with a Midwife.

MARIA   If you will then see the Fruits of the Sport,   210
mark his first Approach before my Lady. He
will come to her in Yellow Stockings, and 'tis
a Colour she abhors, and cross-Garter'd, a
Fashion she detests: and he will smile upon
her, which will now be so unsuitable to her   215
Disposition, being addicted to a Melancholy
as she is, that it cannot but turn him into a
notable Contempt. If you will see it, follow
me.

TOBY   To the Gates of Tartar, thou most excellent   220
Divel of Wit.

ANDREW   I'll make one too.   *Exeunt.*

III.i   This scene takes place in the garden of Olivia's house.

1   **Save thee** God save thee.

2   **Tabor** a small drum of the type carried by jesters. Feste may be
     pretending to hear Viola say 'tabern' (tavern). She appears to
     pick up on that sense in line 10.

4   **Churchman** Viola reciprocates by pretending that 'by the
     Church' (line 3) means 'sustained by your labours on behalf
     of the church as a clergyman'.

8   **lies by a Beggar** Viola plays on 'lies with a beggar' (a mistress
     or prostitute). Viola alludes to a ballad about 'The Beggar and
     the King' (*Richard II*, V.iii.77), popularly known as 'King
     Cophetua and the Beggar Maid'. See *Romeo and Juliet*,
     II.i.13–14, *Love's Labour's Lost*, I.ii.112–13, *Hamlet*,
     IV.iii.22–24, 30–31, and *Measure for Measure*, III.i.476–80,
     for other echoes of the ballad.

10   **stand by** Viola plays on 'is supported or maintained by'.

12   **You have said** you've said it; you are correct.

13   **Sentence** Feste probably means both (a) a maxim (Latin
     sententia), and (b) any kind of utterance.
     Chev'ril soft, stretchable kidskin.

14–15 **how . . . outward** What Feste means is that because of the
     corruption of 'this Age' (line 12), a word or a sentence can be
     reversed (read in an 'opposite' fashion) so that it appears to
     say something other than what the speaker intended or what
     the words would normally convey. By the end of the scene we
     will see that 'wrong Side' out can also have another sense:
     when a character thinks that he or she is saying one thing
     (communicating an 'outward' meaning) but unintentionally
     reveals something else (an 'inward' meaning), usually a secret
     or suppressed desire (as Malvolio has done in his attempts to
     construe the letter in II.v). *Wit* (line 14) echoes II.v.220–21.

16   **dally nicely** play idly. Here *nicely* means 'coyly, subtly', and
     thus with a potential for deception.

17   **Wanton** ungoverned, promiscuous. Viola's point is that when
     words are treated too freely, they can no longer be relied
     upon; having become too 'loose' (equivocal and slippery) to
     be trustworthy, they may cheat and betray you.

24   **Bonds** sworn and written agreements (instead of one's simple
     'word').

ACT III

Scene 1

Enter Viola and Clown.

VIOLA Save thee, Friend, and thy Music. Dost thou
live by thy Tabor?

CLOWN No Sir, I live by the Church.

VIOLA Art thou a Churchman?

CLOWN No such matter, Sir, I do live by the Church: 5
for I do live at my House, and my House dooth
stand by the Church.

VIOLA So thou mayst say the King lies by a Beggar,
if a Beggar dwell near him; or the Church
stands by thy Tabor, if thy Tabor stand by the 10
Church.

CLOWN You have said, Sir. To see this Age: a
Sentence is but a Chev'ril Glove to a good
Wit, how quickly the wrong Side may be turn'd
outward. 15

VIOLA Nay that's certain: they that dally nicely
with Words may quickly make them Wanton.

CLOWN I would therefore my Sister had had no Name,
Sir.

VIOLA Why, Man? 20

CLOWN Why Sir, her Name's a Word, and to dally
with that Word might make my Sister Wanton.
But indeed, Words are very Rascals, since
Bonds disgrac'd them.

VIOLA Thy Reason, Man? 25

27   **loath**   reluctant, unwilling. Compare I.v.186–87.

28   **prove Reason**   both (a) test or probe a proposition (to see whether it accords with reason), and (b) try to prove a proposition valid. *Reason* echoes II.v.174–75.

29   **Merry**   gamesome, given to playful jests and tricks.

30   **car'st for nothing**   have a carefree approach to life. Compare II.iv.72–78.

32   **Conscience**   consciousness, private thoughts.

34   **make you invisible**   cause you to disappear.

35   **Fool**   Viola means professional jester. But Feste mis-takes her to mean a lover, and then, more specifically, a deceived one. The Fool may also be alluding to the common belief that a literal fool (a man with limited intelligence) was endowed with larger than usual genital attributes; see I.v.1–21, where Feste refers to the advantages of being 'well hang'd in this World'. It was proverbial that 'Fools please women best'.

36   **Folly**   Here Feste appears to refer primarily to sexual wantonness. See the note to I.v.16.

38   **Pilchers**   both (a) leather outer garments, and by metaphorical extension, scabbards (as in *Romeo and Juliet*, III.i.83–84, where Mercutio puns on the proverb 'Pitchers have ears'), and (b) pilchards, small fish, similar to herrings. Here as in *Romeo and Juliet*, I.i.30–34, II.iii.41–43, fish (and, by extension, 'Fools') are phallic in implication.

40–41 **Corrupter of Words**   Feste is drawing a distinction between his kind of wantonness (playing with words) and another kind of 'corruption'.

45   **but**   unless.

47   **your Wisdom**   This phrase echoes 'your Honour' or 'your Worship'. Here it implies 'your Folly'.

48   **and thou pass upon me**   if you make a victim of me. Here *pass* either means 'thrust' (from fencing) or 'pass judgement'. Compare *Hamlet*, V.ii.310–12, where the Prince says, 'Laertes, you do but dally. / I pray you pass with your best Violence: / I am sure you make a Wanton of me.'

50   **Commodity**   consignment, allotment for shipping.

CLOWN   Troth, Sir, I can yield you none without
Words, and Words are grown so false I am loath
to prove Reason with them.

VIOLA   I warrant thou art a Merry Fellow, and
car'st for nothing.   30

CLOWN   Not so, Sir, I do care for something: but
in my Conscience, Sir, I do not care for you.
If that be to care for nothing, Sir, I would
it would make you invisible.

VIOLA   Art not thou the Lady Olivia's Fool?   35

CLOWN   No indeed, Sir, the Lady Olivia has no Folly:
she will keep no Fool, Sir, till she be married,
and Fools are as like Husbands as Pilchers
are to Herrings, the Husbands the bigger.
I am indeed not her Fool, but her Corrupter   40
of Words.

VIOLA   I saw thee late at the Count Orsino's.

CLOWN   Foolery, Sir, does walk about the Orb like
the Sun, it shines every where. I would be
sorry, Sir, but the Fool should be as oft with   45
your Master as with my Mistress: I think I saw
your Wisdom there.

VIOLA   Nay, and thou pass upon me, I'll no more
with thee. Hold, there's Expenses for thee.
                                        [*Gives him a Coin.*]

CLOWN   Now Jove in his next Commodity of Hair   50
send thee a Beard.

52–53 **sick for one** overwhelmed with longing for one. 'Cesario'
pretends to be anxious to develop the attributes of a mature
male; but what Viola means privately is that she yearns with
lovesickness for the bearer of Orsino's beard.

56 **put to use** both (a) loaned at interest (usury), and (b) 'kept' to
breed (produce offspring). Coins are wantons too.

57 **Lord Pandarus** the uncle who served as go-between for the
affair between his niece Cressida and the Trojan soldier
Troilus.

61 **Cressida was a Beggar** According to a sequel to Chaucer's
Troilus and Criseyde, Cressida finally degenerated into a
common whore and a begging leper. In line 65, Feste implies
that wanton words can become similarly 'over-worn'. See the
note to line 8.

62 **conster** construe; a wanton way of saying 'explain'.

64 **out of my Welkin** literally, beyond my sphere. *Element* and
Welkin were both used to refer to the sky. Compare I.i.25,
II.iii.60–61.

67 **Wit** intelligence, cleverness. But here as in lines 12–15, *Wit* can
also function in a genital sense (see the note to I.iii.86–87)
that relates to the erotic implications sometimes associated
with *Fool* (see the notes to lines 35, 36).

70 **Haggard** an untrained hawk, and thus one that will 'check at'
(give instant pursuit to) every bird that catches his eye. See the
note to II.v.122. *Time* (line 69) recalls II.iii.99–100.

71 **Practice** profession. In lines 71–74 Viola notes that wise 'Folly'
is an 'Art' that is 'Fit' (appropriate, valid), because it 'shews'
as true folly (tainted judgement) what often passes as the 'Wit'
(good judgement) of 'Wise-men.'

73 **shews** shows, displays. But in this passage, as occasionally
elsewhere, *shews* can function as an aphetic form of *eschews*,
'shuns, avoids'. Compare *Macbeth*, I.iii.52, V.vii.14.

74 **But ... Wit** but once wise men's proclivity to 'Folly' has
befallen them, it thoroughly corrupts their reasoning faculties.
Viola's phrasing can also refer to genital senses of *Folly* and
Wit; see the note to line 67.

77 **Dieu ... Monsieur** God protect you, sir (French). The French
phrases in lines 77–78 (rendered here as they appear in the
Folio) probably represent how the words were spoken on the
Elizabethan stage.

VIOLA   By my troth I'll tell thee, I am almost sick
  for one, though I would not have it grow on
  my Chin. Is thy Lady within?
CLOWN   Would not a Pair of these have bred, Sir?   55
VIOLA   Yes, being kept together, and put to use.
CLOWN   I would play Lord Pandarus of Phrygia, Sir,
  to bring a Cressida to this Troilus.
VIOLA   I understand you, Sir, 'tis well begg'd.
              [*Gives him another Coin.*]
CLOWN   The Matter I hope is not great, Sir;   60
  begging but a Beggar; Cressida was a Beggar.
  My Lady is within, Sir. I will conster to them
  whence you come; who you are, and what you
  would, are out of my Welkin; I might say
  Element, but the Word is over-worn.   *Exit.*   65
VIOLA   This Fellow is wise enough to play the Fool,
  And to do that well craves a kind of Wit:
  He must observe their Mood on whom he jests,
  The Quality of Persons, and the Time,
  And, like the Haggard, check at every Feather   70
  That comes before his Eye. This is a Practice
  As full of Labour as a Wise-man's Art:
  For Folly that he wisely shews is Fit,
  But Wise-men's Folly fall'n, quite taint their
    Wit.

          Enter Sir Toby and Andrew.

TOBY   Save you, Gentleman.   75
VIOLA   And you, Sir.
ANDREW   *Dieu vou guard, Monsieur.*

78   **Et ... Serviture**   And you too; your servant.

80   **incounter**   encounter. Sir Toby means 'enter', of course. But his
      excessively decorative language makes it clear that words
      continue to be wanton in this setting. Like *desirous* and *Trade*
      (line 81), *encounter* was often used with copulative
      (frequently mock-military) implications. Here as elsewhere the
      word plays on a term for the female genitalia. See the note to
      I.iii.107, and compare *Troilus and Cressida*, III.ii.217–19.

83   **bound to**   Viola means 'directing my course towards'. But
      bound to could also mean 'committed to' (as a slave, a
      servant, a debtor, or a lover).

84   **List**   destination, termination point. Viola 'consters' (interprets)
      her first clause.

85   **Taste**   test, feel. Sir Toby picks up on *Voyage* and pretends that
      Viola is still suffering from her sea-legs. Meanwhile he is
      probably mis-taking *bound* (line 83) to mean 'tied' or
      'shackled'.

86   **understand**   stand under. Viola plays on a sense of *understand*
      (see *The Two Gentlemen of Verona*, II.v.23–36) that can be
      related to more than one kind of male 'Legs' (see *Troilus and
      Cressida*, I.ii.15–17).

90   **Gate**   Viola puns on both 'gait' and 'entrance'. Compare
      II.iii.172. One meaning of *gate* is 'right to pasture'.

91   **prevented**   anticipated (rendering it unnecessary for me to
      enter).

93   **Odours**   Viola probably means 'fragrant air'.

96–97 **My ... Ear**   In her deliberately 'rare' (overwrought) style, Viola
      says, 'What I have to convey I can only speak privately into
      your own ear, which I hope you will condescend to make
      ready ("pregnant") for my words.' Sir Andrew takes notes on
      this highfalutin balderdash. *Pregnant* recalls II.ii.29.

99   **already**   both (a) quickly, and (b) all ready. Compare *almost* in
      I.iii.29.

VIOLA *Et vouz ousie, vostre Serviture.*

ANDREW I hope, Sir, you are, and I am yours.

TOBY Will you incounter the House, my Niece is   80
desirous you should enter, if your Trade be to
her.

VIOLA I am bound to your Niece, Sir; I mean she
is the List of my Voyage.

TOBY Taste your Legs, Sir, put them to Motion.   85

VIOLA My Legs do better understand me, Sir, than
I understand what you mean by bidding me taste
my legs.

TOBY I mean to go, Sir, to enter.

VIOLA I will answer you with Gate and Entrance.   90
But we are prevented.

Enter Olivia, and Gentlewoman.

– Most excellent accomplish'd Lady, the Heavens
rain Odours on you.

ANDREW That Youth's a rare Courtier: 'rain Odours',
well.   95

VIOLA My Matter hath no Voice, Lady, but to your
own most pregnant and vouchsafed Ear.

ANDREW 'Odours', 'pregnant', and 'vouchsafed': I'll
get 'em all three already.

107 **lowly Feigning** pretences of lowliness. Olivia has been
encouraging 'Cesario' to act like a courtier in his own right
rather than like a humble servant. Olivia is in a mood to be
'merry' (line 106), wanton, free from customary restraint; but
unlike Malvolio, 'Cesario' is intent on keeping the existing
social boundaries and hierarchical relationships as distinct as
possible. *Feigning* recalls I.v.213.
Complement both (a) compliment (compliance with good
manners), and (b) complement (manners that fit with and
'complete' a particular social context).

111 **For** as for.

112 **Would ... Blanks** I would rather have them be empty. *Blanks*
can be either (a) clean sheets of paper, or (b) metal discs that
are yet to be stamped and thereby minted as coins. Olivia's
phrasing anticipates a sense (empty shells or cartridges) that
entered the language in the nineteenth century.

113 **whet** sharpen, stimulate. By the end of the scene it will be
apparent that 'Cesario' also has the capacity to 'wet' Olivia's
'gentle Thoughts' with erotic arousal.

115 **bad** bade. Compare II.iii.104.

116 **undertake another Suit** Olivia means 'initiate another
courtship'. In a scene in which words tend to be wanton,
however, it seems likely that we are also to read an
unconscious erotic meaning into Olivia's phrasing: *Suit* often
means clothing, and *undertake* can refer to going under or
'taking' a garment in an amorous encounter (I.iii.60).

118 **Music from the Spheres** The planets were thought to revolve
with a harmony too refined for mortal ears to hear.

120 **Enchantment** Olivia refers to 'Cesario's' claim to have been
captivated by Olivia on his last visit. What she is noting
privately is that 'Cesario' bore a real 'Enchantment' in his
own person.
hear claim to have experienced as I answered your questions
(see I.v.252–312). Most editions emend the Folio's *heare* to
here.

121 **abuse** Olivia probably means 'misuse'; but the other sense of
abuse, 'deceive', fits her situation even more aptly.

OLIVIA   — Let the Garden Door be shut, and leave me   100
  to my Hearing.   [*Exeunt all but Olivia and Viola.*]
  — Give me your Hand, Sir.

VIOLA   My Duty, Madam, and most humble Service.

OLIVIA   What is your name?

VIOLA   Cesario is your Servant's name, fair
  Princess.   105

OLIVIA   My Servant, Sir? 'Twas never merry World
  Since lowly Feigning was call'd Complement.
  Y'are Servant to the Count Orsino, Youth.

VIOLA   And he is yours, and his must needs be
  yours:
  Your Servant's Servant is your Servant, Madam.   110

OLIVIA   For him, I think not on him: for his
  Thoughts,
  Would they were Blanks, rather than fill'd with
  me.

VIOLA   Madam, I come to whet your gentle Thoughts
  On his behalf.

OLIVIA   O by your leave I pray you,
  I bad you never speak again of him;   115
  But would you undertake another Suit,
  I had rather hear you, to solicit that,
  Than Music from the Spheres.

VIOLA   Dear Lady.

OLIVIA   Give me leave, beseech you. I did send,
  After the last Enchantment you did hear,   120
  A Ring in chase of you. So did I abuse
  My self, my Servant, and, I fear me, you.

123 **your hard Construction** your unfavourable opinion. Here
      Construction derives from 'construe'. Again, though, Olivia's
      words are wanton in a way that we would now call Freudian.
      Construction (which recalls II.iii.190) can mean 'erection',
      particularly in this context, and *Cunning* (line 124) echoes a
      more 'shameful' word that derives from the Latin *cunnus*; see
      the note to line 80, and compare I.iii.106–7.

125 **Which you knew none of yours** Olivia refers, of course, to the
      ring she sent to 'Cesario' after their previous meeting. Here
      knew hints at carnal knowledge; compare *Measure for
      Measure*, V.i.179–80, 204–5.

126 **set mine Honour at the Stake** Olivia depicts her 'Honour'
      (both her reputation and her chastity, here symbolized by her
      'Ring') as if it were a bear tied to the stake and 'baited' by
      'unmuzzled' dogs. Once again her language has erotic
      undertones. For the genital implications of *Ring* (line 121), see
      The Merchant of Venice, V.i.197, 307, and *Hamlet*,
      II.ii.458–59. *Baited* recalls II.v.9.

128 **tyrannous** both (a) dictatorial, and (b) cruel.
      receiving ability to take in a meaning and understand it. But
      Olivia also refers to 'Cesario' as the recipient of her
      love-token.

129 **a Cypress** Olivia probably refers to a transparent, gauzelike
      material (from Cyprus) that 'shows' her heart rather than
      hiding it like a 'Bosom'. But Olivia's image also reminds us of
      another kind of cypress, the black crepe veil worn by
      mourners. Olivia may still be wearing black; if so, however,
      she is probably more mournful now over her unrequited love
      for 'Cesario' than over her loss of a brother. *Cypress* recalls
      II.iv.50–51. Compare the 'Curtain' imagery of I.v.252–65.

131 **a Degree to** an increment towards.

132 **Grize** Like *Degree* (line 131), this word means 'step',
      gradation, as on a stairway.
      'tis a vulgar Proof it is proven by common experience.

135 **Proud** haughty, aloof. Compare I.v.274, II.v.170–71.

136– **If ... Wolf** If I am destined to be a victim, how much would I
37   have preferred to fall prey to the king of beasts (the lion)
      rather than to a lower predator (the wolf, a 'Poor', inadequate
      pretender to lion-like attributes). Olivia may be thinking of
      Orsino as the 'Lion' and 'Cesario' as the 'Wolf'.

140 **Harvest** the time when they are ripe and ready to be enjoyed.

Under your hard Construction must I sit,
To force that on you in a shameful Cunning
Which you knew none of yours. What might you
   think? 125
Have you not set mine Honour at the Stake,
And baited it with all th' unmuzzled Thoughts
That tyrannous Heart can think? To one of your
   receiving
Enough is shewn; a Cypress, not a Bosom,
Hides my Heart. So let me hear you speak. 130

VIOLA   I pity you.

OLIVIA   That's a Degree to Love.

VIOLA   No not a Grize: for 'tis a vulgar Proof
That very oft we pity Enemies.

OLIVIA   Why then me thinks 'tis time to smile again.
O World, how apt the Poor are to be Proud? 135
If one should be a Prey, how much the better
To fall before the Lion than the Wolf?

                          Clock strikes.

The Clock upbraids me with the waste of Time.
Be not afraid, good Youth, I will not have you,
And yet when Wit and Youth is come to Harvest, 140
Your Wife is like to reap a proper Man.
There lies your Way, due West.

VIOLA   Then Westward hoe.
Grace and good Disposition attend your Ladyship.
You'll nothing, Madam, to my Lord by me?

OLIVIA   Stay: I prethee tell me what thou think'st
   of me? 145

---

142 **Way** route. Olivia's phrasing echoes I.v.220–21; compare
     II.iii.170–71.

143 **hoe** both (a) ho (here meaning 'let us be on our way'), and (b)
     hoe (an agricultural verb that plays on 'Harvest' and 'reap' in
     lines 140–41). Viola's phrase alludes to the shout that
     watermen gave as they set out on the Thames in a westerly
     direction from the City of London to Westminster.

146   **That . . . are** Viola probably means that Olivia thinks that she is not in love with a woman but with a man. Meanwhile, however, she may also mean that Olivia lacks self-knowledge in a broader sense. Among other things, this line relates to what Olivia inadvertently discloses about herself through her choice of words in this scene. Compare I.v.332–33.

148   **think you right** you think correctly.

151   **now I am your Fool** 'Cesario' appears to mean here that it will now be necessary to return empty-handed (and thus looking foolish) from yet another mission to the woman whose hand Orsino seeks. But what Viola is probably thinking privately is that she is Olivia's 'Fool' in a sense analogous to that which applies to Feste: knowing what she does, and knowing that she is unwillingly fooling (deceiving) Olivia, she is in a position to see and comment upon how foolish Olivia's behaviour is. See the notes on erotic folly at I.v.16, III.i.35, 36.

152   **a deal** a large amount. Through linguistic inflation, this phrase has now become 'a great deal'. Olivia probably speaks lines 152–55 as an aside.

155   **Love** Here Olivia refers to herself, and specifically to her inability to hide her love for 'Cesario' despite the 'Scorn' with which he greets it. Love is so luminous, despite itself, that its 'Night' is as bright as 'Noon'. It is therefore pointless for a person in love to try keeping it secret. The word *murd'rous* recalls what Antonio has said to Sebastian in II.i.37–38. And lines 154–55 echo the proverb 'Murder will out'; compare *Hamlet*, II.ii.626–36. *Scorn* (line 152) is a reminder of the curse Viola has wished upon Olivia in I.v.309–12.

158   **maugre** notwithstanding (from French *malgré*). *Pride* echoes line 135.

159   **Wit** cunning, prudence. See the note to line 67.

160–   **Do not . . . Cause** Do not take as a reason for not loving me
61   the following clause: [that] because I woo you, you therefore have no reason to love me. Here as elsewhere, *Cause* can mean 'case', another English word that derives from the Latin *causa*. For *case* as a word that can be used with genital implications, see *Romeo and Juliet*, II.iii.56–58, and *The Merry Wives of Windsor*, IV.i.59–73.

VIOLA   That you do think you are not what you are.

OLIVIA   If I think so, I think the same of you.

VIOLA   Then think you right: I am not what I am.

OLIVIA   I would you were, as I would have you be.

VIOLA   Would it be better, Madam, than I am?   150
I wish it might, for now I am your Fool.

OLIVIA   — O what a deal of Scorn looks
beautiful?
In the contempt and anger of his Lip,
A murd'rous Guilt shews not it self more soon
Than Love that would seem hid: Love's Night is
Noon.   155
— Cesario, by the Roses of the Spring,
By Maidhood, Honour, Truth, and Everything,
I love thee so, that maugre all thy Pride,
Nor Wit nor Reason can my Passion hide.
Do not extort thy Reasons from this Clause: 160
For that I woo, thou therefore hast no Cause.
But rather Reason thus with Reason fetter:
Love sought is good, but given unsought is
better.

VIOLA   By Innocence I swear, and by my Youth,
I have one Heart, one Bosom, and one Truth,   165
And that no Woman has, nor never none
Shall Mistress be of it, save I alone.
And so adieu, good Madam; never more
Will I my Master's Tears to you deplore.

OLIVIA   Yet come again: for thou perhaps may'st
move   170

162– **But . . . better**   But instead bind your Reason with the following
63   reason to love me: [the fact that] the love you seek is good,
       but the love that comes your way without your seeking it is
       even better. *Reason* (lines 159–62) recalls I.v.328–30;
       compare I.v.217, II.iii.156–59, II.v.174–75.

169   **deplore**   lament (as an argument for you to pity and love him).

171 **abhors** loathes, shuns.

III.ii This scene takes place in Olivia's house.

1 **I'll . . . longer** Sir Andrew is discouraged and is telling Sir Toby
and Fabian that he will not waste any more time or money on
his pursuit of Olivia.
iot jot (from the Greek letter *iota*).

2 **Venom** poison. Sir Toby applies this strong epithet to Sir
Andrew with his usual private irony. Not wanting to lose a
lucrative source of income, Sir Toby moves quickly to prevent
Sir Andrew from doing something rash. *Reason* echoes
III.i.159–62.

8 **see** see that you were observing. Most editions insert a *thee*
after *see*.

11–12 **This . . . you** Rather than showing that she doesn't favour you,
this is a clear signal that she loves you indeed.

13 **S'light** God's light.

14 **legitimate** both (a) valid (a logically demonstrable assertion),
and (b) legally admissible and compelling as evidence.

16 **Grand-jurymen** sage elders, authorities in assessing evidence.

19 **onely** only, solely. Compare I.ii.56.
exasperate irritate, incense. Fabian is probably punning on *ass*;
compare II.iii.184–85.

20 **Dormouse** a small, hibernating rodent. Fabian's image
combines two concepts: (a) sleepy, and (b) mousy.

21 **Brimstone** sulphur. Fire and brimstone were both associated
with Hell, of course, and Fabian is mockingly encouraging Sir
Andrew to manifest the demonic fury of a fire-eyed avenger.
Brimstone echoes II.v.55.

22 **accosted her** approached her (with all the passion of an
offended suitor). *Accosted* recalls I.iii.51–61. *Liver* echoes
II.v.104; compare I.i.36, II.iv.100.

25 **look'd for** both (a) desired, and (b) expected.
baulk'd allowed to go undone, neglected.

26 **double Gilt** double-layered gold.

28 **North** northern waters, away from the warmth of the sun
(Olivia's favour) into your Lady's icy dismissal. See the note
on 'cool my Nature' at I.iii.99.

The Heart which now abhors to like his Love.

Exeunt.

Scene 2

Enter Sir Toby, Sir Andrew, and Fabian.

ANDREW   No faith, I'll not stay a iot longer.

TOBY   Thy Reason, dear Venom, give thy Reason.

FABIAN   You must needs yield your Reason, Sir
Andrew.

ANDREW   Marry, I saw your Niece do more Favours   5
to the Count's Servingman than ever she bestow'd
upon me: I saw't i'th' Orchard.

TOBY   Did she see the while, old Boy, tell me
that.

ANDREW   As plain as I see you now.   10

FABIAN   This was a great Argument of Love in her
toward you.

ANDREW   S'light; will you make an Ass o' me.

FABIAN   I will prove it legitimate, Sir, upon the
Oaths of Judgement and Reason.   15

TOBY   And they have been Grand-jurymen since
before Noah was a Sailor.

FABIAN   She did shew Favour to the Youth in your
Sight onely to exasperate you, to awake your
Dormouse Valour, to put Fire in your Heart,   20
and Brimstone in your Liver. You should then
have accosted her, and with some excellent
Jests, Fire-new from the Mint, you should have
bang'd the Youth into Dumbness. This was
look'd for at your hand, and this was baulk'd.   25
The double-Gilt of this Opportunity you let
Time wash off, and you are now sail'd into the
North of my Lady's Opinion, where you will
hang like an Icicle on a Dutchman's Beard,

30–31 **laudable Attempt** praiseworthy exploit.

31 **Policy** strategy, intrigue.

33 **a Brownist** a member of an extreme Puritan sect, the
Congregationalists, founded by Robert Browne. *Politician*
(line 34) echoes II.iii.82, II.v.170–71.

35 **build me** Here *me* exemplifies what grammarians call the 'ethic
dative' (it literally means 'for me'); Shakespeare often uses it
to provide a colloquial touch.

40 **Commendation** reputation, standing.

45 **curst** shrewish, curt. See the note to I.iii.49.

47 **Invention** creativity, originality. *Witty* (line 46) echoes III.i.159
and recalls I.v.28–30.

48 **with Licence of Ink** with the boldness that writing allows you.
Writing could be a metaphor for the activity a virile man
undertook with his genital 'pen' (see *The Merchant of Venice*,
V.i.236–37, and compare *All's Well That Ends Well*,
II.i.69–78), and here Sir Toby's phrasing is another reminder
of Sir Andrew's inability to do anything that smacks of
'Invention' (line 47).
thou'st him call'st him 'thou' (thereby insulting him with a
presumptuous familiarity). The familiar pronouns (here *thou*
rather than *you*) were properly used only with intimates or
social inferiors.

52 **Bed of Ware** a famous Elizabethan four-poster bed more than
ten feet square, probably made for an inn at Ware, Herts, and
now in London's Victoria and Albert Museum. Lines 51–52
recall the imagery of III.i.112.

53 **Gall** both (a) bitterness, and (b) an acidic ingredient (from oak
galls) used in ink.

54 **a Goose-pen** a goose-feather quill. Sir Toby's implication is
that the letter will be just as foolish and cowardly as the
proverbially silly goose. One meaning of *goose* is 'whore';
once again, then, Sir Toby is alluding to Sir Andrew's lack of
manliness.

57 **Cubiculo** cubicle, small private chamber; probably a room in
Olivia's house, perhaps Sir Andrew's own quarters.

unless you do redeem it by some laudable   30
Attempt, either of Valour or Policy.

ANDREW   And't be any way, it must be with Valour,
for Policy I hate: I had as lief be a Brownist
as a Politician.

TOBY   Why then build me thy Fortunes upon the basis   35
of Valour. Challenge me the Count's Youth to
fight with him; hurt him in eleven places. My
Niece shall take note of it, and assure thy
self, there is no Love-broker in the World can
more prevail in Man's Commendation with Woman   40
than Report of Valour.

FABIAN   There is no way but this, Sir Andrew.

ANDREW   Will either of you bear me a Challenge to
him?

TOBY   Go, write it in a Martial Hand, be curst and   45
brief: it is no matter how Witty, so it be
Eloquent, and full of Invention. Taunt him
with the Licence of Ink. If thou *thou*'st him some
thrice, it shall not be amiss, and as many
Lies as will lie in thy sheet of Paper,   50
although the Sheet were big enough for the
Bed of Ware in England, set 'em down, go
about it. Let there be Gall enough in thy Ink,
though thou write with a Goose-pen, no matter:
about it.   55

ANDREW   Where shall I find you?

TOBY   We'll call thee at the Cubiculo. Go.

                              Exit Sir Andrew.

58   **dear Manikin to you**   a puppet (literally, 'little man') who is
        dear (valuable) to you. In the next line Sir Toby uses *dear* to
        mean 'costly' (probably to the tune of two thousand ducats,
        or two-thirds of Sir Andrew's yearly income, to judge from
        I.iii.22). See the note on another kind of 'Manikin' at I.v.38.

63   **then**   if I don't.

64–65 **Wain-ropes**   wagon-ropes.

65   **hale**   haul, drag.

68   **Anatomy**   either (a) body (whether alive or dead), or (b)
        skeleton.

69   **Opposite**   opponent. Compare II.v.156–57, III.iv.74–75.

70   **Presage of Cruelty**   sign that he will prove cruel. *Liver* (line 67)
        recalls line 21.

71   **youngest . . . mine**   my smallest and most youthful wren (a
        diminutive bird). It was said that the last egg hatched would
        yield the tiniest offspring. Most editions emend the Folio's
        mine to *nine*; the alteration is unnecessary.

72   **the Spleen**   uncontrollable laughter. The spleen was regarded as
        one of the seats of the impulsive passions.

74   **is turn'd Heathen**   is acting so strangely that it appears that he
        is no longer recognizable as a member of a Christian
        commonwealth. *Gull* (dupe) echoes II.iii.147.

75   **Renegatho**   renegade; a traitor who has renounced his faith.

76   **can**   that can.

77–78 **such . . . Grossness**   such incredible instances of gross
        behaviour.

80   **Pedant**   schoolmaster.

81   **dogg'd him**   either (a) pursued him like an animal with dogs on
        his trail, or (b) baited him like a bear tied to the stake.
        Compare III.i.126–28.

83   **betray him**   both (a) trick him, and (b) induce him to betray
        himself for what he is.

84   **Lines**   wrinkles. Maria alludes to the rhumb lines (lines
        indicating navigational routes determined by fixed points on a
        compass) on a map. See the note to line 85.

FABIAN   This is a dear Manikin to you, Sir Toby.

TOBY   I have been dear to him, Lad, some two
thousand strong, or so.   60

FABIAN   We shall have a rare Letter from him; but
you'll not deliver't.

TOBY   Never trust me then: and by all means stir on
the Youth to an Answer. I think Oxen and Wain-
ropes cannot hale them together. For Andrew,   65
if he were open'd and you find so much Blood
in his Liver as will clog the Foot of a Flea,
I'll eat the rest of th' Anatomy.

FABIAN   And his Opposite the Youth bears in his
Visage no great Presage of Cruelty.   70

Enter Maria.

TOBY   Look where the youngest Wren of mine comes.

MARIA   If you desire the Spleen, and will laugh
your selves into Stitches, follow me. Yond
Gull Malvolio is turn'd Heathen, a very
Renegatho; for there is no Christian that   75
means to be saved by believing rightly can
ever believe such impossible passages of
Grossness. He's in Yellow Stockings.

TOBY   And cross-Garter'd?

MARIA   Most villainously: like a Pedant that keeps   80
a School i'th' Church. I have dogg'd him like
his Murtherer. He does obey every Point of the
Letter that I dropp'd to betray him: he does
smile his Face into more Lines than is in the

85   **new Map . . . Indies** Maria probably refers to a map printed in 1599 and using Gerhardus Mercator's new principles of projection; this rendering made the East Indies appear larger and in more detail than in previous depictions of the Eastern Hemisphere.

87   **forbear** resist.

89   **Favour** sign of her affection. Compare lines 5–21.

III.iii   This scene takes us to a street in Illyria.

1   **by my Will** willingly.

2   **Pains** effort, trouble. Line 2 echoes II.iv.66–70.

6   **all** merely, entirely, solely.

8   **Jealousy** anxiety, doubt.

9   **skilless in these Parts** unfamiliar with this territory.

10   **unfriended** without friends to call upon for help.

12   **The rather by** made all the stronger and speedier by. Compare II.i.14–15.
    these Arguments of Fear these concerns about your safety. *Arguments* echoes III.ii.11–12.

14   **I can . . . make** I can no reciprocation offer.

16   **shuffled . . . Pay** accepted casually with nothing of any value (monetary currency that is still valid) offered in return. Line 15, which is one metrical foot short of the pentameter norm, provides a prosodic illustration of the insufficiency (mere 'Thanks' rather than current, negotiable 'Pay') Sebastian describes in lines 13–16. The phrase *shuffled off*, 'evaded by a clever shift', parallels *Hamlet*, III.i.64, where it refers to the sloughing off of an outer covering.

17   **were . . . firm** if I had the financial means to match the resolve I feel in my thoughts. Here the primary meaning of *Conscience* is 'consciousness', referring in particular to a sense of obligation. Compare III.i.32.

18   **better Dealing** more appropriate recompense.

19   **Reliques** relics, antiquities.

20   **see** arrange for.

new Map, with the Augmentation of the Indies.   85
You have not seen such a thing as 'tis: I can
hardly forbear hurling things at him, I know
my Lady will strike him. If she do, he'll
smile, and take't for a great Favour.

TOBY   Come bring us, bring us where he is.   *Exeunt.*   90

Scene 3

Enter Sebastian and Antonio.

SEBASTIAN   I would not by my Will have troubled you,
But since you make your Pleasure of your Pains,
I will no further chide you.

ANTONIO   I could not stay behind you: my Desire
(More sharp than filed Steel) did spur me
        forth,   5
And not all love to see you (though so much
As might have drawn one to a longer Voyage),
But Jealousy, what might befall your Travel,
Being skilless in these Parts, which to a
        Stranger,
Unguided and unfriended, often prove   10
Rough and unhospitable. My willing Love,
The rather by these Arguments of Fear,
Set forth in your Pursuit.

SEBASTIAN   My kind Antonio,
I can no other Answer make but Thanks,
And Thanks: and ever oft Good Turns   15
Are shuffled off with such Uncurrent Pay.
But were my Worth as is my Conscience firm,
You should find better Dealing. What's to do?
Shall we go see the Reliques of this Town?

ANTONIO   To morrow, Sir, best first go see your
        Lodging?   20

SEBASTIAN   I am not weary, and 'tis long to Night:

23   **Memorials**   monuments.

24   **Would**   I would request that.

26   **Count his**   Count's.

27   **did some Service**   performed some military exploits. *Note* here
       means both 'distinction' and 'notoriety'.

28   **answer'd**   explained and justified without jeopardy to my life.
       In line 33 *answer'd* means 'made up for, recompensed'.

29   **Belike**   probably, in all likelihood.

31   **quality . . . Quarrel**   the nature of the occasion and the reason
       for the conflict.

32   **Bloody Argument**   a reason for a deadly battle. In V.i.63–66,
       72– 75, Antonio's conflict with Orsino's forces is described in
       more violent terms.

33–35 **It might . . . did**   During the time that has elapsed since, the
       quarrel might have been patched up by our repaying what we
       took from them, which, to restore commerce, most of the
       merchants in our city agreed to do.

35–37 **Onely . . . dear**   I alone refused to go along with the settlement,
       for which reason if I am caught (*lapsed*, taken by surprise)
       here without a good excuse, or the means to defend myself, I
       shall be executed. *Onely* (only) recalls III.ii.19, and here as
       elsewhere it plays on 'one-ly' to reinforce Antonio's message
       that he was the only one who 'stood out' (a phrase that
       suggests the masculine assertiveness *onely* bears in passages
       such as *Macbeth*, I.vii.26, 72–74, and *Julius Caesar*,
       I.ii.153–54). See the notes on *one* at I.v.136, II.v.130.

38   **fit me**   suit me, serve my safety.

39   **Elephant**   In Shakespeare's time an inn of this name stood near
       the Globe playhouse in Bankside, Southwark. (The famous
       Elephant and Castle, at the busy road junction further south,
       was a later coaching inn first mentioned in 1765.)

40   **bespeak our Diet**   order our meals.

41   **beguile the Time**   literally, fool the time; make the time pass
       without its seeming to do so. Compare *A Midsummer Night's
       Dream*, V.i.40–41.

I pray you let us satisfy our Eyes
With the Memorials and the things of Fame
That do renown this City.

ANTONIO   Would you'd pardon me:
I do not without Danger walk these Streets.   25
Once in a Sea-fight 'gainst the Count his
    Galleys
I did some Service, of such Note indeed
That were I ta'en here it would scarce be
    answer'd.

SEBASTIAN   Belike you slew great number of his
    People.

ANTONIO   Th' Offence is not of such a Bloody
    Nature,   30
Albeit the quality of the Time and Quarrel
Might well have given us Bloody Argument;
It might have since been answer'd in repaying
What we took from them, which for Traffic's
    sake
Most of our City did. Onely my self stood out,   35
For which if I be lapsed in this Place
I shall pay dear.

SEBASTIAN   Do not then walk too open.

ANTONIO   It doth not fit me. Hold, Sir, here's my
    Purse.
In the South Suburbs at the Elephant
Is best to lodge; I will bespeak our Diet   40
Whiles you beguile the Time and feed your
    Knowledge

42   **have** find. Antonio's verb suggests that he would wish
Sebastian to 'have' him in a way that Sebastian either ignores
or, more likely, fails to register. Like the Antonio who
sacrifices everything for Bassanio in *The Merchant of Venice*,
Sebastian's friend ends up alone at the end of the action.

44   **Haply** both (a) perchance, and (b) happily.
    Toy trifle, perhaps as a souvenir.

45   **Store** supply of money.

46   **for idle Markets** sufficient for you to spend money idly (on a
whim, and for luxuries rather than necessities).

III.iv This scene takes place in Olivia's garden.

1   **come** make another visit. But see the note on the orgasmic
sense of *coming* at II.iii.47.

2   **bestow of him** give to him. Here *of* means 'on'. It may be that
Olivia speaks lines 1–4 to herself rather than to Maria.

5   **Sad and Civil** grave and civilized (appropriately 'correct').

6   **suits ... Fortunes** is the kind of servant my present difficulties
call for. The phrase *suits well* will turn out to be ironically apt
for a 'Servant' who does indeed aspire to his Lady's
'Fortunes'.

9   **Possess'd** mad; literally, inhabited by a demonic spirit.

13–14 **tainted in's Wits** disordered in his mind. *Tainted* here means
'infected'. But another sense, 'discoloured, stained', will soon
prove pertinent when Malvolio arrives in his yellow stockings.
And that will lead to a third sense, 'disgraced, degraded'.
Compare III.i.74. *Wits* recalls III.ii.46; see the note to
I.iii.86–87.

S.D.   **Enter Malvolio** If the placement of the Folio stage direction
reflects the early performances of the play, Malvolio enters
before Maria can exit to 'call him hither'.

With viewing of the Town; there shall you have
    me.
SEBASTIAN   Why I your Purse?
ANTONIO   Haply your Eye shall light upon some Toy
    You have desire to purchase; and your Store   45
    I think is not for idle Markets, Sir.
SEBASTIAN   I'll be your Purse-bearer, and leave you for
    An Hour.
ANTONIO   To th' Elephant.
SEBASTIAN   I do remember. *Exeunt.*

Scene 4

Enter Olivia and Maria.

OLIVIA   I have sent after him, he says
    he'll come:
  How shall I feast him? What bestow of him?
  For Youth is bought more oft than begg'd or
      borrow'd.
  I speak too loud.
  Where's Malvolio? He is Sad and Civil,   5
  And suits well for a Servant with my Fortunes.
  Where is Malvolio?
MARIA   He's coming, Madam, but in very Strange
  Manner: he is sure Possess'd, Madam.
OLIVIA   Why what's the matter? Does he rave?   10
MARIA   No Madam, he does nothing but smile: your
  Ladyship were best to have some Guard about
  you, if he come, for sure the man is tainted
  in's Wits.
OLIVIA   Go call him hither.

Enter Malvolio.

                    — I am as Mad as he   15

16 **If ... be** if the kinds of madness that make one sombre are equivalent to those that make one jolly.

19 **Sad** serious (not mournful). The 'Occasion' she refers to is the coming visit of 'Cesario' and the need to entertain him properly. See lines 1–6.

22 **Obstruction in the Blood** impediment in my blood circulation. But *Blood* can also mean both (a) passion and (b) nobility (as noted in II.v.154), and Malvolio's 'suit' (line 6) will prove to be an 'Obstruction' to 'the Blood' upon which his lofty ambitions depend. *Obstruction* echoes II.v.126.

25 **Sonnet** lyric poem. Malvolio alludes to a ballad, 'The Crow Sits Upon the Wall', published in 1592. Its theme is that all women want the same thing, and that what pleases one therefore pleases them all. Malvolio's meaning is different: what he implies is that to please one woman (Olivia) is all he wants; whether he pleases anyone else is of no concern to him. Here *one* hints at the erotic sense the word sometimes bears; see the note to III.iii.35–37.

26 **MARIA ... thee?** The Folio text assigns this speech to *Mal.* (Malvolio). Most editions reassign it to Olivia, but it seems more plausible that a speech that should be given to *Mar.* (as Maria's speeches are designated in this scene) would be misprinted as *Mal.* than that one intended for *Ol.* (Olivia) would be. If Maria does in fact speak the line, Malvolio may choose to ignore her, as he does in lines 42–43, and address Olivia as if she had asked the question.

28–29 **Not ... Legs** Malvolio probably means that he is not filled with 'black thoughts', even though the yellow in his legs might suggest that he is suffering from a condition (jealousy) that would cast a man into melancholy (a humour that was thought to result from an excess of black bile in the system). Compare I.v.60–62.

29–31 **it ... Hand** Malvolio now shifts to the third person to refer to the letter, assuming, of course, that Olivia will immediately pick up on his innuendo. The 'sweet Roman Hand' he refers to is an italic calligraphy (rather than the less graceful 'Secretary' script that most Elizabethans employed). *Roman Hand* may also be intended as an allusion to Lucrece; see II.v.99–103. *Hand* echoes III.ii.45.

32 **go to Bed** What Olivia means is that Malvolio appears to be in need of medical attention. In line 33, *I* means both 'I' and 'Ay', as in II.v.130, 140–42.

If sad and merry Madness equal be.
– How now, Malvolio?

MALVOLIO   Sweet Lady, ho, ho.

OLIVIA   Smil'st thou? I sent for thee upon a Sad
Occasion.   20

MALVOLIO   Sad Lady, I could be Sad. This does
make some Obstruction in the Blood, this
cross-Gartering, but what of that? If it please
the Eye of one, it is with me as the very
true Sonnet is: 'Please one, and please all.'   25

MARIA   Why how doest thou, Man? What is the Matter
with thee?

MALVOLIO   Not Black in my Mind, though Yellow in
my Legs: it did come to his Hands, and Commaunds
shall be executed. I think we do know the sweet   30
Roman Hand.

OLIVIA   Wilt thou go to Bed, Malvolio?

MALVOLIO   To Bed? I, sweet Heart, and I'll come to
thee.

OLIVIA   God comfort thee: why dost thou smile so,   35
and kiss thy Hand so oft?

MARIA   How do you, Malvolio?

MALVOLIO   At your Request: yes, Nightingales answer
Daws.

MARIA   Why appear you with this ridiculous Boldness   40
before my Lady?

MALVOLIO   – 'Be not afraid of Greatness': 'twas
well writ.

OLIVIA   What meanst thou by that, Malvolio?

34–35 **come to thee**   join you there. Compare lines 1, 8–9.

36   **kiss thy Hand**   Kissing one's hand was a sign of respect.

38–39 **At . . . Daws**   One way to interpret this speech is 'Shall I answer
you? Yes, in the same way that elegant nightingales
condescend to speak to lowly jackdaws (birds of the crow
family).' Malvolio is being 'surly with Servants' (II.v.157). In
his subsequent lines he quotes from or paraphrases the letter.

45   **borne**   both (a) born, and (b) carried. See the note to II.v.151.

49   **Greatness thrust upon them**   Malvolio's 'Greatness' (his puffed-up hubris or pride) has been thrust upon him, but by means quite different from those he imagines. The phrase itself has sexual implications relevant to the present states of both Malvolio and Olivia ('Greatness' can refer both to male tumescence and to female pregnancy), but of course neither of them picks up on it.

54–55 **And wish'd . . . cross Garter'd?**   Olivia's question suggests that she believes *thee* to be addressed to her. Her bewildered 'Am I made?' (line 58) reflects the same kind of confusion.

56   **Go to**   get to it. See the note to II.v.163.

60   **Midsummer Madness**   The midsummer moon was proverbially associated with outbreaks of lunacy. If the title of the play indicates the time when the action takes place (the first week of January), Malvolio's madness is doubly shocking for its untimeliness.

62   **hardly**   scarcely, only with great difficulty. See the notes to I.iii.107, III.i.123, and compare II.iii.176–77, III.ii.86–87.

63   **he . . . Pleasure**   He awaits your Ladyship's instructions. The Servant has no idea that Olivia's 'Pleasure' (will, command) is focused on the same kind of pleasure that Malvolio fantasizes about. *Come* (line 64) reinforces that sense; compare lines 1, 8–9, 34–35, 69, 88–90.

65   **let . . . look'd to**   What Olivia means is that Malvolio should be put under the care of someone who will nurse him back to health. Malvolio construes her words quite differently. Compare I.v.148–49, where Feste says that 'the Fool shall look to the Madman'.

68   **miscarry**   go utterly insane, be lost completely. Here the word echoes *Care* (line 67).

69   **do you come near me now?**   Just what this line means is uncertain. Malvolio may address it to Olivia as she exits, expressing delight that after pretending to be so distant from Malvolio, she is now saying something that hints at her 'special Care of him'. A more likely possibility is that Malvolio addresses Maria, with the implication that she will soon see that he is too 'great' for someone of her lowly rank to 'come near' (approach or challenge) any longer. A third is that Malvolio is asking all Olivia's subordinates if they are finally coming near a proper appreciation of his special status.

MALVOLIO   'Some are borne Great.'   45
OLIVIA   Ha?
MALVOLIO   'Some achieve Greatness.'
OLIVIA   What say'st thou?
MALVOLIO   'And some have Greatness thrust upon them.'
OLIVIA   Heaven restore thee.   50
MALVOLIO   'Remember who commended thy Yellow
   Stockings.'
OLIVIA   Thy Yellow Stockings?
MALVOLIO   'And wish'd to see thee cross-Garter'd.'
OLIVIA   Cross-Garter'd?   55
MALVOLIO   'Go to, thou art made, if thou desir'st
   to be so.'
OLIVIA   Am I made?
MALVOLIO   'If not, let me see thee a Servant still.'
OLIVIA   Why this is very Midsummer Madness.   60

Enter Servant.

SERVANT   Madam, the young Gentleman of the Count
   Orsino's is return'd, I could hardly entreat him
   back: he attends your Ladyship's Pleasure.
OLIVIA   I'll come to him.   [*Exit Servant.*]
   – Good Maria, let this Fellow be look'd to.   65
   Where's my Cousin Toby? Let some of my People
   have a special Care of him, I would not have
   him miscarry for the half of my Dowry.
                          [*Exeunt Olivia and Maria.*]
MALVOLIO   – Oh ho, do you come near me now?
   – No worse Man than Sir Toby to look to me.   70
   This concurs directly with the Letter, she
   sends him on Purpose, that I may appear
   Stubborn to him: for she incites me to that in the
   Letter. 'Cast thy humble Slough,' says she; 'be
   opposite with a Kinsman, surly with Servants;   75

76   **langer** linger, excuse delays. In the original text of the letter, the phrase corresponding to this reads 'let thy Tongue tang [sound with] Arguments of State' (II.v.158). Modern editors normally assume that *langer* is a compositor's misreading and print *tang* here; but *langer*, a variant spelling of *linger* and a relative of *languor*, fits the context equally well and reinforces *Slow Tongue* in line 79. Compare the situation with *borne*, line 45.

78   **consequently** then (both thereafter and therefore).

79   **Reverend Carriage** solemn bearing.

80   **Habit . . . Note** dress and demeanour of some notable nobleman.

81   **lim'd** caught her with birdlime (a sticky substance). The irony, of course is that it is Malvolio who has been 'lim'd', ensnared. See II.v.91.

83   **Fellow** either (a) servant, or (b) equal (Malvolio's sense). See II.v.68 (where Toby uses the term to mean 'overweening inferior') and 163–67.

86   **Dram of a Scruple** Both words refer to apothecaries' measures for tiny quantities: a dram was an eighth of a fluid ounce, and a scruple was a third of a dram. *Scruple* also means 'doubt', as does *Obstacle* in line 87.

87–88 **no incredulous or unsafe Circumstance** no detail that would suggest any need for incredulity (doubt) or caution.

90   **Prospect** scope or range; but Malvolio means 'realization'. The literal meaning of *prospect* is 'looking forward', and here it reinforces our awareness of Malvolio's jutting 'Hopes'; he believes that they will soon be 'full' (another sense of 'Great', as noted at line 49). See the notes on words with *pro-* prefixes in *Troilus and Cressida*, II.ii.132, 135.

92   **Sanctity** both (a) holiness, and (b) spiritual wholeness, mental well-being. Compare *Hamlet*, I.iii.21, where the Folio text refers to 'The Sanctity and Health of this whole State', and II.ii.219, where the Quarto text contrasts 'Reason and Sanctity' with 'Madness'.

94   **Legion himself** Sir Toby refers to the 'unclean spirit' whom Jesus exorcizes in Mark 5:8–9. The spirit says, 'My name is Legion: for we are many.' *Legion* thus means 'drawn in little' (many squeezed into one).

let thy Tongue langer with Arguments of State;
put thy self into the Trick of Singularity.'
And consequently sets down the Manner how: as
a Sad Face, a Reverend Carriage, a Slow Tongue,
in the Habit of some Sir of Note, and so foorth.   80
I have lim'd her, but it is Jove's doing, and
Jove make me thankful. And when she went away
now, 'Let this Fellow be look'd to.' Fellow?
Not Malvolio, nor after my Degree, but Fellow.
Why every thing adheres together, that no   85
Dram of a Scruple, no Scruple of a Scruple,
no Obstacle, no incredulous or unsafe
Circumstance – What can be said? Nothing
that can be can come between me and the full
Prospect of my Hopes. Well Jove, not I, is the   90
doer of this, and he is to be thanked.

Enter Toby, Fabian, and Maria.

TOBY   Which way is he, in the name of Sanctity? If
    all the Divels of Hell be drawn in little, and
    Legion himself possess'd him, yet I'll speak
    to him.   95
FABIAN   Here he is, here he is. – How is't with you,

97   **Man**   This mode of address can be equivalent to 'Sir'; but it can also be condescending, reminding Malvolio that he is but a servingman. See the note to II.ii.26.

99   **Private**   privacy. Malvolio's phrasing hints at both his own 'Private Part' (*Troilus and Cressida*, II.ii.124) and that of the female object of his aroused infatuation.

100   **hollow**   echoing deeply.

102   **Care**   This word (echoing line 67) can also refer to a 'cure', and in due course Sir Toby and his companions will 'have a Care of' Malvolio indeed.

104   **Go to**   come now, hush. Compare line 56.

105   **Let me alone**   leave it to me to deal with him. Compare lines 119–20 and II.iii.146.

105–6 **How do you, Malvolio?**   Sir Toby probably speaks these words as if he is trying to conjure up the spirit of Malvolio and address that rather than the demonic 'Legion' who has supposedly displaced him in Malvolio's body.

106   **defy**   renounce, repudiate.

109   **La you**   note, observe.
      and   if.

110   **how . . . Heart**   how he is offended by it. Here *he* refers to Malvolio, but with the suggestion that it is the Devil speaking through him.

112   **Carry . . . Wise-woman**   Take a sample of his urine to the 'Wise-woman'. Often a 'wise-woman' was herself a witch (as with the 'Wise Woman of Brainford' in IV.v.26–27 of *The Merry Wives of Windsor*); but Fabian probably refers to a woman with expertise in the application of herbs and other remedies. Often such women were 'white witches' whose charms were thought capable of undoing enchantments. *Water* recalls I.i.28–31, I.iii.129–30, I.v.172–73, II.i.31–34.

114   **loose**   both (a) relinquish, be deprived of, release, and (b) lose. Compare II.v.2.

119   **move**   stir, anger.
      Let me alone with   let me deal with.

121   **Gentleness**   tenderness, solicitous 'Care' (line 102). But here and in lines 104–5 *gentle* also carries reminders of the 'gentleness' (the aristocratic status) to which the 'overweening' Malvolio aspires (see II.v.27–80).

Sir? How is't with you, Man?

MALVOLIO   Go off, I discard you. Let me enjoy my
Private: go off.

MARIA   – Lo, how hollow the Fiend speaks within   100
him; did not I tell you? – Sir Toby, my Lady
prays you to have a Care of him.

MALVOLIO   Ah ha, does she so?

TOBY   – Go to, go to: peace, peace, we must deal
gently with him. Let me alone. – How do you,   105
Malvolio? How is't with you? What, Man, defy
the Divel: consider, he's an Enemy to Mankind.

MALVOLIO   Do you know what you say?

MARIA   – La you, and you speak ill of the Divel,
how he takes it at Heart. Pray God he be not   110
bewitch'd.

FABIAN   Carry his Water to th' Wise-woman.

MARIA   Marry and it shall be done to morrow morning
if I live. My Lady would not loose him for more
than I'll say.   115

MALVOLIO   How now, Mistress?

MARIA   – Oh Lord.

TOBY   Prethee hold thy peace, this is not the way.
Do you not see you move him? Let me alone with
him.   120

FABIAN   No way but Gentleness, gently, gently: the
Fiend is rough, and will not be roughly us'd.

123 **Bawcock** literally, *beau coq*; like *Chuck* (line 124) a term of
endearment equivalent to 'fine fellow'. Here, however, it calls
attention to Malvolio's strutting 'Turkey-cock' plumage (see
II.v.35–37). It also alludes to his sexual ambitions ('cock'
being a term for the male member), an implication furthered
by the reference to 'Cherry-pit' (line 127), a game with
analogies to copulation.

126 **Biddy** chicken (a name often used by children).

126– **'tis not for Gravity** it is not in keeping with a serious
27 demeanour.

127 **Cherry-pit** a child's game in which cherry-stones were tossed
into a hole. See the note to line 123, and compare Lucio's
reference to 'a Game of Tick-tack' in *Measure for Measure*,
I.iii.72–74.

128 **foul Collier** blackened coal-man. Devils were often depicted as
black.

131 **Minx** shameless hussy.

135 **I am not of your Element** What Malvolio means, of course, is
that he is above them in station. What they are trying to teach
him through their merciless baiting is that his 'Place' (II.v.59)
is below theirs. See the notes to lines 97, 121. *Element* echoes
I.i.25–26, III.i.63–65; see the note to II.v.116. *Hang* (line
134) recalls I.v.1–21, II.v.112, III.ii.26–31.

138– **If . . . Fiction** Part of the humour of this line is that what we
39 are witnessing *is* being played upon a stage. The phrase
improbable Fiction refers to a story too far-fetched to be
accepted as plausible (even by an audience that has implicitly
consented to pretend that a dramatic representation is an
imitation of real life).

140– **His . . . Device** His soul itself has caught the 'infection' this
41 trick was intended to implant in his mind. In a sense Malvolio
really *is* possessed, so deeply has he taken to heart the disease
(the *atê* or consuming delusion) the letter was intended to give
him. *Device* echoes II.v.194.

142– **take Air, and taint** become exposed to the air and thus spoiled
43 (by discolouring, rusting, or rotting). Maria probably means
that once the word gets around, someone may spoil the trick
by saying something to expose it. Here as in line 378, *least*
means 'lest'. *Taint* echoes lines 13–14.

TOBY — Why how now, my Bawcock? How dost thou, Chuck?

MALVOLIO   Sir.   125

TOBY   Ay Biddy, come with me. What, Man, 'tis not for Gravity to play at Cherry-pit with Sathan. Hang him, foul Collier.

MARIA   Get him to say his Prayers, good Sir Toby, get him to pray.   130

MALVOLIO   My Prayers, Minx.

MARIA   No, I warrant you, he will not hear of Godliness.

MALVOLIO   Go hang your selves all: you are idle shallow things, I am not of your Element,   135
you shall know more hereafter.   *Exit.*

TOBY   Is't possible?

FABIAN   If this were play'd upon a Stage now, I could condemn it as an improbable Fiction.

TOBY   His very Genius hath taken the Infection of   140
the Device, Man.

MARIA   Nay pursue him now, least the Device take Air, and taint.

FABIAN   Why we shall make him Mad indeed.

MARIA   The House will be the quieter.   145

TOBY   Come, we'll have him in a Dark Room and bound. My Niece is already in the Belief that he's

146   **have him**   have him placed. Compare III.iii.4. The treatment Sir Toby proposes was the one normally prescribed for lunatics in Elizabethan England. *Bound* (line 147) echoes III.i.83–85.

148– **for our Pleasure, and his Penance** This phrase echoes Feste's
49   earlier observation that 'Pleasure will be paid one time or
       another' (II.iv.69–70). Ironically, Malvolio's penance will
       have been earned by no more than the pleasure of fantasizing
       about the pleasure he aspires to. See the note to line 63.

151   **the Bar** the judgement bar (to be found guilty or not guilty).
       Compare I.iii.71–72, I.iv.42.

152   **Finder** both (a) locater, detector, and (b) prover (a legal sense
       that coheres with *Bar* in line 151).

154   **Matter . . . Morning** material for a siege of 'Midsummer
       Madness' (line 60). Fabian refers to the merriment to be
       anticipated from Sir Andrew's letter challenging 'Cesario' to a
       duel.

157   **Saucy** disrespectful, defiant (as in I.v.214). But Fabian puns on
       the culinary sense (spicy) that goes with 'Vinegar and Pepper'
       (line 156).

158   **warrant** assure, guarantee.

162   **admire** marvel.

163– **no Reason** This phrase epitomizes Sir Andrew's letter (and
64   indeed his entire personality). His 'argument' is a ludicrous
       patchwork of non sequiturs (statements that fail to follow
       logically from what precedes them), 'Sense-less' assertions
       (lines 171–72), and self-contradictions. *Reason* recalls
       III.ii.1–4, 14–15.

165– **from the Blow of the Law** away from anything that would
66   make you liable to an accusation that you have slandered
       your opponent and breached the peace. *Blow* can mean both
       (a) violent hit, and (b) wind, breath (see line 177).

168   **uses** treats, receives.

168– **thou . . . Throat** your lies originate in the depths of your being.
69   This phrase was a standard formula for defiance.

173   **waylay** ambush, attack from behind like a coward.

175   **Good** Fabian pretends to be praising Sir Andrew's rhetoric, but
       he is probably implying as well that it would be good for so
       foolish and pusillanimous a knight to be killed.

Mad. We may carry it thus for our Pleasure, and
his Penance, till our very Pastime, tired out of
Breath, prompt us to have Mercy on him: at   150
which time we will bring the Device to the Bar
and crown thee for a Finder of Madmen. But see,
but see.

Enter Sir Andrew.

FABIAN   More Matter for a May Morning.
ANDREW   Here's the Challenge, read it: I warrant   155
  there's Vinegar and Pepper in't.
FABIAN   Is't so Saucy?
ANDREW   Ay is't? I warrant him: do but read.
TOBY   Give me. 'Youth, whatsoever thou art,
  thou art but a Scurvy Fellow.'   160
FABIAN   Good, and Valiant.
TOBY   'Wonder not, nor admire not in thy Mind
  why I do call thee so, for I will shew thee no
  Reason for't.'
FABIAN   A good Note, that keeps you from the Blow   165
  of the Law.
TOBY   'Thou com'st to the Lady Olivia, and in my
  Sight she uses thee kindly: but thou liest in
  thy Throat, that is not the Matter I challenge
  thee for.'   170
FABIAN   Very brief, and to exceeding good Sense-
  less.
TOBY   'I will waylay thee going home, where if it
  be thy chance to kill me.'
FABIAN   Good.   175
TOBY   'Thou kill'st me like a Rogue and a Villain.'

177 **o'th' Windy side** either (a) downwind (so that any scent of you will go undetected by the prey you hunt), or (b) upwind (so that you can retain control of your sails and prevent your ship being driven on to the rocks). The 'Law' referred to in this speech is a prohibition against private duelling to settle matters to be adjudicated by the state.

180– **He . . . better** What Sir Andrew means is 'I may be the one to
81   die, and thus require God's mercy.' But what he says is that he hopes that God will not have mercy on his soul because he has 'Hope' for a 'better' fate.

183– **If . . . cannot** if this letter doesn't send him running away, it
84   will only be because his legs aren't working.

186   **in some Commerce** conducting some business.

187   **by and by** very shortly.

189   **Bum-baily** a bailiff who arrested debtors. The name derives from the notion that the bailiff was always close behind (on the 'bum' or hip of) a potential victim. In *Measure for Measure*, II.i.224–30, *Bum* appears to be phallic (probably by way of such combinations as *bum-blade* or *bum-dagger*), and the references to drawing in lines 189–91 suggest that Toby may be alluding to that sense.

191   **swear horrible** both (a) swear horribly (terrifyingly), and (b) swear a horrifying 'Oath' (line 192) or curse.

193   **twang'd off** delivered with bravado. Compare *tang*, II.v.158.

194   **Approbation** approval, credibility. Compare III.ii.39–41.
      Proof it self an actual display of valour.

196   **let me alone for Swearing** leave it to me to show you some real swearing. Sir Andrew's phrasing echoes lines 119–20.

198– **gives . . . Breeding** reveals that he is a man of intelligence and
99   cultivation. *Capacity* recalls I.i.9–11, II.v.125; the literal meaning of the word relates to 'taking' and 'holding' (capability) as well as to 'containing'. See line 207.

199– **his Employment** the importance of the tasks he is entrusted
200   with. Compare II.v.89–90.

204   **Clodpole** clod-head.

205   **set upon Ague-cheek** confer upon Ague-cheek (give Ague-cheek credit for).

207   **aptly receive it** accept it as an apt report.

FABIAN   Still you keep o'th' Windy side of the
Law: good.

TOBY   'Fare thee well, and God have Mercy upon
one of our Souls. He may have Mercy upon mine,   180
but my Hope is better, and so look to thy self.
Thy Friend as thou usest him, and thy sworn
Enemy, Andrew Ague-cheek.' If this Letter move
him not, his Legs cannot: I'll give't him.

MARIA   You may have very fit Occasion for't: he is   185
now in some Commerce with my Lady, and will
by and by depart.

TOBY   Go, Sir Andrew: scout me for him at the
Corner of the Orchard like a Bum-baily. So
soon as ever thou seest him, draw; and as thou   190
draw'st, swear horrible: for it comes to pass
oft that a terrible Oath, with a swaggering
Accent sharply twang'd off, gives Manhood more
Approbation than ever Proof it self would have
earn'd him. Away.   195

ANDREW   Nay let me alone for Swearing.   *Exit.*

TOBY   — Now will not I deliver his Letter: for the
Behaviour of the young Gentleman gives him out
to be of good Capacity, and Breeding; his
Employment between his Lord and my Niece   200
confirms no less. Therefore this Letter, being
so excellently Ignorant, will breed no Terror
in the Youth: he will find it comes from a
Clodpole. But Sir, I will deliver his Challenge
by word of Mouth, set upon Ague-cheek a notable   205
Report of Valour, and drive the Gentleman (as I
know his Youth will aptly receive it) into a
most hideous Opinion of his Rage, Skill, Fury,
and Impetuosity. This will so fright them both

211 **Cockatrices** The cockatrice, or basilisk, was a mythological
serpent thought capable of killing a victim with one glance
from its eye. It had the head, wings and talons of a cock. See
the note on *Bawcock* at line 123.

212– **give them way** step out of their way (so they won't pay any
13 attention to you).

213 **presently** immediately.

217 **Hart** both (a) stag, and (b) heart. Compare I.i.16–22, 32–38,
II.iii.16, II.v.188.

218 **too unchary** with too little restraint and caution. *Honour* in
this line means both (a) integrity, virtue, and the reputation
for these qualities, and (b) chastity (here maidenhead,
virginity). Compare III.i.126–28, 157–59.

219 **reproves my Fault** scolds my weakness. But here and in lines
220–21, the genital sense of *Fault* is also pertinent. See the
notes to II.iv.77–78, II.v.130, 135.

222 **Haviour** behaviour.

223 **Goes on my Master's Griefs** my Master's sufferings continue.

224 **Jewel** probably a locket with Olivia's picture in miniature.
Compare II.v.64–66.

225 **vex** annoy, distress.

228 **That ... give** that my chastity, consistent with its own
preservation, may give you for the asking.

230 **Honour** truthfulness, fidelity to my vows. Compare line 218.

231 **acquit you** declare you innocent; release you from any claims I
have on your love.

that they will kill one another by the Look,   210
like Cockatrices.

Enter Olivia and Viola.

FABIAN   Here he comes with your Niece; give them
way till he take leave, and presently after
him.
TOBY   I will meditate the while upon some horrid   215
Message for a Challenge.
[*Toby, Fabian, and Maria withdraw*.]
OLIVIA   I have said too much unto a Hart of Stone,
And laid mine Honour too unchary on't.
There's something in me that reproves my Fault:
But such a headstrong potent Fault it is   220
That it but mocks Reproof.
VIOLA   With the same Haviour that your Passion
bears
Goes on my Master's Griefs.
OLIVIA   Here, wear this Jewel for me, 'tis my
Picture:
Refuse it not, it hath no Tongue to vex you.   225
And I beseech you come again to morrow.
What shall you ask of me that I'll deny,
That Honour, sav'd, may upon Asking give?
VIOLA   Nothing but this, your true Love for my
Master.
OLIVIA   How with mine Honour may I give him that   230
Which I have given to you?
VIOLA   I will acquit you.
OLIVIA   Well, come again to morrow. Fare thee well,
A Fiend like thee might bear my Soul to Hell.
Exit.

Enter Toby and Fabian.

TOBY   Gentleman, God save thee.
VIOLA   And you, Sir.   235

236   **Defence**   skill in defending yourself with your sword (your ability to fence).

238   **thy Intercepter**   the man who has asked me to intercept you (to block your path and tell you he intends to cut your life short).

239   **Despight**   spite, malice.
   attends thee   awaits you.

240   **Dismount thy Tuck**   unsheathe your sword.
   yare   speedy, alert, skilful.

241   **quick**   both (a) lively, and (b) dextrous, fast-moving with his sword.

244   **Quarrel to me**   reason to believe that I have wronged him.

249   **betake . . . Guard**   prepare to defend yourself. *Guard* recalls lines 11–13; *Opposite* echoes lines 74–75.

251   **withal**   with.

253–   **dubb'd . . . Consideration**   inducted into the knighthood with
54   an unhacked sword (one never used in combat) and in commemoration of services on the 'carpet' (that is, in peaceful, domestic pursuits or through Court connections) rather than on the battlefield. The word *Consideration* suggests that Sir Andrew may have purchased his title with a 'consideration' (a timely gift or bribe).

255–   **Souls . . . three**   he has killed three men in private duels.
56   *Incensement* means 'hot fury'.

257   **implacable**   incapable of being placated (pacified).
   Satisfaction   honourable resolution of the quarrel.

259   **Hob, Nob**   an expression meaning 'have it, [do] not have it'. This expression refers to a wrath so impetuous and desperate that its agent is totally fearless of any consequences that may befall him.

261   **desire . . . Lady**   request an escort from the Lady.

263   **put . . . others**   deliberately provoke quarrels with others.
   taste   test. Compare III.i.85.

265   **Quirk**   eccentricity, proclivity.

267   **computent Injury**   a slight on his honour that can be computed to a degree of injury that requires duelling for 'Satisfaction'. See *As You Like It*, V.iv.69–110. Most editions emend *computent* to *competent*, 'sufficient'.

TOBY The Defence thou hast, betake thee to't.
Of what nature the Wrongs are thou hast done
him I know not; but thy Intercepter, full of
Despight, Bloody as the Hunter, attends thee
at the Orchard end. Dismount thy Tuck, be yare   240
in thy Preparation, for thy Assailant is quick,
skilful, and deadly.

VIOLA You mistake, Sir, I am sure, no Man hath
any Quarrel to me: my Remembrance is very free
and clear from any Image of Offence done to   245
any Man.

TOBY You'll find it otherwise, I assure you:
therefore if you hold your Life at any Price,
betake you to your Guard: for your Opposite
hath in him what Youth, Strength, Skill, and   250
Wrath can furnish Man withal.

VIOLA I pray you, Sir, what is he?

TOBY He is Knight dubb'd with unhatch'd Rapier,
and on Carpet Consideration, but he is a Divel
in private Brawl. Souls and Bodies hath he   255
divorc'd three, and his Incensement at this
moment is so implacable that Satisfaction can
be none but by Pangs of Death and Sepulchre.
'Hob, Nob' is his Word: give't or take't.

VIOLA I will return again into the House, and   260
desire some Conduct of the Lady. I am no
Fighter. I have heard of some kind of Men
that put Quarrels purposely on others to taste
their Valour: belike this is a Man of that
Quirk.   265

TOBY Sir, no: his Indignation derives it self out
of a very computent Injury; therefore get you
on, and give him his Desire. Back you shall not

269–   **unless . . . him** unless you duel with me, which will be just as
70   dangerous as accepting his challenge. *Undertake* recalls
         I.iii.60, III.i.116.

272   **meddle** fight, mix it up with him. See the note to line 304.

273   **forswear . . . you** give up your sword as a coward.

277   **of my Negligence** I have done without intending it. Compare
         I.iv.5.

283   **a mortal Arbitrement** a trial whose outcome will require at
         least one death.

286   **of that wonderful Promise** that makes you expect wonders of
         him. Line 285 echoes I.v.163–75.

286–   **to read him by his Form** to judge him by his appearance. *Form*
87   recalls I.ii.50 and anticipates V.i.239–40.

287   **like** likely.

289   **Opposite** opponent. Compare lines 249–51. *Proof*
         (demonstration, verification) echoes lines 193–95.

293   **bound** indebted. See lines 146–47.

294–   **go . . . Knight** have a priest for my agent rather than a knight
95   (that is, settle my affairs peacefully rather than by combat).

296   **Mettle** both (a) character, valour, and (b) metal (sword).

298   **Firago** virago (literally, a woman of man-like fierceness). Sir
         Toby doesn't realize how pertinent his facetious term for
         'Cesario' will turn out to be.
         Pass bout. *Pass* derives from *passado*, the Italian word for
         'thrust' or 'stroke'. Compare *Romeo and Juliet*, III.i.88, and
         Hamlet, V.ii.60–62, 311.

299–   **Stuck in** thrust home; *Stuck* is an Anglicization of Italian
300   *stoccado*. See *Romeo and Juliet*, III.i.77, where Mercutio says,
         '*Alla stucatho* carries it away.'

300   **Mortal** deadly. Compare line 283.

301   **inevitable** incapable of being prevented, defended against.
         Answer thrust in reply.
         pays repays, responds to. Here as in *1 Henry IV*, II.iv.211–12,
         pays is a euphemism for 'kills'.

303   **Fencer to the Sophy** a fencer who enjoyed the royal patronage
         of the Shah of Persia.

to the House, unless you undertake that with me
which with as much Safety you might answer him.   270
Therefore on, or strip your Sword stark naked:
for meddle you must, that's certain, or
forswear to wear Iron about you.

VIOLA   This is as Uncivil as Strange. I beseech
you do me this Courteous Office, as to know   275
of the Knight what my Offence to him is: it
is something of my Negligence, nothing of
my Purpose.

TOBY   I will do so. Signior Fabian, stay you by
this Gentleman till my Return.   *Exit.*   280

VIOLA   Pray you, Sir, do you know of this Matter?

FABIAN   I know the Knight is incens'd against you,
even to a mortal Arbitrement, but nothing of
the Circumstance more.

VIOLA   I beseech you what manner of Man is he?   285

FABIAN   Nothing of that wonderful Promise, to read
him by his Form, as you are like to find him
in the Proof of his Valour. He is indeed, Sir,
the most skilful, bloody, and fatal Opposite
that you could possibly have found in any part   290
of Illyria. Will you walk towards him, I will
make your Peace with him if I can.

VIOLA   I shall be much bound to you for't. I am
one that had rather go with Sir Priest than
Sir Knight: I care not who knows so much of   295
my Mettle.   *Exeunt.*

Enter Toby and Andrew.

TOBY   Why, Man, he's a very Divel, I have not seen
such a Firago: I had a Pass with him, Rapier,
Scabbard, and all, and he gives me the Stuck
in with such a Mortal Motion that it is   300
inevitable; and on the Answer he pays you as
surely as your Feet hits the Ground they step
on. They say he has been Fencer to the Sophy.

304 **meddle** literally, 'mingle'. Compare line 272. Sir Andrew's verb is frequently used to describe those who engage in, or desire to engage in, erotic activity (see the notes to *Measure for Measure*, V.i.127, 144, and compare *Romeo and Juliet*, II.i.35–36); in this case it reminds us both of Sir Andrew's own incapacity to 'meddle' (see I.iii.65–82) and of Viola's desire to 'meddle' with her master and evade the misdirected meddling of Olivia.

306 **can scarce hold him yonder** Sir Toby says this with concious irony, implying that Fabian can scarcely hold him back, but knowing that Fabian must hold him to keep him from fleeing.

307 **and** if.

308 **Cunning in Fence** skilled in fencing (see the note to line 236). *Cunning* recalls III.i.123–25, and here it relates to what Viola says in lines 327–29.

311 **Capilet** a name that literally means 'little horse'. This name recurs in *All's Well That Ends Well*, where it is applied to Diana Capilet, the maiden Bertram believes himself to have mounted in a nocturnal assignation. Meanwhile it is a variant of *Capulet* (which also derives from *capul* or *caple*), a surname that accords with *Mountague* (Mount-ague) in *Romeo and Juliet*.

312 **make the Motion** propose the terms you offer.

314 **Perdition** literally, loss or damnation.

316 **take up the Quarrel** resolve (make up) the quarrel without duelling.

318 **He ... him** The youth has as frightening a concept of Sir Andrew.

322 **for's Oath sake** to maintain his oath of honour as a knight.

322– **better bethought him of** reconsidered the grounds for.
23

325 **for ... Vow** to allow him to uphold his vow.

327– **A ... Man** A small trifle would bring me to confess to them
29 how unmanly I am. The words *little thing* and *how much I lack of a Man* are meant to remind us that 'Cesario's' 'fault' is that 'he' has 'no thing'. See the references cited in the note to line 219. In *The Merchant of Venice*, III.iv.59–62, when Portia and Nerissa disguise themselves as men, Portia says that they will go 'in such a Habit / That they shall think we are accomplished / With that we lack.'

ANDREW   Pox on't, I'll not meddle with him.

TOBY   Ay but he will not now be pacified, Fabian   305
can scarce hold him yonder.

ANDREW   Plague on't, and I thought he had been
Valiant, and so Cunning in Fence, I'd have
seen him damn'd ere I'd have challeng'd him.
Let him let the Matter slip, and I'll give him   310
my Horse, grey Capilet.

TOBY   I'll make the Motion: stand here, make a
good Shew on't, this shall end without the
Perdition of Souls. — Marry I'll ride your
Horse as well as I ride you.   315

Enter Fabian and Viola.

— I have his Horse to take up the Quarrel:
I have persuaded him the Youth's a Divel.

FABIAN   He is as horribly conceited of him, and
pants and looks pale, as if a Bear were at his
Heels.   320

TOBY   — There's no Remedy, Sir, he will fight with
you for's Oath sake. Marry he hath better
bethought him of his Quarrel, and he finds
that now scarce to be worth talking of:
therefore draw for the supportance of his Vow,   325
he protests he will not hurt you.

VIOLA   Pray God defend me — A little thing
would make me tell them how much I lack of
a Man.

FABIAN   Give ground if you see him furious.   330

331 **no Remedy** no 'Satisfaction' (line 257) or escape.

333 **Duello** the code duello, the rules governing the conduct of a duel to resolve a dispute.

339 **Put up** put away. So also in line 349.

340 **take . . . me** assume full responsibility for defending his honour against any blemish ('Fault') it is alleged to have. *Fault* echoes line 219; it is also pertinent to lines 308, 327–29.

341 **defy you** challenge you and declare you to have wronged him in the name of honour. Antonio believes, of course, that he is coming to the rescue of Sebastian. Compare lines 343–44 with II.i.47–51, III.iii.4–13, and see the note to III.iii.42.

342 **what** what man, who.

345 **Undertaker** adversary; here one who undertakes another's challenge. Compare lines 269–70.
for you prepared to accept your challenge.

348 **– I'll . . . anon** I'll proceed to duel with you as soon as the Officers depart [and allow us to engage in a 'private Brawl' (line 255) forbidden by law].

350– **for that I promis'd you** Sir Andrew refers to his promise to
51 surrender his horse Capilet to resolve the quarrel. Sir Toby has said nothing to 'Cesario' about this part of the bargain, however (since Toby plans to keep the horse for himself, as he notes in lines 314–15), so this and Sir Andrew's next sentence are completely mystifying to Viola.

351– **He . . . well** Capilet will carry you gently, and he is readily
52 reined in.

353 **Office** duty, job.

354 **at the Suit** under the legal authority.

356 **mistake** both (a) mis-identify, and (b) mis-take (erroneously arrest).

357 **iot** jot.
Favour face.

TOBY   Come, Sir Andrew, there's no Remedy, the
   Gentleman will for his Honour's sake have one
   Bout with you. He cannot by the Duello avoid
   it: but he has promis'd me, as he is a
   Gentleman and a Soldier, he will not hurt   335
   you. Come on, to't.
ANDREW   Pray God he keep his Oath.

Enter Antonio.

VIOLA   I do assure you 'tis against my Will. [*They draw.*]
ANTONIO   Put up your Sword: if this young
   Gentleman
   Have done Offence, I take the Fault on me. [*He draws.*]   340
   If you offend him, I for him defy you.
TOBY   You Sir? Why, what are you?
ANTONIO   One, Sir, that for his Love dares yet do
   more
   Than you have heard him brag to you he will.
TOBY   Nay, if you be an Undertaker, I am for you.   345
                                                [*He draws.*]

Enter Officers.

FABIAN   O good Sir Toby, hold: here come the
   Officers.
TOBY   — I'll be with you anon.
VIOLA   Pray Sir, put your Sword up if you please.
ANDREW   Marry will I, Sir: and for that I promis'd   350
   you, I'll be as good as my Word. He will bear
   you easily, and reins well.
1 OFFICER   This is the Man, do thy Office.
2 OFFICER   Antonio, I arrest thee at the Suit
   of Count Orsino.   355
ANTONIO   You do mistake me, Sir.
1 OFFICER   No Sir, no iot: I know your Favour
   well,
   Though now you have no Sea-cap on your Head.

360 **This . . . you**   this is a result of my coming to look for you. Antonio mistakes 'Cesario' for Sebastian, her twin brother. Since Viola is unaware that Sebastian has survived the shipwreck and is in Illyria too, she has no idea what Antonio is talking about.

361 **answer it**   give my life (as a result of my intervention on your behalf). Compare lines 301–3. *Remedy* echoes line 331.

363 **my Purse**   Antonio refers to the purse he gave Sebastian in III.iii.38–48.
grieves   saddens. But soon the other sense of *grieves* (aggrieves, wrongs) will be applicable to Antonio's feelings.

365 **amaz'd**   astonished, as if you were lost in a maze.

373 **My having**   what I possess.

374 **my Present**   my present fortune. Viola's next line suggests that she carries her entire 'Coffer' (treasure-chest) in her pitiful purse.

376 **my Deserts to you**   what I deserve at your hands because of my favours.

377 **Can lack Persuasion**   can fail to persuade you (to return my purse to me).
tempt my Misery   try my patience by putting yet another burden on me.

378 **unsound**   both (a) unhealthy, broken-down, uncontrollably distraught, and (b) unsound theologically (not forgiving and praying for one who uses me despitefully, but returning evil for evil). See Matthew 5:44–48. Here as in line 142 *Least* means 'lest', but it reminds us that Antonio believes that the youth he has just jeopardized his life for is doing the least he can in reciprocation.

383 **Vainness**   foolish vainglory, the vaunting arrogance that precipitates a fall.
babbling   both (a) loose-talking, and (b) incoherent.

389 **sanctity of Love**   pure, devoted love. *Sanctity* echoes line 92.

390 **his Image**   Antonio describes the 'Youth' as if he were a graven image, an 'Idol' (line 393) who will prove false and 'vild' (vile, worthless).

– Take him away, he knows I know him well.

ANTONIO – I must obey. This comes with seeking you; 360
But there's no Remedy, I shall answer it.
What will you do: now my Necessity
Makes me to ask you for my Purse. It grieves me
Much more for what I cannot do for you
Than what befalls my self. You stand amaz'd, 365
But be of Comfort.

2 OFFICER Come Sir, away.

ANTONIO I must entreat of you some of that Money.

VIOLA What Money, Sir?
For the fair Kindness you have shew'd me here, 370
And part being prompted by your present
   Trouble,
Out of my lean and low Ability
I'll lend you something. My having is not much:
I'll make Division of my Present with you.
Hold, there's half my Coffer.   [*Proffers Money.*]

ANTONIO   Will you deny me now, 375
Is't possible that my Deserts to you
Can lack Persuasion? Do not tempt my Misery,
Least that it make me so unsound a Man
As to upbraid you with those Kindnesses
That I have done for you.

VIOLA   I know of none, 380
Nor know I you by Voice, or any Feature.
I hate Ingratitude more in a Man
Than Lying, Vainness, babbling Drunkenness,
Or any taint of Vice whose strong Corruption
Inhabits our frail Blood.

ANTONIO   Oh Heavens themselves. 385

2 OFFICER Come Sir, I pray you go.

ANTONIO Let me speak a little. This Youth that
   you see here
I snatch'd one half out of the Jaws of Death,
Reliev'd him with such sanctity of Love;
And to his Image, which me thought did promise 390
Most venerable Worth, did I Devotion.

394 **done good Feature Shame** brought shame not only to your
own beautiful features but to 'good Feature' ('Beauty', line
397) in general.

395 **Blemish** blot of ugliness.

396 **the Unkind** those who fail to be the 'kind' of moral, caring
creatures they were ordained to be.

398 **Trunks** both (a) soul-less bodies arrayed in finery by the Devil,
and (b) hollow chests carved or painted with elaborate designs
(devilish 'flourishes'). *O'er-flourish'd* can also mean 'guarded
by the brandished sword of'; compare *Julius Caesar*,
III.ii.193–94, where Mark Antony says that 'all of us fell
down, / Whilst bloody Treason flourish'd over us.' The phrase
empty Trunks alludes to Viola's claim to have an empty coffer
(see the note to line 374).

403 **believes himself** believes to be well founded (referring to the
'Passion' from which Antonio's words emanate or 'fly').
so do not I In the Folio this clause concludes with a colon
(often the equivalent of a full stop in modern usage). It may
be, however, that a question mark belongs here. It is clear
from the previous clause that Viola believes in the sincerity of
Antonio's 'Passion' (expression of deep feeling). And from the
sentence that follows (lines 404–5), it is equally clear that she
is not flatly rejecting the possibility that Antonio's outburst
has a basis in reality.

404 **Imagination** Here Viola means 'hopeful speculation'. Her
mood is what a modern news report would describe as
'cautious optimism'.

405 **ta'en** mistaken. Compare lines 243, 356.

406 **Knight** Sir Andrew.

408 **sage Saws** wise sayings.

409– **I ... Glass** I perceive what appears to be my brother's living
10 image every time I look at myself in the mirror. The next
clause amplifies this idea.

411 **Favour** feature, appearance (with particular reference to the
face).

412 **Still** always.
Fashion mode of dress.

413 **if it prove** if what I imagine to be true turns out to be so in
reality.

1 OFFICER   What's that to us? The Time goes by:
    away.
ANTONIO   But oh how vild an Idol proves this God.
— Thou hast, Sebastian, done good Feature
    Shame.
In Nature there's no Blemish but the Mind;   395
None can be call'd Deform'd but the Unkind.
Virtue is Beauty, but the beauteous Evil
Are empty Trunks, o'er-flourish'd by the Devil.
1 OFFICER   The Man grows Mad, away with him.
— Come, come, Sir.   400
ANTONIO   Lead me on.   *Exit [led by the Officers].*
VIOLA   — Me thinks his Words do from such
    Passion fly
That he believes himself; so do not I.
Prove true, Imagination, oh prove true,
That I, dear Brother, be now ta'en for you.   405
TOBY   Come hither, Knight, come hither, Fabian:
We'll whisper o'er a Couplet or two of most
sage Saws.
VIOLA   — He nam'd Sebastian. I my Brother
    know
Yet living in my Glass: even such, and so   410
In Favour, was my Brother, and he went
Still in this Fashion, Colour, Ornament,
For him I imitate. Oh if it prove,

414 **salt Waves fresh in Love** Viola plays on the idea that salt water may prove to be fresh water. What she means is that waves that would appear to have drowned her brother may instead have given him a 'fresh' new life. The image suggests baptism, and it echoes such previous passages as I.i.9, 25–31, I.ii.27, I.v.283, II.v.156.

415 **dishonest** dishonourable, unfaithful.
     paltry worthless.

416 **Hare** Hares were proverbial for cowardice.

417 **in Necessity** in his time of direst need.

418 **denying him** both (a) refusing to acknowledge that he knew him, and (b) refusing to assist him. See line 375.

421 **'Slid** God's [eye] lid.

424 **And** if.

425 **the Event** the outcome of this provocation.

426 **'twill . . . yet** there will still be no 'Event'.

Tempests are kind, and salt Waves fresh in
   Love. *Exit.*

TOBY A very dishonest paltry Boy, and more a 415
Coward than a Hare. His Dishonesty appears
in leaving his Friend here in Necessity, and
denying him: and for his Cowardship, ask Fabian.

FABIAN A Coward, a most devout Coward, religious
in it. 420

ANDREW 'Slid, I'll after him again, and beat him.

TOBY Do, cuff him soundly, but never draw thy
Sword.

ANDREW And I do not. *Exit.*

FABIAN Come, let's see the Event. 425

TOBY I dare lay any Money, 'twill be nothing yet.
          Exeunt.

IV.i This scene takes place in a street.

1–2 **Will . . . you?** Do you expect me to believe that you are not the man I am sent to bring to my mistress? Just as Viola was mistaken for Sebastian in the previous scene, Sebastian is mistaken for Viola ('Cesario') in this one.

3 **Go to** an expression of dismissal, here equivalent to 'Get lost'. Compare III.iv.104.

4 **clear** rid.

5 **held out** maintained, pretended, sustained.

9 **Nothing that is so is so** In a sense unknown to Feste, what he says is so. Compare I.v.332–35, III.i.145–51, IV.ii.14–19.

10 **vent thy Folly** air and release your foolishness. Sebastian appears to be assuming that Feste is putting on an act too, that of a professional jester inventing a situation comedy about mistaken identity. *Vent* can refer to the discharge of flatulence, excrement, or urine (compare *The Tempest*, II.ii.115), and one or more of those senses may apply to its use in lines 10–18. But by lines 15–18 Feste also appears to be alluding to seminal emissions. *Coming* (line 18) recalls III.iv.1, 8–9, 63–64, and its hint at the orgasmic sense is supported by *Great* in line 13 (see the note to III.iv.49), *Folly* in line 14 (see the notes to I.v.16, III.i.35, 36), and *Cockney* in line 15 (see the notes to III.iv.123, 211).

14 **Lubber** dolt, country bumpkin.

15 **Cockney** effeminate fop. In Shakespeare's time, *Cockney* normally referred to someone who had been coddled or pampered; the word originally meant 'small egg'. Feste's implication is that instead of being as ignorant as a rural lout, the world is now becoming as affected as a London gallant. See the notes to line 10.

16 **ungird thy Strangeness** remove this disguise and stop acting like a stranger to me.

17 **vent** say. Feste harps on the verb Sebastian used in line 10.

19 **foolish Greek** Here the epithet implies that Feste is being frivolous ('merry Greek' was a common phrase); but there may also be a suggestion that what the Fool says is merely nonsense (as in Casca's 'was Greek to me' in *Julius Caesar*, I.ii.286–87).

ACT IV

Scene 1

Enter Sebastian and Clown.

CLOWN Will you make me believe that I am not sent
  for you?

SEBASTIAN Go to, go to, thou art a Foolish Fellow,
  Let me be clear of thee.

CLOWN Well held out i'faith. No, I do not know   5
  you, nor I am not sent to you by my Lady, to
  bid you come speak with her; nor your name is
  not Master Cesario, nor this is not my Nose
  neither. Nothing that is so is so.

SEBASTIAN I prethee vent thy Folly somewhere else,   10
  Thou know'st not me.

CLOWN Vent my Folly: he has heard that Word of
  some Great Man and now applies it to a Fool.
  Vent my Folly: I am afraid this great Lubber
  the World will prove a Cockney. I prethee now   15
  ungird thy Strangeness, and tell me what I
  shall vent to my Lady? Shall I vent to her
  that thou art coming?

SEBASTIAN I prethee, foolish Greek, depart from me.
  There's Money for thee; if you tarry longer,   20
  I shall give worse Payment.

22   **By . . . Hand** Feste's implication is 'My, but you are generous!'
      Payment (line 21) echoes III.iv.301–3.

24   **Report . . . Purchase** reputation, but at their rate it takes them
      fourteen years to buy it.

31   **straight** immediately (with the warning that they are going to
      be in deep trouble).

34–35 **I'll . . . him** I'll find another way to hurt him. Here *let him
      alone* means 'leave him undisturbed'. Compare III.iv.196.

35   **I'll . . . Battery** I'll have him charged with assault and battery.

37   **stroke** struck. Even though he is no longer on the 'Windy Side
      of the Law' (III.iv.177–78), Sir Andrew will now resort to a
      coward's way of pursuing 'Satisfaction' (III.iv.257).

41   **put up your Iron** put away your sword.

42   **flesh'd** initiated and incited (here, over-excited) by your first
      taste of combat (like a hunting dog or falcon that has been
      given a morsel of meat to make him eager to pursue the prey).
      Sir Toby is trying to restrain Sebastian by telling him he is
      unnecessarily agitated.

44   **tempt** provoke. Compare III.iv.377.

46   **malapert** upstart, saucy.

49   **Ungracious Wretch** Olivia means that Sir Toby is acting with
      no more 'grace' (civilized manners) than a brute.

CLOWN   By my troth, thou hast an open Hand. These
Wise-men that give Fools Money get themselves
a good Report, after fourteen years' Purchase.

Enter Andrew, Toby, and Fabian.

ANDREW   Now Sir, have I met you again: there's for   25
you.   [*Strikes him.*]
SEBASTIAN   Why there's for thee, and there,
    and there.   [*Strikes him back.*]
        Are all
the People mad?   [*Draws his Dagger.*]
TOBY   Hold, Sir, or I'll throw your Dagger o'er
the House.   30
CLOWN   This will I tell my Lady straight, I would
not be in some of your Coats for two Pence.   [*Exit.*]
TOBY   Come on, Sir, hold.
ANDREW   Nay let him alone, I'll go another way to
work with him. I'll have an Action of Battery   35
against him, if there be any Law in Illyria:
though I stroke him first, yet it's no matter
for that.
SEBASTIAN   Let go thy Hand.
TOBY   Come, Sir, I will not let you go. Come, my   40
young Soldier, put up your Iron: you are well
flesh'd. Come on.
SEBASTIAN   I will be free from thee. What wouldst thou
    now?
If thou dar'st tempt me further, draw thy Sword.
                                        [*Draws his Sword.*]
TOBY   What, what? Nay then I must have an Ounce   45
or two of this malapert Blood from you.   [*Draws.*]

Enter Olivia.

OLIVIA   Hold, Toby, on thy Life I charge thee hold.
TOBY   Madam.
OLIVIA   Will it be ever thus? Ungracious Wretch,

50 **Fit ... Mountains** People who lived in the Welsh mountains were proverbial for their uncouth, violent behaviour.

53 **Rudesby** rude, coarse fellow.

54 **sway** rule, prevail. Before long Toby will 'sway' in another sense: reel, totter. Compare II.v.116, IV.iii.17.

55 **Extent** encroachment, violent seizure, assault.

57 **fruitless** irresponsible, time-wasting. Olivia's adjective probably derives from biblical parables about bad fruit (such as Matthew 7:16–20).

58 **botch'd up** pieced together. *Pranks* (line 57) are 'mischiefs'.

60 **Beshrew** curse. Here *deny* means 'refuse'. See III.iv.375, 418.

61 **He ... thee** he made my heart leap with fear when he threatened your heart with his sword. Olivia probably puns on both *Heart* ('Hart', a stag) and *started*, which can mean 'sent running'. Compare III.iv.217.

62 **Relish** taste, flavour. Sebastian probably pauses to speak lines 63–66 as an aside. What he means in line 62 is 'What is going on here?'

63 **Or** either.

64 **Let ... steep** Let the power of Love ('Fancy') keep my Reason ('Sense') continually submerged in the River of Forgetfulness.

65 **still** forever.

66 **prethee** Here the metre calls for this word to be glided over as if it were a single syllable.

67 **say so** Olivia means 'Say "I will" in a wedding with me.'

IV.ii **This scene takes place inside Olivia's house.**

2–3 **Sir Topas the Curate** The priest that Feste becomes in this scene probably derives his name from 'The Rime of Sir Thopas' in Chaucer's *Canterbury Tales*. 'Sir' was a common designation for priests and parsons.

5 **dissemble** disguise. In line 7 *dissembled* means 'deceived'.

Fit for the Mountains, and the barbarous Caves,   50
Where Manners ne'er were preach'd: out of my
    sight.
– Be not offended, dear Cesario.
– Rudesby, be gone.
                    [*Exeunt Toby, Andrew, and Fabian.*]
                    – I prethee, gentle Friend,
Let thy fair Wisdom, not thy Passion, sway
In this uncivil and unjust Extent   55
Against thy Peace. Go with me to my House,
And hear thou there how many fruitless Pranks
This Ruffian hath botch'd up, that thou thereby
May'st smile at this. Thou shalt not choose
    but go:
Do not deny. Beshrew his Soul for me,   60
He started one poor Heart of mine, in thee.
SEBASTIAN   What Relish is in this? How runs the
    Stream?
Or I am Mad, or else this is a Dream.
Let Fancy still my Sense in Lethe steep,
If it be thus to Dream, still let me Sleep.   65
OLIVIA   Nay come, I prethee: would thou'dst be
    rul'd by me.
SEBASTIAN   Madam, I will.
OLIVIA   O say so, and so be.   *Exeunt.*

Scene 2

Enter Maria and Clown.

MARIA   Nay, I prethee put on this Gown, and this
Beard; make him believe thou art Sir Topas the
Curate, do it quickly. I'll call Sir Toby the
whilst.
CLOWN   Well, I'll put it on, and I will dissemble   5
my self in't, and I would I were the first

8   **tall ... well**   of sufficient stature to do justice to the duties of a priest. It may be that the gown is too long for Feste; or it may be that he is suggesting that he is too short to stand tall in the pulpit. But *tall* can also mean 'valiant' (as in I.iii.20), and here it may mean 'stout' or 'full-bodied', as opposed to *lean* (line 9) and pale.

9   **Studient**   student, scholar.

10–11 **Good House-keeper**   both (a) conscientious manager of a household, and (b) gracious and generous host (a sense illustrated by *Love's Labour's Lost*, II.i.104, where the Princess of France tells Navarre, who refuses to entertain her and her company in his castle, 'I hear your Grace has sworn out Housekeeping').

11   **Careful**   conscientious, caring for his parishioners and performing his office with care (concern) for its details.

12   **Competitors**   colleagues, confederates. In Shakespeare's time, this word normally meant the opposite of what it means today. In the interlude that follows 'Sir Topas' speaks to the imprisoned Malvolio, who probably cannot hear most of what Sir Toby and Maria say.

14   **Bonos dies**   good day (*bonus dies* in Latin).

15   **Prage**   Prague, now the capital of the Czech Republic.

16   **Gorbodacke**   Feste probably means 'Gorboduc', a legendary king of Britain and the subject of a tragedy by Sackville and Norton (1562).

17   **That that is is**   This tautology is typical of the mock logic that Feste will use throughout the scene. Compare the reflections on being and non-being in III.i.145–51, III.iv.402–3, IV.i.5–9, 62–65, V.i.221.

21   **Peace ... Prison**   Feste echoes the Elizabethan Prayer Book's instruction that 'The Priest, entering into the sick person's house, shall say "Peace be in this house, and to all that dwell in it." '

29   **Out, Hyperbolical Fiend**   Feste pretends to believe that the Devil is speaking, and in an exaggerated, boisterous manner.

30   **Talkest ... Ladies**   Feste accuses the 'Fiend' of inciting Malvolio to dwell solely on lust. Given Malvolio's behaviour in II.v, 'Sir Topas' has a point.

36   **Modest**   both (a) moderate, and (b) polite.

that ever dissembled in such a Gown. I am not
tall enough to become the Function well, nor
lean enough to be thought a good Studient; but
to be said an Honest Man and a Good House-   10
keeper goes as fairly as to say a Careful Man
and a Great Scholar. The Competitors enter.

Enter Toby.

TOBY   Jove bless thee, Master Parson.
CLOWN   *Bonos dies*, Sir Toby: for as the old Hermit
of Prage, that never saw Pen and Ink, very   15
wittily said to a Niece of King Gorbodacke,
'That that is is.' So I, being Master Parson,
am Master Parson: for what is 'that' but
'that', and 'is' but 'is'?
TOBY   To him, Sir Topas.   20
CLOWN   — What ho, I say, Peace in this Prison.
TOBY   The Knave counterfeits well: a good
Knave.   *Malvolio within.*
MALVOLIO   Who calls there?
CLOWN   Sir Topas the Curate, who comes to visit   25
Malvolio the Lunatic.
MALVOLIO   Sir Topas, Sir Topas, good Sir Topas, go
to my Lady.
CLOWN   Out, Hyperbolical Fiend, how vexest thou
this Man? Talkest thou nothing but of Ladies?   30
TOBY   Well said, Master Parson.
MALVOLIO   Sir Topas, never was man thus wrong'd;
good Sir Topas, do not think I am Mad. They
have laid me here in hideous Darkness.
CLOWN   Fie, thou dishonest Sathan: I call thee by 35
the most Modest Terms, for I am one of those
Gentle Ones that will use the Divel himself

38 **Curtesy** courtesy. See the note to I.v.227.

41 **Barricadoes** barricades, barriers.
   Clerestores clerestories, windows near the ceiling, especially in a church or cathedral.

42 **as lustrous as Ebony** as luminous as black wood.

43 **Obstruction** the light being shut out. 'Obstruction' is the key to Malvolio's role in the play. Having tried to stifle the healthy impulses of others by denying them their cakes and ale, Malvolio has now had his own unruly aspirations exposed and barred. The self-contradictions in phrases such as 'South North' (line 42) and 'transparent as Barricadoes' are linguistic and logical obstructions that burlesque the physical impediments represented by Malvolio's 'Prison'. What they all symbolize is the blocking humour that incarcerates Malvolio in a cell of self-love and self-delusion. *Obstruction* echoes II.v.126, III.iv.22.

47 **Ignorance** Malvolio is ignorant (a) of the kind of man he is, (b) of how transparent he is to others, (c) of how he got into the situation in which he finds himself, and (d) of what is now happening to him.

48 **puzzled** lost in a maze, bewildered.
   the Egyptians in their Fog Feste probably refers to the 'thick darkness' visited upon the Egyptians during one of the plagues described in Exodus 10:21–23. In large measure the Egyptians' 'Ignorance' was wilful, a consequence of Pharaoh's determination to ignore exhortations and warnings he preferred not to hear or heed. Malvolio's 'Ignorance' derives in a related way from a will that has impeded the operations of his reason. See the notes to II.v.96–97, 125, 174. For other instances of the ignorance that derives from ignoring the obvious, see *Macbeth*, I.v.58–60, *Romeo and Juliet*, III.iii.129–33, and *King Lear*, IV.v.9–10.

51 **abus'd** Malvolio means 'mistreated'. What he doesn't realize is that the other sense of *abus'd* (deceived) is equally relevant.

53 **constant Question** interrogation based on a test of a person's ability to reason consecutively. Compare *Hamlet*, III.iv.134–41.

54 **Pythagoras** a Greek philosopher best known in the Renaissance for his doctrine that 'Souls of Animals infuse themselves / Into the Trunks of Men' (*The Merchant of Venice*, IV.i.132–33) and vice versa.

with Curtesy. Say'st thou that House is dark?

MALVOLIO As Hell, Sir Topas.

CLOWN Why it hath bay Windows transparent as   40
Barricadoes, and the Clerestores toward the
South North are as lustrous as Ebony: and yet
complainest thou of Obstruction?

MALVOLIO I am not Mad, Sir Topas, I say to you
this House is dark.   45

CLOWN Madman, thou errest: I say there is no
Darkness but Ignorance, in which thou art more
puzzled than the Egyptians in their Fog.

MALVOLIO I say this House is as dark as Ignorance,
though Ignorance were as dark as Hell; and I   50
say there was never man thus abus'd. I am no
more Mad than you are: make the Trial of it in
any constant Question.

CLOWN What is the Opinion of Pythagoras concerning
Wild-fowl?   55

MALVOLIO That the Soul of our Grandam might happily
inhabit a Bird.

CLOWN What think'st thou of his Opinion?

MALVOLIO I think nobly of the Soul, and no way
approve his Opinion.   60

CLOWN Fare thee well: remain thou still in
Darkness; thou shalt hold th' Opinion of
Pythagoras ere I will allow of thy Wits, and

---

56 **Grandam** grandmother.
   happily both (a) haply, perhaps, and (b) contentedly. Compare
      I.ii.47–56, III.iii.44.

63 **allow of thy Wits** acknowledge that your reasoning powers are
      sound. Compare I.ii.52–54, V.i.300.

64   **Woodcock**   Feste implies that the kind of 'Wild-fowl' most likely to house the soul of Malvolio's grandmother is a bird proverbial for its ignorance, puzzlement, and general stupidity. See the notes to II.v.91, III.iv.81, and compare *Hamlet*, I.iii.114, V.ii.318–20.

68   **for all Waters**   ready to try anything now. *Waters* recalls III.iv.112, and one of Feste's meanings is that he is now prepared to put any 'Waters' (urine samples) to a diagnostic test. Feste may also be using *Water* in the sense that pertains to the relative lustres of precious stones such as topaz or opal; see II.iv.72–74. Meanwhile he alludes to the proverb 'a cloak for all waters', which referred to being shielded against any kind of weather; compare V.i.395–414.

72   **how thou find'st him**   what condition he is in. See the note to III.iv.152.

73   **rid of this Knavery**   finished with this trick.

74   **conveniently deliver'd**   released without our being put in danger. *Deliver'd* recalls I.ii.37.

75   **so far in Offence**   so deeply out of favour with Olivia because of my past indiscretions.

77   **the Upshot**   to the upshot (the concluding round in an archery competition).
    by and by   right away.

78–79   **'Hey ... does'**   Feste quotes, and perhaps sings, an old ballad directed to a man whose 'leman' (sweetheart) 'loveth an other'. The song is pertinent to Malvolio's situation, of course, since his 'unkind' Lady (line 81) is in love with 'Cesario'. The 'Jolly Robin' addressed in the lyrics may be the singer's male member, and *does* hints at the copulative sense of *do*; if so, Feste's song is yet another instrument for mocking Malvolio's sexual frustrations.

81   **perdy**   to be sure (literally 'by God', from the French *par Dieu*). For several lines Feste pretends that he doesn't hear Malvolio call him. Then he expresses surprise to find Malvolio in a madman's cell.

86–87   **as ... hand**   if you wish to assure yourself of a generous reward from me.

fear to kill a Woodcock, lest thou dispossess
the Soul of thy Grandam. Fare thee well.   65

MALVOLIO   Sir Topas, Sir Topas.

TOBY   My most exquisite Sir Topas.

CLOWN   Nay, I am for all Waters.

MARIA   Thou mightst have done this without
thy Beard and Gown, he sees thee not.   70

TOBY   To him in thine own Voice, and bring
me word how thou find'st him: I would we
were well rid of this Knavery. If he may be
conveniently deliver'd, I would he were, for
I am now so far in Offence with my Niece that   75
I cannot pursue with any Safety this Sport
the Upshot. Come by and by to my Chamber.   *Exit.*

CLOWN   'Hey Robin, Jolly Robin,
      Tell me how thy Lady does.'

MALVOLIO   Fool.   80

CLOWN   'My Lady is unkind, perdy.'

MALVOLIO   Fool.

CLOWN   'Alas, why is she so?'

MALVOLIO   Fool, I say.

CLOWN   'She loves another.' – Who calls, ha?   85

MALVOLIO   Good Fool, as ever thou wilt deserve well
at my hand, help me to a Candle, and Pen, Ink,
and Paper. As I am a Gentleman, I will live to
be thankful to thee for't.

CLOWN   Master Malvolio?   90

---

88   **As . . . Gentleman**   Malvolio's claim to this title does not
depend on his winning Olivia's hand. His responsibilities as a
steward would entitle him to the status of a gentleman. His
chief offence is that he aspires to the ranks of the noble; see
the notes to II.v.34, 36, 57, III.iv.6, 22, 97.

88–89 **to be thankful to thee**   to show you proper gratitude.

91   **I**   both 'I' and 'Ay'.

92   **fell you besides**   came you to be bereft of. The *five Wits* Feste
      refers to are common sense (often called 'common wit'),
      memory, judgement, imagination, and fantasy.

97–98 **then . . . Fool**   While pretending to show compassion, Feste is
      implicitly reminding Malvolio of his remarks about fools in
      I.v.79–98.

99   **propertied me**   stored me as if I were no more than a piece of
      unwanted stage property (furniture) in a theatre. The root of
      propertied is *proper*, a word that frequently means 'own' (see
      V.i.324) and refers to that which pertains to one's self. Here
      that sense is a reminder that Malvolio's malady derives from
      excessive 'Self-love' (I.v.99). Isolation in 'Darkness' is thus a
      proper (fitting) treatment for his condition.

101   **to face me out of my Wits**   to persuade me that their pretence
      about my insanity is well-founded. See the note on *Wit* at
      III.i.67.

102   **Advise you**   consider carefully. The 'Minister' is Sir Topas, in
      whose voice the next sentence is spoken.

105   **vain Bibble-babble**   empty and vainglorious nonsense. This line
      echoes I.v.297, III.iv.383. Here *Babble* alludes to the Tower
      of Babel (see Genesis 11:1–9), and to the story of an erection
      by which an overweening human race sought to 'reach unto
      heaven'; in response 'the Lord did there confound the
      language of all the earth: and from thence did the Lord scatter
      them abroad upon the face of all the earth.' See the notes to
      lines 88, 89.

107   **– Maintain . . . Fellow**   Speak with him no further, my friend.
      'Sir Topas' addresses this line to 'the Fool'.

108   **God buy you**   God be with you. The Fool pretends to be saying
      goodbye as Sir Topas exits.

112   **shent**   rebuked. Feste speaks this line in his own voice as the
      Fool.

116   **Well-a-day . . . were**   Alas, if only you were.

120   **bearing of Letter**   transporting of messages. But Malvolio's
      phrasing can also refer to the kind of 'bearing' (and baring)
      that relates to the Fool's 'good Hanging' (I.v.20). See the
      notes to I.v.21 and II.v.130, and compare *The Two
      Gentlemen of Verona*, I.i.96–156, I.ii.50–104.

MALVOLIO   I, good Fool.

CLOWN   Alas Sir, how fell you besides your five
Wits?

MALVOLIO   Fool, there was never man so notoriously
abus'd: I am as well in my Wits, Fool, as thou   95
art.

CLOWN   But as well: then you are Mad indeed, if you
be no better in your Wits than a Fool.

MALVOLIO   They have here propertied me: keep me in
Darkness, send Ministers to me, Asses, and do   100
all they can to face me out of my Wits.

CLOWN   Advise you what you say: the Minister is
here. – Malvolio, Malvolio, thy Wits the
Heavens restore: endeavour thy self to sleep,
and leave thy vain Bibble-babble.   105

MALVOLIO   Sir Topas.

CLOWN   – Maintain no Words with him, good Fellow.
– Who, I, Sir? Not I, Sir. God buy you, good
Sir Topas. Marry, amen. I will, Sir, I will.

MALVOLIO   Fool, Fool, Fool, I say.   110

CLOWN   Alas, Sir, be patient. What say you, Sir?
I am shent for speaking to you.

MALVOLIO   Good Fool, help me to some Light, and
some Paper, I tell thee I am as well in my
Wits as any man in Illyria.   115

CLOWN   Well-a-day, that you were, Sir.

MALVOLIO   By this Hand, I am: good Fool, some Ink,
Paper, and Light. And convey what I will set
down to my Lady: it shall advantage thee more
than ever the bearing of Letter did.   120

CLOWN   I will help you to't. But tell me true,

123   **counterfeit** feign madness. Feste's verb echoes lines 22–23.
       In the process it provides a reminder of the kind of
       'counter-fitting' Malvolio is being punished for his desire to
       undertake. See the notes to III.i.80, 123, and compare the
       wordplay on *counterfeit* in *Romeo and Juliet*, II.iii.50–73.
       One meaning of *Mad* (line 122) is 'heated with wanton
       passion' (see *Love's Labour's Lost*, II.i.254, and *Othello*,
       IV.i.243). Meanwhile *indeed* frequently means 'in deed' (see
       Hamlet, I.ii.83–84, 178) and alludes to what Shylock calls
       'the Deed of Kind' in *The Merchant of Venice*, I.iii.86.

125–   **I'll ... Brains** Feste varies a proverb, 'You will not believe he is
26   bald till you see his brain.'

128   **requite** reward.

133   **Trice** moment. It is not clear from the Folio whether lines
       130–41 are to be recited or sung; unlike similar lines in
       II.iii.40–122, they are printed in roman rather than italic type.

136   **Dagger of Lath** The 'Old Vice' (a comic character in the
       late-medieval morality plays) normally wielded a ludicrous
       wooden dagger, and at times he would offer to pare the nails
       of the Devil with it (line 140). The court Clown was a relative
       (if not a descendant) of the Vice, so it is in character for Feste
       to invoke the Vice in a scene in which the Clown is trying to
       shame and ridicule the 'Devil'.

141   **Goodman Divel** By calling the Devil 'Goodman' (yeoman, a
       title below the rank of gentleman), the Vice insults the Prince
       of Darkness. By implication, Feste does the same to the 'Divel'
       (the mad humour) in possession of Malvolio.

IV.iii This scene takes place in Olivia's garden.

3   **enwraps** surrounds, encloses.

6   **this Credit** basis for this belief. Sebastian may be referring to
       what was reported to him by the innkeeper at the Elephant.
       Another possibility is that he is citing a note that Antonio has
       left for him at the Elephant.

7   **range** walk about.

9–10   **though ... Madness** though my innermost being argues well
       against the counsel of my Reason, [persuading me] that what
       has happened may result from some mistake but is not to be
       explained by madness. *Flood* (line 11) echoes IV.i.62.

are you not Mad indeed, or do you but
counterfeit?

MALVOLIO   Believe me, I am not, I tell thee true.

CLOWN   Nay, I'll ne'er believe a Madman till I see   125
his Brains. I will fetch you Light and Paper
and Ink.

MALVOLIO   Fool, I'll requite it in the highest
Degree: I prethee be gone.

CLOWN   I am gone, Sir,   130
                And anon, Sir,
                      I'll be with you again;
                In a Trice,
                Like to the Old Vice,
                      Your Need to sustain.   135

                Who with Dagger of Lath,
                In his Rage and his Wrath,
                      Cries 'Ah ha' to the Divel:
                'Like a Mad Lad,
                Pare thy Nails, Dad,   140
                      Adieu, Goodman Divel.'   *Exit.*

Scene 3

Enter Sebastian.

SEBASTIAN   This is the Air, that is the glorious
      Sun;
   This Pearl she gave me, I do feel't, and see't,
   And though 'tis Wonder that enwraps me thus,
   Yet 'tis not Madness. Where's Antonio then?
   I could not find him at the Elephant,   5
   Yet there he was, and there I found this Credit,
   That he did range the Town to seek me out.
   His Counsel now might do me golden Service:
   For though my Soul disputes well with my Sense
   That this may be some Error, but no Madness,   10

| 12 | **Instance** precedent, prior example. |
| | **Discourse** logic, reasoning. |

| 14 | **wrangle** contend, wrestle. |

| 15 | **Trust** belief, faith. |

| 17 | **sway** rule, oversee. Compare IV.i.54. |
| | **Followers** servants and other subordinates. |

18 **Take . . . Dispatch** receive and respond to (dispatch) business affairs and the dispatch (haste) they require. *Bearing* (demeanour), line 19, echoes IV.ii.120.

19 **discreet** intelligent (showing discretion, stable judgement). Compare I.v.105–6.

21 **deceivable** deceiving, deceptive; incompatible with what my eyes and other senses are telling me.

22 **mean well** are sincere in your intentions.

24 **Chantry** chapel, specifically one where prayers were chanted and services conducted on behalf of the souls of dead members of the family. Here *by* means 'nearby'.

26 **Plight** vow. Olivia's verb is an unintended reminder of the 'plight' (situation) in which Sebastian and others find themselves in this topsy-turvy world; compare *King Lear*, I.i.102–3.

27 **jealous** jealous. Here the word is synonymous with *doubtful*; it means 'anxious, fearful'.

29 **Whiles . . . Note** until you are ready to have it [our marriage] made known.

30 **What . . . keep** at which time we will have a formal solemnization of our marriage, which is now assured (line 26) but not yet ratified in a public ceremony.

31 **According to my Birth** in accordance with the customs befitting my native station in life.

33 **And . . . True** And once I have vowed fidelity to you, I will ever be loyal to my promise.

35 **fairly note** observe with favour, lend their approval to.

Yet doth this Accident and Flood of Fortune
So far exceed all Instance, all Discourse,
That I am ready to distrust mine Eyes,
And wrangle with my Reason that persuades me
To any other Trust but that I am Mad,   15
Or else the Lady's Mad; yet if 'twere so,
She could not sway her House, command her
   Followers,
Take and give back Affairs, and their Dispatch,
With such a smooth, discreet, and stable
   Bearing
As I perceive she does. There's something in't   20
That is deceivable. But here the Lady comes.

Enter Olivia, and Priest.

OLIVIA   Blame not this Haste of mine: if you mean
   well,
Now go with me, and with this Holy Man,
Into the Chantry by. There before him,
And underneath that consecrated Roof,   25
Plight me the full Assurance of your Faith,
That my most jealous and too doubtful Soul
May live at Peace. He shall conceal it,
Whiles you are willing it shall come to Note,
What Time we will our Celebration keep   30
According to my Birth. What do you say?
SEBASTIAN   I'll follow this good Man, and go with
   you,
And having sworn Truth, ever will be True.
OLIVIA   Then lead the way, good Father, and Heavens
   so shine
That they may fairly note this Act of mine.   35
                          Exeunt.

V.i   This scene takes place in front of Olivia's house.

1   **his** Malvolio's.

7–8   **This . . . again** This exchange may well be an allusion to an incident recorded in the diary of a Middle Temple law student named John Manningham. 'Mr. Francis Curle told me how one Dr. Bullein, the Queen's kinsman, had a dog which he doted on, so much that the Queen, understanding of it, requested he would grant her one desire, and he should have what soever he would ask. She demanded his dog; he gave it, and "Now Madam," quoth he, "you promised to give me my desire." "I will," quoth she. "Then I pray you give me my dog again".'

10   **Trappings** paraphernalia, belongings. Feste takes 'Belong you to' (line 9) in the most literal sense. Compare *propertied* in IV.ii.99.

20   **profit** benefit.

22   **abused** both (a) deceived, and (b) misused. Compare IV.ii.51, 95.

       Conclusions to be as Kisses if conclusions are like kisses. The 'Four Negatives' that Feste refers to may be the four lips that have to consent to a kiss; if so, the 'two Affirmatives' are the two mouths that overcome any resistance the four lips may put up. Feste also is playing on the grammatical rule that (in the words of Sir Philip Sidney's *Astrophil and Stella*, Sonnet 63) 'two negatives affirm'. In *Lust's Dominion*, a poem that seems to have been written by John Marston and Thomas Dekker, we read that when coy maidens answer men, ' "No, no" says "aye", and twice "away" says "stay".' Compare *Richard II*, IV.i.200–1.

ACT V

Scene 1

Enter Clown and Fabian.

FABIAN Now as thou lov'st me, let me see his
Letter.
CLOWN Good Master Fabian, grant me another
Request.
FABIAN Any thing.   5
CLOWN Do not desire to see this Letter.
FABIAN This is to give a Dog, and in Recompense
desire my Dog again.

Enter Duke, Viola, Curio, and Lords.

DUKE Belong you to the Lady Olivia, Friends?
CLOWN Ay Sir, we are some of her Trappings.   10
DUKE I know thee well: how doest thou, my good
Fellow?
CLOWN Truly Sir, the better for my Foes, and the
worse for my Friends.
DUKE Just the contrary: the better for thy Friends.   15
CLOWN No Sir, the worse.
DUKE How can that be?
CLOWN Marry Sir, they praise me, and make an Ass
of me. Now my Foes tell me plainly I am an
Ass. So that by my Foes, Sir, I profit in the   20
Knowledge of my Self, and by my Friends I am
abused: so that, Conclusions to be as Kisses, if
your four Negatives make your two Affirmatives,
why then the Worse for my Friends, and the
Better for my Foes.   25

27–28 **By . . . Friends** The Duke has called Feste's 'fooling' excellent. Feste pretends, however, that *Excellent* refers to the fact that it is 'the Worse for my Friends, and the Better for my Foes'. That, he says, is not a good thing, though he hopes it will not discourage the Duke from being a 'friend'.

31 **double Dealing** here both (a) duplicity, and (b) giving a second gratuity. Compare III.i.49–61, III.iii.17–18.

34–35 **Put . . . it** Feste is telling the Duke to put his Grace (both his generous impulses and that virtuous part of him that would resist 'Ill Counsel') into his pocket and obey his 'Flesh and Blood' (both his hand and his sinful nature). What Feste means is 'yield to temptation and engage in "double-dealing" '.

38 **Prima, Secundo, Tertio** Latin for 'first, second, third'. In lines 38–42 Feste is probably alluding to the proverb that in games of chance the third try ('Throw', line 44) is the one that will prove to be the winner.

40 **Triplex** triple-time in music.

41 **Saint Bennet** Saint Benedict. This is probably a reference to St Benet Hithe, a church just across the Thames from the Globe playhouse.

44 **Throw** toss of the dice.

47 **Lullaby to your Bounty** Feste pretends to sing the Duke's generosity to sleep. He plays on *awake* in line 46.

50 **Covetousness** desire for another's goods. Feste alludes to the commandment in Exodus 20:17.

56 **Vulcan** the blacksmith of the gods, here associated with the 'smoke' (battle heat) of the weapons he has made.

57 **baubling** tiny, like a bobbing bauble or plaything.

58 **For . . . unprizable** contemptible for its shallow draught (the amount of water it displaces) and size.

59 **scathful Grapple** destructive battle.

60 **Bottom** ship.

DUKE   Why this is Excellent.

CLOWN   By my troth, Sir, no: though it please you
to be one of my Friends.

DUKE   Thou shalt not be the worse for me: there's
Gold.   [*He hands him a Coin.*]   30

CLOWN   But that it would be double Dealing, Sir,
I would you could make it another.

DUKE   O you give me Ill Counsel.

CLOWN   Put your Grace in your Pocket, Sir, for this
once, and let your Flesh and Blood obey it.   35

DUKE   Well, I will be so much a Sinner to be a
double Dealer: there's another.

CLOWN   *Primo, Secundo, Tertio* is a good Play, and
the old Saying is 'The Third pays for all':
the Triplex, Sir, is a good tripping Measure,   40
or the Bells of Saint Bennet, Sir, may put
you in mind, one, two, three.

DUKE   You can fool no more Money out of me at this
Throw. If you will let your Lady know I am
here to speak with her, and bring her along   45
with you, it may awake my Bounty further.

CLOWN   Marry Sir, Lullaby to your Bounty till I
come again. I go, Sir, but I would not have
you to think that my desire of having is the
Sin of Covetousness: but, as you say, Sir,   50
let your Bounty take a Nap, I will awake it
anon.   *Exit.*

Enter Antonio and Officers.

VIOLA   Here comes the Man, Sir, that did rescue me.

DUKE   That Face of his I do remember well,
Yet when I saw it last, it was besmear'd   55
As Black as Vulcan, in the Smoke of War:
A baubling Vessel was he Captain of,
For shallow Draught and Bulk unprizable,
With which such scathful Grapple did he make
With the most noble Bottom of our Fleet   60

61–62 **That . . . him**   that he was praised even by those who envied and hated him most and had lost most as a result of his valour.

64 **Fraught**   freight (cargo).
Candy   Candia (Crete).

65 **boord**   board.

67 **desperate of Shame and State**   with complete disregard for the shame he brought to the dignity of his name. See the note to III.iv.259.

68 **In private Brabble**   in an ordinary street brawl. Compare III.iv.254–55.

69 **on my Side**   to defend me.

70 **But . . . me**   but when it was over [he] spoke very strangely to me (as if I had suddenly become a stranger again).

71 **but Distraction**   unless it was a seizure of madness. Compare II.ii.20–22.

73 **to their Mercies**   to put yourself at the mercy of those. Lines 72–75 recall, and appear to contradict, what Antonio has said in III.iii.29–37.

76 **shake off**   disregard. *Shake* recalls I.v.79–82, II.iii.135.

78 **on Base and Ground enough**   for sufficient reasons (not for piracy). *Base* and *Ground* are synonyms.

79 **A Witchcraft**   a power beyond my control. Compare Olivia's language in III.i.119–21.

82 **redeem**   rescue.
Wrack   wreck, here the victim of a shipwreck.

84 **Retention**   reservation (holding anything back). Compare II.iv.96.

85 **in Dedication**   in complete devotion.

86 **pure**   both (a) absolute, totally sanctified, and (b) solely, only.

87 **adverse**   hostile, enemy.

88 **beset**   set upon by enemies.

That very Envy and the Tongue of Loss
Cried Fame and Honour on him. What's the matter?
1 OFFICER   Orsino, this is that Antonio
That took the *Phoenix* and her Fraught from
     Candy,
And this is he that did the *Tiger* boord   65
When your young Nephew Titus lost his Leg;
Here in the Streets, desperate of Shame and
     State,
In private Brabble did we apprehend him.
VIOLA   He did me Kindness, Sir, drew on my Side,
But in conclusion put Strange Speech upon me: 70
I know not what 'twas, but Distraction.
DUKE   — Notable Pirate, thou salt-water Thief,
What foolish Boldness brought thee to their
     Mercies
Whom thou in Terms so Bloody and so Dear
Hast made thine Enemies?
ANTONIO   Orsino, Noble Sir,   75
Be pleas'd that I shake off these Names you
     give me:
Antonio never yet was Thief, or Pirate,
Though I confess, on Base and Ground enough,
Orsino's Enemy. A Witchcraft drew me hither:
That most ingrateful Boy there by your Side   80
From the rude Sea's enrag'd and foamy Mouth
Did I redeem. A Wrack past Hope he was:
His Life I gave him, and did thereto add
My Love without Retention or Restraint,
All his in Dedication. For his sake   85
Did I expose my self (pure for his Love)
Into the Danger of this adverse Town,
Drew to defend him when he was beset:
Where being apprehended, his false Cunning
(Not meaning to partake with me in Danger)   90

91 **face . . . Acquaintance** brazenly put on a face that suggested he
didn't recognize me. *Face* echoes IV.ii.99–101. *Acquaintance*
recalls I.ii.15, I.iii.54–55, II.v.171–72. And *Cunning* (line 89)
harks back to I.v.262, II.ii.23–24, III.i.124, III.iv.308. Here
the words *Cunning* and *Acquaintance*, echoing the Latin term
for the female pudendum, keep us mindful of the basis for the
'false' behaviour of the 'Boy' (line 80) Antonio is now
upbraiding for ingratitude; see the note to III.i.123.

92 **And . . . thing** and became someone who supposedly hadn't
seen me in twenty years.

93 **While . . . wink** as quickly as one could blink.

94 **recommended** commended, conferred, made available.

98 **Vacancy** interval, absence, interim.

103 **anon** shortly. So also in line 52.

104 **but . . . have** except for my love, which you cannot have.

105 **seem Serviceable** be of assistance to you.

106 **you . . . me** What Olivia probably means is that, as her
husband, 'Cesario' should no longer be serving Orsino.

108 **Good my Lord** Olivia may address this sentence to 'Cesario',
believing him to be the 'Lord' to whom she has secretly
pledged herself in matrimony. An alternative possibility
(endorsed by most editors of the play) is that Olivia speaks
instead to Orsino, requesting his indulgence to permit
'Cesario' to answer first. In either case, 'Cesario' then replies
that his own 'Lord' (master, as noted in lines 102–3) must be
heard before a servant's 'Duty' will allow him to respond.

110 **ought to the Old Tune** anything pertaining to your old tune
(your wooing 'song'). This line recalls the 'Music' with which
the play commenced.

111 **Fat and Fulsome** distasteful and nauseating. *Fulsome* can also
mean 'lustful' or 'impassioned' (as in *The Merchant of Venice*,
I.iii.87, and *Othello*, IV.i.37). That is unlikely to be a part of
Olivia's intended implication, but it is pertinent to the
character of Orsino's 'Old Tune'.

114 **Uncivil** barbarous.

115 **ingrate and unauspicious** ungrateful and unrewarding.
Orsino's point is that he has offered many a sacrifice on the
altar of this unrelenting goddess and he has received nothing
in return but scorn.

Taught him to face me out of his Acquaintance,
And grew a twenty years removed thing
While one would wink; denied me mine own Purse,
Which I had recommended to his use
Not half an Hour before.   95
VIOLA   How can this be?
DUKE   When came he to this Town?
ANTONIO   To day, my Lord; and for three Months
      before,
No Int'rim, not a Minute's Vacancy,
Both Day and Night did we keep company.

Enter Olivia and Attendants.

DUKE   Here comes the Countess, now Heaven walks
      on Earth;   100
But for thee, Fellow, Fellow, thy Words are
      Madness;
Three Months this Youth hath tended upon me,
But more of that anon. – Take him aside.
OLIVIA   What would my Lord, but that he may not
      have,
Wherein Olivia may seem Serviceable?   105
– Cesario, you do not keep Promise with me.
VIOLA   Madam –
DUKE   Gracious Olivia.
OLIVIA   What do you say, Cesario? Good my Lord.
VIOLA   My Lord would speak, my Duty hushes me.
OLIVIA   If it be ought to the Old Tune, my Lord,   110
It is as Fat and Fulsome to mine Ear
As Howling after Music.
DUKE   Still so Cruel?
OLIVIA   Still so Constant, Lord.
DUKE   What, to Perverseness? You Uncivil Lady,
To whose ingrate and unauspicious Altars   115
My Soul the faithfull'st Off'rings have
      breath'd out

117 **ere** both (a) before, and (b) e'er, ever. Compare I.i.12.
tender'd offered (here with tenderness).

120 **th' Egyptian . . . Death** Orsino refers to an episode in
Heliodorus' *Ethiopica* (a Greek romance). Here Thyamis, an
Egyptian bandit, is on the point of capture by a rival band of
robbers. Rather than allow his beloved Chariclea to fall into
their hands, he tries to slay her first. As it happens, in the
darkness he kills another woman by mistake. Orsino's words
echo the plight of Othello, another victim of 'savage Jealousy'
(line 121) who kills what he loves.

122 **savours nobly** has a noble flavour. *Jealousy* (line 121) recalls
IV.iii.27.

123 **non-Regardance** disregard, scorn.

125 **screws** forces out, wrenches.

127 **Minion** spoiled favourite, darling. The phrase *Marble-breasted
Tyrant* (line 126) recalls Olivia's reference to 'Cesario's'
'tyrannous Heart' (III.i.128) and Viola's description of
'Patience on a Monument' (II.iv.114).

128 **tender dearly** regard as most precious. Compare line 117.

132 **sacrifice the Lamb that I do love** Orsino now proposes to offer
Olivia a real sacrifice rather than the figurative ones he
referred to in lines 115–17. Orsino's imagery recalls both the
sacrifice of Isaac (Genesis 22) and the sacrifice of 'the Lamb of
God, which taketh away the sin of the world' (John 1:29).

133 **Raven's Heart within a Dove** a predatory, black heart within
the white breast of a beautiful dove. Doves symbolized both
peace and love. Here *spight* (spite) means 'thwart' and 'injure
grievously'.

134 **jocund** joyous.
apt ready, eager.

135 **To do you rest** to give you contented repose. Viola plays on
the sense of *rest* that refers to a man's achieving what he
resolves to do; compare *Romeo and Juliet*, IV.iii.92–93,
where *set up his Rest* alludes to the practice of deploying a
'rest' (support) for the barrel of a musket or cannon to be
fired. She also uses *do* in the sense that pertains to copulation;
compare *Measure for Measure*, II.i.148–51, 210–13.

That ere Devotion tender'd. What shall I do?
OLIVIA   Even what it please my Lord, that shall
  become him.
DUKE   Why should I not (had I the Heart to do it),
  Like to th' Egyptian Thief, at Point of Death   120
  Kill what I love (a savage Jealousy
  That sometime savours nobly)? But hear me this:
  Since you to non-Regardance cast my Faith,
  And that I partly know the Instrument
  That screws me from my True Place in your
    Favour,   125
  Live you the Marble-breasted Tyrant still.
  But this your Minion, whom I know you love,
  And whom, by Heaven, I swear I tender dearly,
  Him will I tear out of that cruel Eye
  Where he sits crowned in his Master's Spight.   130
  – Come, Boy, with me, my Thoughts are ripe in
    Mischief:
  I'll sacrifice the Lamb that I do love,
  To spight a Raven's Heart within a Dove.
VIOLA   And I, most jocund, apt, and willingly,
  To do you rest, a thousand Deaths would die.   135
OLIVIA   Where goes Cesario?
VIOLA   After him I love
  More than I love these Eyes, more than my Life,
  More by all Mores than e'er I shall love Wife.
  – If I do feign, you Witnesses above
  Punish my Life, for tainting of my Love.   140

---

135 **a thousand Deaths would die** Here *die* can relate both to
      execution (the meaning 'Cesario' intends for public
      consumption) and to orgasm (the meaning Viola hopes will
      prove applicable). See the note to II.iv.41.

141 **beguil'd** deceived, cheated. *Tainting* (soiling, discrediting) recalls III.iv.142–43, 384–85.

145 **Whether** whither.
Husband Even though Olivia and Sebastian (whom she mistakes for 'Cesario') have yet to solemnize their vows publicly, the commitment they have made to each other entitles Olivia to use this designation for her espoused.

147 **Sirrah** a form of address for a social inferior.

149 **strangle thy Propriety** both (a) choke your own identity and the privileges it entitles you to [by denying that you are now the Lord of a Countess], and (b) stifle your right to act in accordance with the manners of a nobleman. Viola's reluctance to seize her 'Fortunes' is in marked contrast to the eagerness Malvolio has displayed in his efforts to win his Lady's hand.

150 **take thy Fortunes up** claim your fortunes publicly. Olivia's phrasing echoes the exhortations to Malvolio in Maria's forged letter from his 'Mistress'; see II.v.153–54, 163–67. Compare the Steward's words to 'Cesario' in II.ii.13–17.

152 **As . . . fear'st** Olivia means that as her Lord, 'Cesario' will be able to quell his worst fears (such as the threats of a Count who will now be a social equal rather than a superior).

153 **charge** appeal to, entreat.

154 **unfold** disclose. Compare I.ii.17.
lately a short while ago.

156 **'tis Ripe** its proper time has arrived.

159 **Joinder** joindure; joining, uniting.

160 **Attested** ratified.
holy . . . Lips both (a) the sacred vows your lips have uttered, and (b) the kiss by which you have ratified your pledges to each other. Compare lines 20–25.

162 **Compact** agreement, contract. What the Priest refers to is a binding commitment to marry. In Elizabethan law this was tantamount to marriage itself.

163 **in my Function** through my office, under my authority.

165 **travail'd** both (a) travelled, and (b) laboured. See I.ii.21, II.v.58.

OLIVIA   Ay me Detested, how am I beguil'd?
VIOLA   Who does beguile you? Who does do you wrong?
OLIVIA   Hast thou forgot thy self? Is it so long?
  – Call forth the Holy Father.
DUKE   Come, away.
OLIVIA   Whether, my Lord? – Cesario, Husband, stay.   145
DUKE   Husband?
OLIVIA   Ay Husband. Can he that deny?
DUKE   Her Husband, Sirrah?
VIOLA   No, my Lord, not I.
OLIVIA   Alas, it is the baseness of thy Fear
  That makes thee strangle thy Propriety.
  Fear not, Cesario, take thy Fortunes up,   150
  Be that thou know'st thou art, and then thou
    art
  As great as that thou fear'st.

Enter Priest.

                       – O welcome, Father:
  Father, I charge thee by thy Reverence
  Here to unfold, though lately we intended
  To keep in Darkness what Occasion now   155
  Reveals before 'tis Ripe, what thou dost know
  Hath newly pass'd between this Youth and me.
PRIEST   A Contract of eternal Bond of Love,
  Confirm'd by mutual Joinder of your Hands,
  Attested by the holy Close of Lips,   160
  Strength'ned by Interchangement of your Rings,
  And all the Ceremony of this Compact
  Seal'd in my Function, by my Testimony;
  Since when, my Watch hath told me, toward my Grave
  I have travail'd but two Hours.   165
DUKE   – O thou dissembling Cub: what wilt thou be

---

166   **dissembling**   lying, masquerading. Compare IV.ii.5–7.
     Cub   Orsino is thinking specifically of a cunning young fox.

167   **sow'd . . . Case**   sprinkled a coating of grey hair on your skin. *Case* was a word that referred specifically to a fox's skin. What no one yet realizes, of course, is that 'Cesario' is in fact 'dissembling' in a way that neither Orsino nor Olivia suspects, and the reference to his 'Case' (a term often applied to the female genitalia) is an oblique reminder of the Viola beneath 'Cesario's' outer casing. See the note to III.i.160–61, and compare *Romeo and Juliet*, III.iii.84–85, IV.iii.184–86.

169   **Trip**   craftiness. The word referred specifically to an attempt to trip (throw) an opponent through a quick leg movement in wrestling, a sense that Orsino may be hinting at in the phrase 'direct thy Feet' in line 170. Compare II.iii.45.

173   **Hold little Faith**   maintain a little fidelity and trust; retain your grip on the small amount of faith you have. Elizabethans might have heard an allusion to Mark 9:23–24, where Jesus tells an apprehensive father, 'If thou canst believe, all things are possible to him that believeth. And straightway the father . . . cried out, and said with tears, Lord, I believe; help thou mine unbelief.'

174   **Surgeon**   doctor.

175   **presently**   immediately.

177   **H'as**   he has; so also with *has* in line 198.

178   **bloody Coxcomb**   a scalp that resembles the red crest of (a) a rooster, and (b) a court Fool. See the note to II.iii.203.

184   **incardinate**   Sir Andrew's malapropism for 'incarnate' (in the flesh, in human form). For related variations on this word, see *The Merchant of Venice*, II.ii.28–29 ('the very Devil incarnation'), *Henry V*, II.iii.35 ('Carnation'), and *Measure for Measure*, II.i.82 ('a Woman cardinally given').

186   **'Od's Lifelings**   a diminutive oath ('God's little life') in keeping with Sir Andrew's diminutive manhood.

191   **bespake you fair**   spoke only courteous words to and about you. *Cause* (justification), line 190, recalls III.i.160–61. Compare *Case* (line 167 and see line 360).

193   **set nothing by**   place no value on, regard as unimportant. *Coxcomb* (lines 192, 194, echoing lines 177–78) can mean 'fool's cap' and 'fool', and both senses fit Sir Andrew perfectly.

194   **halting**   limping.

When Time hath sow'd a Grizzle on thy Case?
Or will not else thy Craft so quickly grow
That thine own Trip shall be thine Overthrow?
Farewell and take her, but direct thy Feet   170
Where thou and I henceforth may never meet.

VIOLA   My Lord, I do protest.

OLIVIA   O do not swear,
Hold little Faith, though thou hast too much Fear.

Enter Sir Andrew.

ANDREW   For the love of God, a Surgeon, send one
presently to Sir Toby.   175

OLIVIA   What's the matter?

ANDREW   H'as broke my Head across, and has given
Sir Toby a bloody Coxcomb too: for the love of
God, your Help, I had rather than forty Pound
I were at Home.   180

OLIVIA   Who has done this, Sir Andrew?

ANDREW   The Count's Gentleman, one Cesario.
We took him for a Coward, but he's the very
Divel incardinate.

DUKE   My Gentleman Cesario?   185

ANDREW   'Od's Lifelings, here he is. – You broke my
Head for nothing; and that that I did, I was
set on to do't by Sir Toby.

VIOLA   Why do you speak to me, I never hurt you:
You drew your Sword upon me without Cause,   190
But I bespake you fair and hurt you not.

Enter Toby and Clown.

ANDREW   If a bloody Coxcomb be a Hurt, you have
hurt me: I think you set nothing by a bloody
Coxcomb. Here comes Sir Toby halting, you shall
hear more: but if he had not been in Drink, he   195

196   **tickled** a euphemism for a less pleasant form of entertainment. Compare II.v.25–26.

       other gates in another manner, otherwise.

198   **That's all one** it's no matter. Sir Toby doesn't want to talk about how he is. See line 378, and compare I.v.140.

199   **Sot** fool, one of Sir Toby's names for Feste. Compare I.v.132. The phrase *th' end on't* recalls II.iii.202–3.

       Dick Surgeon evidently the name for the doctor.

201   **agone** both (a) ago, and (b) gone.

202   **set** inoperative, and probably closed. It is ironically fitting that a man of Sir Toby's lifestyle should suffer because of the unavailability of a 'drunken Rogue' (line 204).

203   **passy-measures Panyn** a paynim (pagan, non-Christian, especially a Muslim) who walks like someone performing the *passamezzo*, a slow-paced Italian dance whose swaying steps could be thought to resemble the unsteady motions of a drunk. Because the passamezzo was often combined with the pavan (a somewhat more stately dance), most editors emend this phrase to 'passy-measures pavin'. The *passamezzo pavana* commonly featured strains of eight bars in duration, and it has been suggested that what prompts Sir Toby's reference to the dance is the phrase 'set at eight' in line 202. *Panyn* recalls I.iii.84–86, III.ii.72–78.

207–8   **be dress'd** have our wounds tended. Compare the use of *dress'd* in other pertinent senses in II.v.121.

209   **Coxcomb** fool, 'asshead'. See the note to line 193.

216   **a Strange Regard** an odd expression. Sebastian's phrasing is unintentionally apt: what he interprets as a disapproving look is in fact a look that casts him as a stranger. *Regard* recalls II.v.58, 72. And *Strange* echoes such previous passages as II.v.180–81, III.iv.8–9, 274, and V.i.70; compare I.iii.112–13, I.iv.3–4, III.iii.9–11, IV.i.15–16.

219   **so late ago** so recently.

220   **Habit** suit of clothes. Compare III.iv.80.

would have tickled you other gates than he did.

DUKE   How now, Gentleman? How is't with you?

TOBY   That's all one, has hurt me, and there's
th' end on't. — Sot, didst see Dick Surgeon,
Sot?   200

CLOWN   O he's Drunk, Sir Toby, an Hour agone; his
Eyes were set at eight i'th' morning.

TOBY   Then he's a Rogue, and a passy-measures Panyn:
I hate a drunken Rogue.

OLIVIA   Away with him? Who hath made this Havoc   205
with them?

ANDREW   I'll help you, Sir Toby, because we'll be
dress'd together.

TOBY   Will you help, an Asshead, and a Coxcomb,
and a Knave: a thin-fac'd Knave, a Gull?   210

OLIVIA   Get him to Bed, and let his Hurt be look'd
to.   [*Exeunt Clown, Fabian, with Toby and Andrew.*]

Enter Sebastian.

SEBASTIAN   I am sorry, Madam, I have hurt your
Kinsman:
But had it been the Brother of my Blood,
I must have done no less with Wit and Safety.   215
You throw a Strange Regard upon me, and by
that
I do perceive it hath offended you:
Pardon me, Sweet One, even for the Vows
We made each other but so late ago.

DUKE   One Face, one Voice, one Habit, and two
Persons,   220

221   **A Natural . . . not** Orsino is probably thinking of a 'perspective glass' by means of which one could distort an image or even make it appear to be two or more objects; but he may also be thinking of perspective paintings, which depicted one image when viewed straight on and a different image when viewed from an angle. See the note to II.iii.17, and compare *Richard II*, II.ii.14–27. In either case, he is here referring to what seems to be an optical illusion produced by natural rather than artificial means. *Perspective* is accented on the first syllable. The phrase *is, and is not* recalls IV.ii.17–19.

223   **Hours** here to be treated metrically as a two-syllable word.
       rack'd Sebastian alludes to an instrument of torture whereby the victim was tied to a rack and stretched unmercifully. But *rack'd* can also be heard as *wrack'd*; see line 82, where Antonio describes Sebastian as 'A Wrack past Hope', and compare *King Lear*, V.iii.311, where the Folio's *Wrack* is usually emended to *rack* in modern editions. Also see *The Merchant of Venice*, I.i.181, where *rack'd* means 'put on your shelf (rack)' and thereby 'transferred to your inventory'.

229   **wonderful** astonishing, to be wondered at.

231–   **Nor . . . every where** Nor am I a god with the capacity to be
32   omnipresent. Hamlet uses the Latin version of 'here and every where' (*hic et ubique*) in one of his references to the Ghost (*Hamlet*, I.v.149).

234   **Of Charity** as an act of kindness [please tell me].

238   **So . . . suited** both (a) thus, wearing that name and identity, and (b) so attired as you now see me (compare III.iv.409–13).

241–   **am . . . participate** Sebastian means that he is attired in the
42   same 'gross' (fleshly and thus corrupt) garment (a human body) that he has participated in (shared with other mortals) since conception.

243   **as the rest goes even** since all the other circumstances are in keeping with the hypothesis that you must be my sister.

245   **Thrice** most. Here *thrice* parallels the French adverb *très*.

249   **Record** memory; here *Record* is accented on the second syllable.
       lively living, alive.

250   **finished** In this line the word is trisyllabic.
       his Mortal Act his life (here compared to a dramatic action).

252   **lets** forbids; hinders, prevents.

A Natural Perspective, that is, and is not.

SEBASTIAN   Antonio: O my dear Antonio,
How have the Hours rack'd and tortur'd me
Since I have lost thee?

ANTONIO   Sebastian are you?

SEBASTIAN   Fear'st thou that, Antonio?   225

ANTONIO   How have you made Division of your Self?
— An Apple cleft in two is not more Twin
Than these two Creatures. Which is Sebastian?

OLIVIA   Most wonderful.

SEBASTIAN   — Do I stand there? I never had a
Brother,   230
Nor can there be that Deity in my Nature
Of here and every where. I had a Sister,
Whom the blind Waves and Surges have devour'd:
Of Charity, what Kin are you to me?
What Countryman? What Name? What Parentage?   235

VIOLA   Of Messaline: Sebastian was my Father,
Such a Sebastian was my Brother too;
So went he suited to his watery Tomb.
If Spirits can assume both Form and Suit,
You come to fright us.

SEBASTIAN   A Spirit I am indeed,   240
But am in that Dimension grossly clad
Which from the Womb I did participate.
Were you a Woman, as the rest goes even,
I should my Tears let fall upon your Cheek,
And say 'Thrice welcome, drowned Viola.'   245

VIOLA   My Father had a Mole upon his Brow.

SEBASTIAN   And so had mine.

VIOLA   And died that Day when Viola
From her Birth had number'd thirteen Years.

SEBASTIAN   O that Record is lively in my Soul:
He finished indeed his Mortal Act   250
That Day that made my Sister thirteen Years.

VIOLA   If nothing lets to make us happy both

253 **usurp'd** assumed (even though it didn't fit my gender). Compare I.v.202.

255 **cohere and jump** Both words mean hold together, agree, coincide.

256 **confirm** prove by means of a witness.

258 **Weeds** clothes.

259 **preserv'd** both (a) rescued, and (b) sustained, taken care of. Viola's verb recalls the imagery of I.i.25–31, III.iv.413–14.

262 **mistook** both (a) mistaken, deceived; and (b) mis-taken (wrongly taken). Sebastian plays on the verb *take* as it is employed in the wedding ceremony of the Book of Common Prayer; his point is that Olivia has been wrongly taken in marriage. Compare *Hamlet*, III.ii.269–76.

263 **But . . . that** Sebastian's image comes from the game of bowls, in which a bowl (ball) is weighted on one side so that it curves as it rolls towards its destination; a skilful player takes the bias (the curvature) into account when aiming the bowl. What Sebastian means, then, is that (a) Nature put a bias on your (Olivia's) straightforward intentions so as to give you what you aimed for despite your lack of skill (knowledge), and (b) Nature took into account the bias in your human nature and 'drew' you to the destination (husband) proper to you.

266 **Maid** Sebastian refers to his own virginity.

268 **as . . . true** given that up to this point the 'Glass' appears to be providing us with true likenesses rather than deceptions. *Glass* can mean either (a) mirror, or (b) perspective glass (see line 221). Compare IV.iii.9–21.

269 **happy Wrack** fortunate misfortune (wreck). See the second note to line 223.

274 **orbed Continent** Viola refers to the Sun. Here *Continent* literally means 'container', and *orbed* alludes to the orb or sphere that houses the Sun.

278 **Action** legal accusation.

279 **in Durance at Malvolio's Suit** in prison under Malvolio's authority.

281 **enlarge** free, release. Olivia's verb is an unwitting reminder of Malvolio's obsession with enlarging himself: both (a) becoming 'Great', and (b) getting out of his 'Dark House' (line 347).

But this my masculine usurp'd Attire,
Do not embrace me till each Circumstance
Of Place, Time, Fortune do cohere and jump   255
That I am Viola, which to confirm
I'll bring you to a Captain in this Town,
Where lie my Maiden Weeds: by whose gentle Help
I was preserv'd to serve this Noble Count.
All the Occurrence of my Fortune since   260
Hath been between this Lady and this Lord.

SEBASTIAN   — So comes it, Lady, you have been
    mistook:
But Nature to her Bias drew in that.
You would have been contracted to a Maid,
Nor are you therein (by my Life) deceiv'd: 265
You are betroth'd both to a Maid and Man.

DUKE   Be not amaz'd: right Noble is his Blood.
If this be so, as yet the Glass seems true,
I shall have share in this most happy Wrack.
— Boy, thou hast said to me a thousand times   270
Thou never should'st love Woman like to me.

VIOLA   And all those Sayings will I over swear,
And all those Swearings keep as true in Soul
As doth that orbed Continent, the Fire,
That severs Day from Night.

DUKE   Give me thy Hand,   275
And let me see thee in thy Woman's Weeds.

VIOLA   The Captain that did bring me first on Shore
Hath my Maid's Garments; he upon some Action
Is now in Durance at Malvolio's Suit,
A Gentleman and Follower of my Lady's.   280

OLIVIA   He shall enlarge him. Fetch Malvolio
    hither —
And yet alas, now I remember me,

283   **Distract** distracted, seized with madness. Compare line 71.

284   **extracting Frenzy** distracting madness; a seizure of my own that took my 'Remembrance' (memory) of him out of my mind. Olivia refers to her infatuation with 'Cesario'.

285   **clearly** completely.

287   **Belzebub** Beelzebub, one of the names of the Devil (Matthew 12:24).

287–   **at the Stave's end** at the end of a pole [to keep him at a safe
88   distance].

288   **Case** condition. But Feste may also be alluding to the cell in which Malvolio is now holding the Devil at bay. *Case* echoes line 167.

290   **to day morning** this morning (earlier today).

291   **Epistles are no Gospels** Feste puns on the two primary categories of New Testament books (and liturgical readings). His meaning is that a madman's letters are so unreliable that they could never be confused with either epistles or gospels in the theological sense. They are not to be taken as 'gospel' (absolute truth). Compare the imagery in I.v.240–55.
    it skills not it matters not, it makes no difference.

294   **edified** instructed; literally, 'built up'.

295   **delivers** Feste puns on (a) reads, (b) presents, and (c) releases. Compare IV.ii.73–74.

300   **allow Vox** permit an imitation of the voice of the speaker presented. Feste's point is that the only proper way to 'deliver the Madman' dramatically is to adopt all his characteristics in the presentation of his words. *Vox* recalls II.iii.56, 96–99, III.i.96–97, III.iv.380–81, IV.ii.71, V.i.220. Compare I.v.116–17, where Olivia says 'he speaks nothing but Madman'.

302   **to read his Right Wits** to give a proper rendering of the present state of his wits. Feste makes *Right* mean (a) true, rather than (b) sound.

303   **perpend** pay attention, consider. Compare *Hamlet*, II.ii.104–5.

305   **Read it you, Sirrah** Having run out of patience with Feste, Olivia tells Fabian to read the letter.

312   **Semblance** appearance. Malvolio refers to the costume and manner commended in the letter.

They say, poor Gentleman, he's much Distract.

Enter Clown with a Letter, and Fabian.

A most extracting Frenzy of mine own
From my Remembrance clearly banish'd his.   285
– How does he, Sirrah?
CLOWN Truly Madam, he holds Belzebub at the
Stave's end as well as a Man in his Case may do:
has here writ a Letter to you, I should have
given't you to day morning. But as a Madman's   290
Epistles are no Gospels, so it skills not much
when they are deliver'd.
OLIVIA Open't, and read it.
CLOWN Look then to be well edified, when the Fool
delivers the Madman. 'By the   295
Lord, Madam.'
OLIVIA How now, art thou Mad?
CLOWN No Madam, I do but read Madness: and
your Ladyship will have it as it ought to be, you
must allow *Vox*.   300
OLIVIA Prethee read i' thy Right Wits.
CLOWN So I do, Madonna: but to read his Right Wits
is to read thus. Therefore, perpend, my Princess,
and give Ear.
OLIVIA – Read it you, Sirrah.   305
FABIAN 'By the Lord, Madam, you wrong me,
and the World shall know it. Though you have
put me into Darkness, and given your drunken
Cousin rule over me, yet have I the Benefit
of my Senses as well as your Ladyship. I have   310
your own Letter, that induced me to the
Semblance I put on; with the which I doubt
not but to do my self much Right, or you much

314–   **I . . . Injury**   What Malvolio means is that he employs
16   somewhat less respectful ceremony than he normally would,
      since he speaks as one who feels grievously mistreated.

319   **savours . . . Distraction**   doesn't have the flavour of a madman's
      ravings. Compare line 122.

320   **deliver'd**   released. See line 295.

321–   **My Lord . . . Cost**   Olivia says that if, on further reflection,
24   Orsino is willing to love her as a sister-in-law rather than as a
      wife, then both weddings (and thus the new relationship
      between Orsino and Olivia) can be celebrated on the same
      day, at Olivia's house and at her own (*proper*) expense. See
      the note to IV.ii.99. *Crown* echoes I.v.145, where Olivia says,
      'Go thou and seek the Crowner.'

325   **apt**   ready, pleased. Compare I.iv.36–37, I.v.27, III.i.135,
      V.i.134–35.

326   **quits**   both (a) releases, and (b) leaves (in his old role as
      'Master' to a page). Orsino addresses this line to 'Cesario',
      who will be delivered from her 'case' (her 'masculine usurp'd
      Attire' and the servant role that went with it) at the same time
      that Malvolio is being released from his 'Dark Room'
      (III.iv.146).

327   **Mettle**   character, virtues; metal, composition. Compare
      III.iv.296.

331   **Your Master's Mistress**   Orsino means both (a) your Master's
      wife, and (b) the 'Mistress' your Master serves as his Lady.
      Orsino's image suggests that this will be a marriage based on
      mutuality rather than one in which the husband rules his wife
      with an overbearing hand.

336   **must not**   are not able to.

337   **Write from it**   write in a way that is different from this.

338   **Invention**   phrasing, style. Malvolio may also mean 'devising',
      'conception' (referring to the idea of the letter, not merely its
      execution). Compare III.ii.47.

    Shame; think of me as you please. I leave my
    Duty a little unthought of, and speak out of   315
    my Injury.   The madly us'd Malvolio.'

OLIVIA   Did he write this?

CLOWN   Ay Madam.

DUKE   This savours not much of Distraction.

OLIVIA   See him deliver'd, Fabian, bring him hither.   320

                                  [*Exit Fabian.*]

     – My Lord, so please you, these things further
       thought on,
    To think me as well a Sister as a Wife,
    One Day shall crown th' Alliance on't, so
       please you,
    Here at my House, and at my proper Cost.

DUKE   Madam, I am most apt t' embrace your Offer.   325
     – Your Master quits you; and for your Service
       done him,
    So much against the Mettle of your Sex,
    So far beneath your soft and tender Breeding,
    And since you call'd me Master for so long,
    Here is my Hand; you shall from this time be   330
    Your Master's Mistress.

OLIVIA   A Sister, you are she.

Enter Malvolio.

DUKE   Is this the Madman?

OLIVIA   Ay my Lord this same.
     – How now, Malvolio?

MALVOLIO   Madam, you have done me Wrong,
    Notorious Wrong.

OLIVIA   Have I, Malvolio? No.

MALVOLIO   Lady, you have, pray you peruse that
    Letter.   335
    You must not now deny it is your Hand,
    Write from it if you can, in Hand or Phrase,
    Or say 'tis not your Seal, not your Invention:
    You can say none of this. Well, grant it then,

340 **in the Modesty of Honour** in keeping with the sense of propriety that guides a woman of honour. *Modesty* recalls I.iii.8–9, I.v.195, II.i.11–13, IV.ii.35–36.

341 **Lights** signals, indications.

342 **bad** bade. Compare III.i.115.

344 **the Lighter People** those lower subordinates of yours whose lives are marked by levity (a lack of gravity).

345 **acting . . . Hope** while I was carrying out your instructions in an obedient, hopeful manner. *Hope* echoes such previous passages as I.ii.12, 17, I.iii.102–3, II.v.139, III.i.60, 79, III.iv.180–81, and V.i.82; it anticipates line 363.

346 **suffer'd** permitted.

348 **Geck and Gull** Both words refer to a dupe. *Gull* echoes line 210. *Priest* recalls III.iv.293–96.

351 **much like the Character** very similar to the way I form my characters (letters of the alphabet).

355– **And . . . thee** and in the very manners (*Forms*, ways) that were
56 previously suggested to you.

357 **This . . . thee** this trick has most cunningly and cursedly taken you in.

358 **Grounds and Authors** motives and perpetrators.

360 **Cause** case. *Cause* and *case* both derive from the same word in Latin, *causa*. See the note to line 167.

361 **Brawl to come** future duel. *Brawl* recalls III.iv.254–55, V.i.67–68.

362 **Taint the Condition** spoil the [happy] disposition or mood. *Taint* echoes lines 139–40.

363 **wond'red** marvelled. Compare I.v.214–16, IV.iii.3–4.

364– **my self . . . Malvolio** Fabian's account of the 'Device' (trick)
65 attributes to Fabian and Sir Toby an 'Invention' whose author was actually Maria (see II.iii.160–93). He thus protects Maria's position of trust as Olivia's waiting gentlewoman.

And tell me in the Modesty of Honour,   340
Why you have given me such clear Lights of
   Favour,
Bad me come Smiling and cross-Garter'd to you,
To put on Yellow Stockings, and to frown
Upon Sir Toby, and the Lighter People:
And acting this in an obedient Hope,   345
Why have you suffer'd me to be imprison'd,
Kept in a Dark House, visited by the Priest,
And made the most notorious Geck and Gull
That e'er Invention play'd on? Tell me why?
OLIVIA   Alas Malvolio, this is not my Writing,   350
Though I confess much like the Character:
But out of question 'tis Maria's Hand.
And now I do bethink me, it was she
First told me thou wast Mad; then cam'st in
   Smiling,
And in such Forms which here were presuppos'd   355
Upon thee in the Letter. Prethee be content,
This Practice hath most shrewdly pass'd upon
   thee:
But when we know the Grounds and Authors of it,
Thou shalt be both the Plaintiff and the Judge
Of thine own Cause.
FABIAN   Good Madam, hear me speak,   360
And let no Quarrel, nor no Brawl to come,
Taint the Condition of this present Hour,
Which I have wond'red at. In hope it shall not,
Most freely I confess my self and Toby
Set this Device against Malvolio here,   365

366–   **Upon . . . him**   as a result of some rude and uncivilized grudges
67   we had generated against him. Fabian magnanimously implies
       that the principal fault was in himself and Toby rather than in
       Malvolio. The Steward, after all, was at least as 'Stubborn'
       (inflexible, obstinate) and 'Uncourteous' as his detractors.
       Parts (both 'attitudes' and 'roles') recalls II.v.191–93.

368   **Importance**   importunity, urging.

371   **then**   than. What modern editions spell *than* is normally rendered *then* in the early texts of Shakespeare. Occasionally, as here, the usual modern sense of *then* is also applicable – if not to what the speaker intends, to what the action of the play will unfold. See lines 383–84. For other instances of *then/than* ambiguity, compare *Macbeth*, III.ii.7, III.iv.13.

374   **baffled**   degraded (as by depicting a knight hanging by his heels in shame) and displayed as a 'Fool' (thus answering Feste's prayer in I.v.84–88 and turning upon Malvolio a wish he had hoped to visit upon Sir Toby, II.v.171).

375   **borne**   both (a) born, and (b) carried.

377   **Interlude**   Once again Feste compares the 'Device' (line 365) to a brief play.

378   **that's all one**   that's of no consequence. Feste also means that he and 'Sir Topas' were 'all one' (identical). In other contexts, *all one* has copulative implications (see *The Two Gentlemen of Verona*, II.v.30–31, where Launce notes that ' "stand-under" and "under-stand" is all one', and Feste may be hinting derisively at that sense here. Compare lines 198, 413, and see the note to I.v.136.

378–   **'By . . . gag'd**   Feste paraphrases I.v.90–95. See the note to
81   I.v.95.

382   **Whirligig of Time**   A whirligig is a spinning top. Feste uses it as a metaphor for Time's way of bringing things full circle in retribution. What the suffering Malvolio has endured is a consequence of forces he himself set in motion. In his next speech, moreover, he threatens to initiate a new round of 'Revenges'. The word *gig* frequently carries phallic import (see *Love's Labour's Lost*, IV.iii.168–73, V.i.70–74, and compare *Hamlet*, III.i.147), and here it provides yet another reminder of Malvolio's lust not only for 'Greatness' but for his Lady's 'Day-bed' (II.v.53–54). See the note on 'Parish Top' at I.iii.43–44.

Upon some Stubborn and Uncourteous Parts
We had conceiv'd against him. Maria writ
The Letter, at Sir Toby's great Importance,
In Recompense whereof he hath married her.
How with a sportful Malice it was follow'd   370
May rather pluck on Laughter then Revenge
If that the Injuries be justly weigh'd
That have on both Sides pass'd.

OLIVIA   Alas poor Fool, how have they baffled thee?

CLOWN   Why 'some are borne Great, some achieve   375
Greatness, and some have Greatness thrown upon
them'. I was one, Sir, in this Interlude, one
Sir Topas, Sir, but that's all one. 'By the
Lord, Fool, I am not Mad.' But do you remember,
'Madam, why laugh you at such a barren Rascal,   380
and you smile not, he's gag'd': and thus the
Whirligig of Time brings in his Revenges.

MALVOLIO   I'll be reveng'd on the whole Pack of
you?   [*Exit.*]

OLIVIA   He hath been most notoriously abus'd.   385

DUKE   Pursue him, and entreat him to a Peace.

---

383   **Pack**   both (a) conspiring gang, and (b) cluster of baying dogs
      (such as the mastiffs used in bear-baitings). See I.iii.92–95,
      II.v.9, 12, III.i.126–28.

385   **abus'd**   both (a) deceived, and (b) mistreated. Compare
      IV.ii.51, 95. The Folio question mark at the end of lines
      383–84 is usually emended to an exclamation point. But
      Malvolio's exit line may not carry as much bravado as is
      usually assumed; at this point he is probably so baffled that he
      has no idea of how to obtain the vengeance he so fervently
      desires.

386   **entreat him to a Peace**   beg him to forgive and be reconciled.
      Fabian has already begun this process (see the note to lines
      366–67), and it would thus be appropriate for him to take the
      lead in restoring Malvolio to the society that has now
      re-crystallized in Illyria.

388 **When . . . convents**   when time has ripened to a harvest gold.
Here *convents* means 'suits' or 'comes together'. And the
word *Golden* suggests a higher realm (echoing the Golden
Age and anticipating an eternal Paradise) that transforms
'Time' from an avenger into an agent of redemption and
harmony ('solemn Combination'). *Golden* recalls I.i.32–36.

394 **his Fancy's Queen**   the ruler of his affections. Here *Fancy*
means 'love'. *Habits* echoes line 220.

395 **tine**   tiny.

397 **A Foolish Thing was but a Toy**   Here *Toy* means 'trifle'
(something of no consequence). *Foolish Thing* may refer to
(a) a naughty or silly deed, (b) a foolish person, or (c) the male
member (epitomizing Man's unruly will). See the notes to
I.v.16, III.i.35–36, IV.i.10.

401 **'Gainst . . . Gate**   What this line suggests is that, whereas a
'little tine Boy' suffers no dire consequences for a 'Foolish
Thing', a person who has grown to 'Man's Estate'
(adulthood) will find that his pranks get him branded as a
knave or a thief. He will thus be shut out to face 'the Wind
and the Rain' without the shelter a boy can take for granted.
This is one of the major themes of *King Lear*, and in that play
the Fool sings a version of this song to the suffering King
during the Storm Scene on the heath (III.ii). *Gate* recalls
I.iv.16, I.v.109, 127–28, 136–37, 214–16, 292, II.iii.172,
III.i.90.

405 **Swaggering**   carousing, boasting, and quarrelling.

407 **when I came unto my Beds**   This line, and this stanza, can be
interpreted in various ways. The 'Beds' referred to may be
those in inns the song's singer has had to resort to after being
thrown out by his wife; or they may be hospital beds that
anticipate deathbeds.

409 **Tosspots**   drunkards. The defective syntax in this line may be a
reflection of the inebriated state the singer describes.

He hath not told us of the Captain yet;
When that is known, and Golden Time convents,
A solemn Combination shall be made
Of our dear Souls. Mean time, sweet Sister,   390
We will not part from hence. – Cesario, come
(For so you shall be while you are a Man:
But when in other Habits you are seen,
Orsino's Mistress, and his Fancy's Queen).

       Exeunt [all but the Clown].

   Clown Sings.

When that I was and a little tine Boy,   395
 With hey, ho, the Wind and the Rain,
A Foolish Thing was but a Toy,
 For the Rain it raineth every Day.

But when I came to Man's Estate,
 With hey, ho, the Wind and the Rain,   400
'Gainst Knaves and Thieves Men shut their
  Gate,
For the Rain it raineth every Day.

But when I came alas to Wive,
 With hey, ho, the Wind and the Rain,
By Swaggering could I never thrive,   405
 For the Rain it raineth every Day.

But when I came unto my Beds,
 With hey, ho, the Wind and the Rain,
With Tosspots still had Drunken Heads,
 For the Rain it raineth every Day.   410

411   **begon**   began (to be rhymed with *done* in line 413).

413   **that's all one**   that's all the same. But as usual, the Fool's words allude to the at-one-ment that normally occurs in the concluding act of a Shakespearean comedy. Compare lines 198, 378.

414   **we'll strive to please you every Day**   These words state the credo of an Elizabethan acting company. But coming where they do in the song, they imply that the pleasure a play can bring is at best a temporary respite from 'the Rain' that 'raineth every Day'. Compare II.iv.66–70. The 'Rain' in this passage is, among other things, a symbol of the 'Revenges' that 'Time' visits upon those who disregard good counsel. For an Elizabethan audience it would have called to mind such passages as Matthew 7:24–27, where Jesus says that 'whosoever heareth these sayings of mine, and doeth them, I will liken him unto a wise man, which built his house upon a rock: And the rain descended, and the winds blew, and beat upon that house; and it fell not: for it was founded upon a rock. And everyone that heareth these sayings of mine, and doeth them not, shall be likened unto a foolish man, which built his house upon the sand: And the rain descended, and the floods came, and the winds blew, and beat upon that house; and it fell: and great was the fall of it.'

A great while ago the World begon,
  With hey, ho, the Wind and the Rain,
But that's all one, our Play is done,
  And we'll strive to please you every Day.

FINIS

PERSPECTIVES ON
Twelfth Night

The earliest surviving critical response to *Twelfth Night* dates from a Candlemas celebration on 2 February 1602, when Shakespeare and his acting colleagues presented the playwright's comedy at London's Middle Temple Hall. The audience, in all likelihood, was a sophisticated gathering of lawyers and law students, and one of the barristers in attendance, a young man named John Manningham, recorded a perceptive entry in his diary:

> At our feast wee had a play called 'Twelve Night, or What You Will', much like the Commedy of Errores, or Menechmi in Plautus, but most like and neere to that in Italian called *Ingnanni*. A good practise in it to make the Steward believe his Lady widdowe was in love with him, by counterfeyting a letter as from his Lady in generall termes, telling him what shee liked best in him, and prescribing his gesture in smiling, his aparaile, &c., and then when he came to practise making him beleeue they tooke him to be mad.

A century later, in the commentary accompanying the first multi-volume collection of Shakespeare's dramatic works (London, 1709), Nicholas Rowe asserted that there was 'something singularly ridiculous and pleasant in the fantastical Steward Malvolio'.

A few decades after Rowe, in the notes to his own edition of Shakespeare's plays and poems (London, 1765), Samuel Johnson wrote that *Twelfth Night*

> is in the graver part elegant and easy, and in some of the lighter scenes exquisitely humorous. Ague-cheek is drawn with great propriety, but his character is in a great measure that of natural fatuity, and is therefore not the proper prey of a satirist. The soliloquy of Malvolio is truly comic; he is betrayed to ridicule merely by his pride. The marriage of Olivia and the succeeding perplexity, though well enough

contrived to divert on the stage, wants credibility, and fails to produce the proper instruction required in the drama, as it exhibits no just picture of life.

At the height of the nineteenth-century Romantic movement, the eminent German critic A. W. Schlegel found the play's comic scenes to be 'as admirably conceived and significant as they are laughable'. In *A Course of Lectures on Dramatic Literature*, 1809–11 (translated by John Black and published in London in 1846), Schlegel remarked that

> This comedy unites the entertainment of an intrigue, contrived with great ingenuity, to the richest fund of comic characters and situations, and the beauteous colours of an ethereal poetry. In most of his plays Shakespeare treats love more as an affair of the imagination than the heart; but here we are particularly reminded by him that, in his language, the same word, *fancy*, signified both fancy and love. The love of the music-enraptured Duke to Olivia is not merely a fancy, but an imagination; Viola appears at first to fall arbitrarily in love with the Duke, whom she serves as a page, although she afterwards touches the tenderest chords of feeling. The proud Olivia is entangled by the modest and insinuating messenger of the Duke, in whom she is far from suspecting a disguised rival, and at last, by a second deception, takes the brother for the sister. To these, which I might call ideal follies, a contrast is formed by the undisguised absurdities to which the entertaining tricks of the ludicrous persons of the piece give rise, in like manner under pretence of love.

Writing a short time later in *Characters of Shakespear's Plays* (London, 1817), William Hazlitt observed that *Twelfth Night*

> is justly considered as one of the most delightful of Shakespear's comedies. It is full of sweetness and pleasantry. It is perhaps too good-natured for comedy. It has little satire, and no spleen. It aims at the ludicrous rather than the ridiculous. It makes us laugh at the follies of mankind, not despise them, and still less bear any ill-will towards them. Shakespear's comic genius resembles the bee rather in its power of extracting sweets from weeds or poisons than in leaving a sting behind it. He gives the most amusing exaggeration of the prevailing foibles of his characters, but in a way that they themselves, instead of being offended at, would almost join in the humour; he rather contrives opportunities for them to show themselves off in the happiest lights, than renders them contemptible in the perverse construction of the wit or malice of others.

Within a few years of Hazlitt's comments, in an essay that

signalled a shift of opinion about the gulling of Lady Olivia's trusted Steward, Charles Lamb wrote that 'Malvolio is not essentially ludicrous. He becomes comic but by accident.' Focusing on 'Some of the Old Actors' in various Shakespearean roles, and assembling his reflections in *The Essays of Elia* (London, 1822), Lamb went on to say that Malvolio

> is cold, austere, repelling; but dignified, consistent, and for what appears, rather of an over-stretched morality. Maria describes him as a sort of Puritan; and he might have worn his gold chain with honour in one of our old round-head families, in the service of a Lambert, or a Lady Fairfax. But his morality and his manners are misplaced in Illyria. He is opposed to the proper *levities* of the piece, and falls in the unequal contest. Still his pride, or his gravity (call it which you will) is inherent, and native to the man, not mock or affected, which latter only are the fit objects to excite laughter. His quality is at the best unlovely, but neither buffoon nor contemptible. His bearing is lofty, a little above his station, but probably not much above his deserts. We see no reason why he should not have been brave, honourable, accomplished. His careless committal of the ring to the ground (which he was commissioned to restore to Cesario), bespeaks a generosity of birth and feeling. His dialect on all occasions is that of a gentleman, and a man of education. We must not confound him with the eternal old, low steward of comedy. He is master of the household to a great Princess; a dignity probably conferred upon him for other respects than age or length of service. Olivia, at the first indication of his supposed madness, declares that she 'would not have him miscarry for half of her dowry'. Does this look as if the character was meant to appear little or insignificant? Once, indeed, she accuses him to his face – of what? – of being 'sick with self-love' – but with a gentleness and considerateness which could not have been, if she had not thought that this particular infirmity shaded some virtues. His rebuke to the knight, and his sottish revellers, is sensible and spirited; and when we take into consideration the unprotected condition of his mistress, and the strict regard with which her state of real or dissembled mourning would draw the eyes of the world upon her house-affairs, Malvolio might feel the honour of the family in some sort in his keeping; as it appears not that Olivia had any more brothers, or kinsmen, to look to it – for Sir Toby had dropped all such nice respects at the buttery hatch. That Malvolio was meant to be represented as possessing estimable qualities, the expression of the Duke in his anxiety to have him reconciled, almost infers. 'Pursue, and entreat him to a peace.' Even in his abused state of chains and darkness, a sort of greatness seems never to desert him. He argues highly and well with the

supposed Sir Topas, and philosophises gallantly upon his straw. There must have been some shadow of worth about the man; he must have been something more than a mere vapour – a thing of straw, or Jack in office – before Fabian and Maria could have ventured sending him upon a courting-errand to Olivia. There was some consonancy (as he would say) in the undertaking, or the jest would have been too bold even for that house of misrule.

Towards the end of the century (in *Macmillan's Magazine*, August 1884) William Archer confessed that

Malvolio has always been to me one of the most puzzling of Shakespeare's creations. The theory, so popular with German, and with some English, commentators, which makes of him a satirical type of the Puritan as Shakespeare conceived him, will not hold ground for a moment. It is founded on one or two detached speeches wrested from their context. . . . If I may hazard a theory, I should say that he is not a Puritan, but a Philistine. The radical defect of his nature is a lack of that sense of humour which is the safety-valve of all our little insanities, preventing even the most expansive egoism from altogether over-inflating us. He takes himself and the world too seriously. He has no intuition for the incongruous and grotesque. . . . His face, not only smileless itself, but contemptuous of mirth in others, has acted as a damper upon the humour of the sprightly Maria and the jovial Sir Toby; he has taken a set pleasure in putting the poor Clown out of countenance by receiving his quips with a stolid gravity. Hence the rancour of the humorists against a fundamentally antagonistic nature; hence, perhaps, their whim of making him crown his absurdities by a forced smile, a grimace more incongruous with his pompous person-ality than even cross-garters or yellow stockings. He is a being, in short, to whom the world, with all its shows and forms, is intensely real and profoundly respectable. He has no sense of its littleness, its evanescence, without which he can have no true sense of its greatness and its mystery.

One of the most acute Shakespearean interpreters in the first half of the twentieth century was Mark Van Doren. In his ever-rewarding *Shakespeare* (New York, 1939), Van Doren began his chapter on the last of the playwright's romantic comedies with a comparison:

If so absorbing a masterpiece as 'Twelfth Night' permits the reader to keep any other play in his mind while he reads, that play is 'The Merchant of Venice.' Once again Shakespeare has built a world out of music and melancholy, and once again this world is threatened by an alien voice. The opposition of Malvolio to Orsino and his class parallels the opposition of Shylock to Antonio and his friends. The parallel is not precise, and the contrast is more subtly contrived; Shakespeare holds the balance in a more delicate hand, so that the ejection of Malvolio is perhaps less painful to our sense of justice than the punishments heaped upon Shylock until *he* is crushed under their weight. But the parallel exists, and nothing provides a nicer opportunity for studying the way in which Shakespeare, returning to a congenial theme, could ripen and enrich it.

Orsino's opening speech is not merely accompanied by music; it discusses music, and it is music in itself. Furthermore, a suggestion of surfeit or satiety occurs as early as the second line: this suggestion, so consonant with Orsino's melancholy tone, to be developed throughout a speech of considerable complexity.... The music of 'The Merchant of Venice' is freer than this, more youthful and less tangled with ideas of sickness; and the bank of violets has aged beyond the simple sweetness of Lorenzo's bank whereon the moonlight slept. Orsino's love for Olivia turns in upon him and torments him. He is as mannerly in his sadness as Antonio was, but he knows, or thinks he knows, the origin of his state. He may not wholly know; his melancholy is in part a fine convention of his class, like the preference he feels for olden days and the gentle idiom of an outmoded music.... Orsino is indeed an exquisitely finished portrait of his type. His is the luxury of a 'secret soul' (I, iv, 14), and it is natural that he should so easily understand the young gentleman who is Viola in disguise, and who lets concealment, like a worm i' the bud, feed on her damask cheek (II, iv, 114–15). Viola's variety of melancholy is green and yellow. Olivia's is 'sad and civil' (III, iv, 5–6). But all of them are graced with sadness....

Sir Toby Belch is a gentleman too, or at any rate he belongs. He is an old relation and retainer in the somewhat cluttered household of Olivia.... The household of Olivia is old-world, it is Merry England. At its center sits the Lady Olivia, but there is room for every other kind of person here for whom a changing age has still not made existence impossible. There is the clown Feste and the clever servant Fabian; and there is the still cleverer Maria, whose extreme smallness is rendered clear to us, in the perverse language of a good-natured people, by such terms as 'giant' and 'Penthesilea,' though she is also a 'wren' and a 'little villain.' Chiefly, however, there is Sir Toby. He is gluttonous and drunken, and must be kept out of sight as much as possible; but Olivia would no more turn him away than she would refuse to hear an excellent old song sung to the lute. For one thing there is no place for Sir Toby to go. He is as old-fashioned as Falstaff, and as functionless in the modern world. 'Am not I consanguineous? Am I not of her blood?' (II, iii, 82–3). He even talks like Falstaff, puffingly and explosively, as he reminds Maria that he is Olivia's uncle. And for another thing he belongs. Old households harbor such old men. They are nuisances to be endured because they are symbols of enduringness, signs of the family's great age. Sir Toby has another parasite on him – Sir Andrew Aguecheek, whose foolish devotion to Olivia he makes use of to keep himself in money. . . .

It is to Sir Toby that Malvolio is most alien. 'Dost thou think, because thou art virtuous, there shall be no more cakes and ale?' This most famous sentence in the play is more than Sir Toby disposing of his niece's steward; it is the old world resisting the new, it is the life of hiccups and melancholy trying to ignore latter-day puritanism and efficiency. On the occasion when it is spoken there is danger for Sir Toby in the fact that Olivia is moody with her new love for Cesario; she has lost patience with her kinsman's misdemeanors. . . . But Malvolio is the last man on earth to come with the message. [For] the sight of Malvolio, like the sound of his voice, threatens death to [Sir Toby and Maria's] existence. His own existence somehow challenges their right to be freely what they are. He is of a new order – ambitious, self-contained, cold and intelligent, and dreadfully likely to prevail. That is why Sir Toby and his retinue hate him. . . .

. . . Modern audiences have bestowed more sympathy upon Malvolio than Shakespeare perhaps intended, so that the balance is now not what it was. It can scarcely be overthrown, however, whatever changes the whirligig of time brings in.

In what has proven to be a frequently cited if much debated attempt to establish the precise occasion for the play in *The First Night of 'Twelfth Night'* (London, 1955), Leslie Hotson argued that for Shakespeare and his early seventeenth-century audiences 'the connotations of *Illyria*', far from 'the lyric, the idyll, or the illusion which the romantic sound of the name so often suggests in a modern ear', were more likely to be 'thoughts of wild riot and drunkenness, and the lawless profession of piracy'. No, Hotson suggested, the never-never land of Illyria would have signified 'a boisterous coast', and one that provided 'A fit stage for what Dowden happily called "the reeling heights of Sir Toby's bacchanals" '.

But the prime aura of suggestion clinging to Sir Toby's name and nature is the Biblical one, from the Apocrypha: in itself an affront to Puritan sympathizers such as '*Mal*'-*voglio*. . . . For the Puritans vehemently rejected the Apocryphal books. . . . Queen Elizabeth nevertheless had the objectionable Toby – Tobias, son of Tobit or Tobias – actively displayed before the courtiers' eyes. At Hampton

Court hung 'two pieces of rich arras of the story of Thobie,' and at Westminster a dozen more 'pieces of tapestry of the story of Tobie.' . . . Aside from the Angel, and the Devil – who killed his bride's seven previous grooms – the salient points in Toby's story were two: (a) his fish, and (b) his postponed wedding-night.

First, the fish. Not forgetting the fumigatory power of the very ancient and fish-like smell, the fish fume which the devil himself couldn't abide, the fish is firmly held by all devout can-suckers, bang-pitchers, and elbow-lifters to be the happiest of living things – for it can drink at will. It is no accident that the drunken coachman in Fletcher's *Night-walker*, with his 'Give me the bottle! I can drink like a fish,' is called Toby; or that Lady Olivia's cousin, who 'is in the third degree of drink – he's drowned,' is that deboshed fish, Sir Toby.

As for the Biblical Toby's postponed wedding-night, it became a rule of the Church A.D. 398 – marital abstinence for the first night or nights after marriage. The 'Toby-night' custom was so well known to the Elizabethans that Chapman brought it into his play *Alphonsus, Emperor of Germany*. Here the groom is encouraged to console himself on his Toby-night by drinking 'a dozen or two of these bowls,' for 'it is the use That the first night the bridegroom spares the bride.'

The trouble with Sir Toby Belch, from Mistress Maria's leap-year point of view, is that this Toby will hardly stop drinking long enough to let her jockey him into the Toby-night situation – turn him from fish into flesh. Feste condoles with her: 'If Sir Toby would leave drinking, thou wert as witty a piece of Eve's flesh as any in Illyria.' . . . But the marriage does not take place until poetic justice, in the shape of bloody coxcombs given them by Sebastian, has sobered both the drunkards, Sir Toby and Sir Andrew. How neatly their punishment fits their crime appears by the contemporary euphemism 'cut in the head' for *drunk*. . . .

If Shakespeare fitted [such characters as] Toby with such well-tailored and significant names, he suited the Illyrian gentleman-reveller who joined them in the mad jest on Malvolio equally well: for we find *Fabian* as a favourite current nickname for 'a riotous, lavish roister, a careless fellow' – 'a flaunting fabian.'

Wise men hold that there is no great wit without a mixture of madness. Further, that 'there is a pleasure sure in being mad which none but madmen know.' 'Wild, madding, jocund, and irregular,' the world of *Twelfth Night* is a very mad world, exceeding mad. Small wonder that the epithet *mad* appears here more often than in any other play of Shakespeare's. Sir Toby in drink speaks nothing but madman; witty Maria is a finder of madmen; self-loving Malvolio, both sad-mad and madly-used; Lady Olivia in love, merry-mad; the startled Sebastian not only asks 'Are all the people mad?' but is forced to the conclusion, 'I am mad, or else the lady's mad.' And *Feste*, mad by vocation, seconds the notion by calling her *Mad-donna*. . . .

Twelfth Night's high spirits irresistibly call to mind 'that merry man Rablays.' . . . Certainly Rabelais had meaning even in his strangest locutions. And so had Shakespeare. . . .

'For what says *Quinapalus*?' Surely the Fool's guide and philosopher, whom he consults for sage corroboration, can be no other than his inseparable bauble, his *marotte*, the absurd little figure on a stick. *That* is Quinapalus. And the form suggests derivation from an Italianate *Quinapalo* – 'There on the stick' – on the model of *quinavalle* and *quinamonte*. On his stick, *Quinapalo* is of course in the best position to leap nimbly *di palo in frasca* – from pole to bush – which is the Italian for 'cock-and-bull,' skipping, disconnected talk, the Fool's stock-in-trade. As for *Pigrogromitus*, he seems to be compounded of the Italian for *lazy* and *scab or scruf*. . . .

Can we do better with the *Vapians* passing the equinoctial of *Queubus*? A *Va-pian* should be an Easy-goer, a Leisurely, a Fair-and-softly – from *Chi va pian piano va lontano*: 'Fair and softly goes far in a day.' And the astonishing distance these *Va-pians* cover is beyond the Equinoctic or Equator of *Cubus* – which, in Plato's cosmology, is the Earth: The Easygoers passing the Earth's Equator – below the burning Line. Inevitably there is an ingeniously indecent meaning as well. . . . Stripped of scholarly whimsy, Feste's *festina lente* [make haste slowly] embodies a sound maxim of statecraft. Queen Elizabeth herself told the French ambassador that 'one should go gently and do nothing in haste.' . . .

[Maria's insistence that 'thought is free' brings us to] the very door of [the Rabelaisian character] Gargantua's House of Will or Pleasure. . . . For Shakespeare's title issues the saturnalian invitation, Twelfth Night, or *Fay ce que vouldras*, What you will – Liberty Hall. . . . No excuse is left for the shallow opinion that the play has no connection with Twelfth Night, or that the added title shows a carelessness of the main one. On the contrary, *What You Will* defines and drives home its rollicking message. . . .

Sovereign for a night, Maria receives us into her holiday realm – a land teeming with Christmas and Epiphany legend, folk custom, and traditional feasting, dance, jesting, and game. For Twelfth Night is not only the joyful Feast of Light for the returning sun, but also *Le Jour des Rois*, the anniversary of the Three Kings [in Matthew's gospel who visit the Christ child]. . . . According to Florio, the name *Maria* signifies *Illumination*: not inappropriate for the queen of the Feast of Light.

Sir Toby brings in a well-known piece of Twelfth Day folklore by hailing the neat little sovereign's approach with 'Look where the youngest Wren of mine comes.' For the tiny Wren is both universally known as King of the Birds, and connected with this feast in a fashion as familiar as it is baffling. Under 'Wren' in the *Encyclopaedia Britannica*, Alfred Newton writes,

> The curious association of this bird with the Feast of the Three Kings, on which day in South Wales – or in Ireland and in the South of France on or about Christmas Day – men and boys used to 'hunt the wren,' addressing it in a song as 'the king of the birds,' is remarkable. . . .
>
> . . . At all events, it is certain that the ancients called the people of Araby-the-blest 'Troglodytes' or cave-dwellers. Furthermore, the country 'abounds in small birds,' and the name of the Wren is *Troglodytes parvulus*, 'the tiny cave-dweller.' However far we may still be from fathoming the mysterious relation of King Wren the cave-dweller to the Three Kings of cave-dwelling Saba and Mine, we can now begin to see light in Sir Toby's 'Wren of Mine.'

Wren Maria discharges her role as mock ruler, Twelfth Night queen, to admiration. But Shakespeare does not therefore neglect two other features of the ancient Christmas folk-play – the sword-dance or sham combat, and the mumming. . . .

Another Twelfth Night custom of high antiquity which heralds the wassail is *Hunt the Fox*. Obviously a process of 'killing the old Devil for good luck,' in former times it was accomplished by the hullabaloo of hunting down and killing a fox or a cat released in the Court. . . . The death of the devil-fox gave the joyful signal for wassail so notoriously that drunkards were termed *fox-catchers*, and to be drunk was called *to whip the cat, to hunt the fox*, or to be *foxed*. . . . *Hunt the Fox* gives point to Feste's defiance of Malvolio: 'Sir Toby will be sworn that I am no *fox*; but he will not pass his word for twopence that you are no fool.' As much as to say, 'I am no Twelfth Night fox to be hunted out; if you are so anxious to chase out a fool, begin with yourself.' . . .

Once the wassail and catch-singing have been well launched, the natural course is to stretch to the limit the last gaudy night of the holidays, mocking the midnight bell. But Sir Toby's 'Not to be abed after midnight is to be up betimes' and ''Tis too late to go to bed now' inevitably bring the thought of the morning after, when the world will go back to work. . . .

Turning . . . to Twelfth Night guessing games, we learn from Drayton and Jonson that the latter included Purposes and Riddles. . . . Purposes (a sort of 'Guess what I'm thinking of') receives only passing reference in Maria's admission, 'My purpose is indeed a horse of that colour.' But the Riddle takes centre-stage in *Twelfth Night* with Maria's cunningly-prepared 'dish o' poison' for Malvolio: '*M.O.A.I. doth sway my life.*'

Clearly, this fustian riddle must have a simple solution, obvious both to the audience and to all the characters except that dullard,

Malvolio. . . . Query, what is the most obvious group of four? Answer, the Four Elements – which in her 'Armada' prayer Queen Elizabeth defined as 'serving to continue in orderly government the whole of all the mass' – and the word *element* comes more frequently into *Twelfth Night* than into any other play of Shakespeare's. '*M.O.A.I. doth sway my life.*' Maria has cleverly chosen those 'fustian' designations of the elements whose initials appear in his name: *Mare*-Sea, *Orbis*-Earth, *Aer*-Air, and *Ignis*-Fire. . . . Her 'dish o'

poison' dupes the self-loved MALVOLIO into imagining himself Controller of Lady Olivia, although every fool knows that she is swayed only by *Mare*, *Orbis*, *Aer*, and *Ignis*. And the order of Maria's arrangement of the elemental four is thoroughly appropriate. According to accepted theory, Woman is cold and moist, Man, hot and dry; in the elements swaying Olivia, therefore, *Mare* must take first place. . . .

This riddle is an essential part of the practical joke on Malvolio. Elaborate plots to make somebody look like a fool constituted a principal Court pastime in the holidays. The current courtier's slang for the jest was to *dor* someone – 'that villain *dors* me' – or to give someone the *dor*. Like Malvolio's *geck*, the term is obviously borrowed from the Dutch: *een door*, a fool. . . . Shakespeare . . . brings in the *dor*-ing, but so lightly and deftly that we have failed to notice it – in the foolish Sir Andrew's innocent echo of Sir Toby's boast of Maria's love for him: 'She's a beagle true bred, and one that adores me: what o' that?'

Sir Andrew: 'I was a-*dor*'d once too.'

To close up the Illyrian revel with music and moral, Shakespeare gives us Feste's celebrated song, *When that I was and a little tiny boy*. For lack of understanding of its drift, this song has naively been received as a tale in rime but little reason. . . .

[But] must we really be reminded that ribaldry was the proper and age-old function of the Fool? Shakespeare's colleague Robert Armin played not only Feste but Lear's Fool as well. Knavish, licentious speech is common to both roles; and Armin's rendering of Feste's song proved so popular that an additional stanza was sung in *Lear* – *He that has and a little tiny wit*. Historically, the Fool and indecency cannot be parted. To make up for his mental shortcomings, Nature was commonly believed to have endowed the Fool with an excess of virility, symbolized by his *bauble*. 'Fools please women best.' 'A fool's bauble is a lady's playfellow.' 'A foolish bed-mate, why, he hath no peer.' Priapus used to be described as *that foolish god*; and Mercutio's cynical notion of Love is *a great natural* with his *bauble*.

As for Lear's Fool, he advertises the Fool's characteristic advantage by announcing, 'Marry, here's grace and a codpiece: that's a wise man and a fool.' To this he adds a complacent boast of his physical

irresistibility to the other sex: 'ladies too, they will not let me have all
the fool to myself, they'll be snatching.' And he closes the first act of
the tragedy with the witty and bawdy tag

> She that's a maid now, and laughs at my *deporter*,
> Shall not be a maid long, unless things be cut shorter.

The text has *departure*, a word unacceptable both for the rime and for
the sense. I suggest that Shakespeare must have written *deporter*,
which Cotgrave gives as the French for 'a sporting bauble.' . . . *Thing*
in its bauble sense is the key word, not only here, but also in the first
stanza of Feste's song. In the Fool's childish state as a little tiny boy, a
foolish thing was no more than a harmless trifle. Far otherwise,
however, when he was grown 'fit for breed' – a lecherous knave and
thief of love, on the prowl for other men's wives:

> 'Gainst knaves and thieves men shut their gate.

[Feste] has already told Lady Olivia – as they contemplate the
condition of Sir Toby – that a drunken man is like a fool, a madman,
and a drowned man: 'One draught above heat makes him a fool, the
second mads him, and a third drowns him.' Now he proceeds to
illustration, with a dramatic lyric of rueful reminiscence leading us
through the same three familiar degrees – goat-drunk, lion-drunk, and
swine-drunk: 'now goatishly to whore, now lion-like to roar, now
hoggishly in the mire' – whose attendant deadly sins, appropriated to
the three ages of manhood (youth, prime, and old age), are Lechery,
Wrath, and Sloth.

During the same year that saw the appearance of Hotson's
book, Joseph H. Summers published an important article on 'The
Masks of *Twelfth Night*' (*University Review*, 1955).
Summers commenced with a reminder that

> Love and its fulfillment are primary in Shakespeare's comedies. Its
> conflicts are often presented in terms of the battle of the generations.
> At the beginning of the plays the bliss of the young lovers is usually
> barred by an older generation of parents and rulers, a group which has
> supposedly experienced its own fulfillment in the past and which is
> now concerned with preserving old forms or fulfilling new ambitions.
> The comedies usually end with the triumph in which the lovers make
> peace with their elders and themselves assume adulthood and often
> power. The revolutionary force of love becomes an added element of
> vitality in a reestablished society.
> *Twelfth Night* does not follow the customary pattern. In this play
> the responsible older generation has been abolished, and there are no
> parents at all. In the first act we are rapidly introduced into a world in

which the ruler is a love-sick Duke – in which young ladies, fatherless and motherless, embark on disguised actions, or rule, after a fashion, their own households, and in which the only individuals possibly over thirty are drunkards, jokesters, and gulls, totally without authority. All the external barriers to fulfillment have been eliminated in what becomes almost a parody of the state desired by the ordinary young lovers, the Hermias and Lysanders – or even the Rosalinds and Orlandos. According to the strictly romantic formula, the happy ending should be already achieved at the beginning of the play: we should abandon the theater for the rites of love. But the slightly stunned inhabitants of Illyria discover that they are anything but free. Their own actions provide the barriers, for most of them know neither themselves, nor others, nor their social worlds.

For his festival entertainment, Shakespeare freshly organized all the usual material of the romances – the twins, the exile, the impersonations – to provide significant movement for a dance of maskers. Every character has his mask, for the assumption of the play is that no one is without a mask in the seriocomic business of the pursuit of happiness. The character without disguises who is not ridiculous is outside the realm of comedy. Within comedy, the character who thinks it is possible to live without assuming a mask is merely too naive to recognize the mask he has already assumed. He is the chief object of laughter. As a general rule, we laugh with the characters who know the role they are playing and we laugh at those who do not: we can crudely divide the cast of *Twelfth Night* into these two categories.

But matters are more complicated than this, and roles have a way of shifting.

At the opening of the play Orsino and Olivia accept the aristocratic (and literary) ideas of the romantic lover and the grief-stricken lady as realities rather than as ideas. They are comic characters exactly because of that confusion. . . .

[Viola] is the one character active in the intrigue who provides a measure for the comic excesses of all the others. (Feste's role as observer is analogous to Viola's role as 'actor.') Although Viola chooses to impersonate Cesario from necessity, she later plays her part with undisguised enjoyment. She misses none of the opportunities for parody, for confession, and for *double entendre* which the mask affords, and she never forgets or lets us forget the biological distance between Viola and Cesario. Except in the fencing match with Sir Andrew Aguecheek, she anticipates and directs our perception of the ludicrous in her own role as well as in the roles of Orsino and Olivia.

Sebastian is the reality of which Cesario is the artful imitation. Viola's twin assumes no disguises; Viola and the inhabitants of Illyria have assumed it for him. . . . When he truly enters the action of the play in Act IV he is certainly the object of our laughter, not because he has confused himself with an ideal or improper mask, but because he so righteously and ineffectually insists on his own identity in the face of unanimous public opposition. . . .

The other characters in the play do not truly belong to an aristocracy of taste and leisure. For some of them, that is the chief problem. Malvolio and Sir Andrew Aguecheek are ruled by their mistaken notions of the proper role of an upper-class gentleman, and they fail to perceive the comic gaps between themselves and their ideal roles, and between those ideals and the social reality. . . .

In the business of masking, Feste is the one professional among a crowd of amateurs; he does it for a living. He never makes the amateur's mistake of confusing his personality with his mask – he wears not motley in his brain. . . . But though Feste may have deliberately chosen his role, society determines its conditions. . . . While all the other characters are concerned with gaining something they do not have, Feste's struggle is to retain his mask and to make it again ingratiating. He is able to penetrate all the masks of the others, and he succeeds in retaining his own. . . .

The entrance of Sebastian is 'what we will.' It is the most dramatic moment of the play. The confrontation of Sebastian and Cesario-Viola, those identical images, concludes the formal plot and provides the means for the discarding of all the lovers' masks. The moment must be savored and fully realized. As Viola and Sebastian chant their traditional formulas of proof, both the audience and the other characters on the stage undistractedly view the physical image of the duality which has made the confusion and the play. The masks and the play are to be abandoned for a vision of delight beyond delight, in which lovers have neither to wear nor to penetrate disguises since they are at last invulnerable to error and laughter.

Yet the play does not resolve into a magic blessing of the world's fertility as does *A Midsummer Night's Dream*. We have been promised a happy ending, and we receive it. We are grateful that the proper Jacks and Jills have found each other, but the miracle is a limited miracle, available only to the young and the lucky. . . .

It is Feste rather than Malvolio who finally reminds us of the limitations and the costs of the romantic vision of happiness with which we have been seduced. However burdensome, masking is his career, and romantic love provides no end for it. Alone on the stage at the end of the play, he sings a song of unfulfilled love which shows the other side of the coin. For Feste, as for the audience, the mask can never be finally discarded: the rain it raineth every day. . . . As the fictional lovers have unmasked to reveal or realize their 'true' identities, it is only proper that the clown, the only character who might move freely in the environs of Bankside, as well as in the realm of Illyria, should unmask the whole proceeding for the imitation of a desired world which it has been. The audience must be returned from 'What You Will' to its own less patterned world where the sea rarely disgorges siblings given up for lost, where mistaken marriages rarely turn out well, where Violas rarely catch Dukes, and where Malvolios too often rule households with disturbing propriety. . . .

Twelfth Night is the climax of Shakespeare's early achievement in comedy. The effects and values of the earlier comedies are here subtly embodied in the most complex structure which Shakespeare had yet created. But the play also looks forward: the pressure to dissolve the comedy, to realize and finally abandon the burden of laughter, is an intrinsic part of its 'perfection.' . . . After *Twelfth Night* the so-called comedies require for their happy resolutions more radical characters and devices – omniscient and omnipresent Dukes, magic, and resurrection. More obvious miracles are needed for comedy to exist in a world in which evil also exists, not merely incipiently but with power.

Four years after Summers' essay, C. L. Barber came out with what is perhaps the most influential book ever published on the playwright's comedies. In *Shakespeare's Festive Comedy* (Princeton, 1959) Barber said that

The title of *Twelfth Night* may well have come from the first occasion when it was performed, whether or not Dr. Leslie Hotson is right in arguing that its first night was the court celebration of the last of the twelve days of Christmas on January 6, 1600–1601. The title tells us that the play is like holiday misrule – though not just like it, for it adds 'or what you will.' . . .

The most fundamental distinction the play brings home to us is the difference between men and women. To say this may seem to labor the obvious; for what love story does not emphasize this difference? But the disguising of a girl as a boy in *Twelfth Night* is exploited so as to renew in a special way our sense of the difference. Just as a saturnalian reversal of social roles need not threaten the social structure, but can serve instead to consolidate it, so a temporary, playful reversal of sexual roles can renew the meaning of the normal relation. One can add that with sexual as with other relations, it is when the normal is secure that playful aberration is benign. This basic security explains why there is so little that is queasy in all Shakespeare's handling of boy actors playing women, and playing women pretending to be men. . . .

Over against the Olivia–Cesario relation, there are Orsino–Cesario and Antonio–Sebastian. Antonio's impassioned friendship for Sebastian is one of those ardent attachments between young people of the same sex which Shakespeare frequently presents, with his positive emphasis, as exhibiting the loving and lovable qualities later expressed in love for the other sex. Orsino's fascination with Cesario is more complex. . . . The delight he takes in Cesario's fresh youth and graceful responsiveness, in conversation and in service, is one part of the spectrum of love for a woman, or better, it is a range of feeling that is common to love for a youth and love for a woman. For the audience, the woman who is present there, behind Cesario's disguise, is brought to mind repeatedly by the talk of love and of the differences of men and women in love. . . . The effect of moving back and forth from woman to sprightly page is to convey how much the sexes differ yet how much they have in common, how everyone who is fully alive has qualities of both. . . . The countess marries the man in this composite, and the count marries the maid. He too has done he knows not what while nature drew him to her bias, for he has fallen in love with the maid without knowing it.

We have seen how each of the festive comedies tends to focus on a particular kind of folly that is released along with love – witty masquerade in *Love's Labour's Lost*, delusive fantasy in *A Midsummer Night's Dream*, romance in *As You Like It*, and, in *The Merchant of Venice*, prodigality balanced against usury. *Twelfth Night* deals with the sort of folly which the title points to, the folly of misrule. . . . As in *The Merchant of Venice* the story of a prodigal is the occasion for an exploration of the use and abuse of wealth, so here we get an exhibition of the use and abuse of social liberty.

What enables Viola to bring off her role in disguise is her perfect courtesy, in the large, humanistic meaning of that term as the Renaissance used it, the *corteziania* of Castiglione. Her mastery of courtesy goes with her being the daughter of 'that Sebastian of Messalina whom I know you have heard of': gentility shows through her disguise as does the fact that she is a woman. . . . We think of manners as a mere prerequisite of living decently, like cleanliness. For the Renaissance, they could be almost the end of life, as the literature of courtesy testifies. . . . People in *Twelfth Night* talk of courtesy constantly. But the most important expression of courtesy of course is in object lessons. It is their lack of breeding and manners which makes the comic butts ridiculous, along with their lack of the basic, free humanity which, be it virile or feminine, is at the center of courtesy and flowers through it. . . .

. . . The festive spirit shows up the kill-joy vanity of Malvolio's decorum. The steward shows his limits when he calls misrule 'this uncivil rule.' But one of the revellers is Sir Andrew, who reminds us that there is no necessary salvation in being a fellow who delights 'in masques and revels sometimes altogether' (I iii 106). . . . The thin creature's motive is self-improvement: he is a version of the stock type of prodigal who is gulled in trying to learn how to be gallant. . . .

Sir Toby is gentlemanly liberty incarnate, a specialist in it. He lives at his ease, enjoying heritage, the something-for-nothing which this play celebrates. . . . In his talk as in his clothes, he has the ease of a gentleman whose place in the world is secure, so that, while he can find words like *consangineous* at will, he can also say 'Sneck up!' to Malvolio's accusation that he shows 'no respect of persons, places, nor time' (II iii 90). . . . Falstaff makes a career of misrule; Sir Toby uses misrule to show up a careerist. . . .

Throughout the play a contrast is maintained between the taut, restless, elegant court, where people speak a nervous verse, and the free-wheeling household of Olivia where, except for the intense moments in Olivia's amorous interview with Cesario, people live in an easy-going prose. The contrast is another version of pastoral. . . .

All of the merrymakers show a fine sense of the relations of people, including robust Fabian, and Sir Toby, when he has need. The fool, especially, has this courtly awareness. We see in the first scene that he has to have it to live: he goes far enough in the direction of plain speaking to engage Olivia's unwilling attention, then brings off his thesis that *she* is the fool so neatly that he is forgiven. . . . [W]hat Feste chiefly does is sing and beg – courtly occupations – and radiate in his songs and banter a feeling of liberty based on accepting disillusion. . . .

. . . There is no way to settle just how much of Malvolio's pathos should be allowed to come through when he is down and out in the dark hole. Most people now agree that Charles Lamb's sympathy for the steward's enterprise and commiseration for his sorrows is a romantic and bourgeois distortion. But he is certainly pathetic, if one thinks about it, because he is so utterly cut off from everyone else by his anxious self-love. He lacks the freedom which makes Viola so perceptive, and is correspondingly oblivious. . . .

Malvolio has been called a satirical portrait of the Puritan spirit, and there is some truth in the notion. But he is not hostile to holiday because he is a Puritan; he is like a Puritan because he is hostile to holiday. Shakespeare even mocks, in passing, the thoughtless, fashionable antipathy to Puritans current among gallants. . . . Shakespeare's two great comic butts, Malvolio and Shylock, express basic human attitudes which were at work in the commercial revolution, the new values whose development R. H. Tawney described in *Religion and the Rise of Capitalism*. But both figures are conceived at a level of esthetic abstraction which makes it inappropriate to identify them with specific social groups in the mingled actualities of history: Shylock, embodying ruthless money power, is no more to be equated with actual bankers than Malvolio, who has something of the Puritan ethic, is to be thought of as a portrait of actual Puritans. Yet, seen in the perspective of literary and social history, there is a curious appropriateness in Malvolio's presence, as a kind of foreign body to be expelled by laughter, in Shakespeare's last free-and-easy festive comedy. He is a man of business, and, it is passingly suggested, a hard one; he is or would like to be a rising man, and to rise he *uses* sobriety and morality. One could moralize the spectacle by observing that, in the long run, in the 1640s [when the Puritan revolution overthrew the aristocratic social order and closed the theatres], Malvolio *was* revenged on the whole pack of them.

But Shakespeare's comedy remains, long after 1640, to move audiences through release to clarification, making distinctions between false care and true freedom and realizing anew, for successive generations, powers in human nature and society which made good the risks of courtesy and liberty. And this without blinking the fact that 'the rain it raineth every day.'

For L. G. Salingar, the thematic key to *Twelfth Night* was its imitation of 'a feast of misrule, when normal restraints and relationships were overthrown'. In 'The Design of *Twelfth Night*' (*Shakespeare Quarterly*, 1958) Salingar noted that

The subplot shows a prolonged season of misrule, or 'uncivil rule,' in Olivia's household, with Sir Toby turning night into day; there are drinking, dancing, and singing, scenes of mock wooing, a mock sword fight, and the gulling of an unpopular member of the household, with Feste mumming it as a priest and attempting a mock exorcism in the manner of the Feast of Fools. Sir Andrew and Malvolio resemble Ben Jonson's social pretenders; but Shakespeare goes beyond Jonson in ringing the changes on the theme of Folly and in making his speakers turn logic and courtesy on their heads. A girl and a coward are given out to be ferocious duellists; a steward imagines that he can marry his lady; and finally a fool pretends to assure a wise man that darkness is light. In Feste, Shakespeare creates his most finished portrait of a professional fool; he is superfluous to the plot, but affects the mood of the play more than any other of Shakespeare's clowns.

Moreover, this saturnalian spirit invades the whole play. In the main plot, sister is mistaken for brother, and brother for sister. Viola tells Olivia 'That you do think you are not what you are' – and admits that the same holds true for herself. The women take the initiative in wooing, both in appearance, and in fact; the heroine performs love-service for the lover. The Duke makes his servant 'your master's mistress' and the lady who has withdrawn from the sight of men embraces a stranger. The four main actors all reverse their desires or break their vows before the comedy is over; while Antonio, the one single-minded representative of romantic devotion, is also the only character in the main plot who tries to establish a false identity and fails (III.iv.341–343); and he is left unrewarded and almost disregarded. Such reversals are, as Johnson says, devices peculiar to the stage, but Shakespeare makes them spring, or seem to spring, from the very nature of love. . . . Love here will 'be clamorous, and leap all bounds,' like a lord of misrule; 'love's night is noon,' like Sir Toby's carousals. Love seems as powerful as the sea, tempestuous, indifferent, and changeable as the sea. And fortune, or fate, reveals the same paradoxical benevolence in this imbroglio of mistakes and disguises: 'Tempests are kind, and salt waves fresh in love.'

Like L. G. Salingar, John Hollander interpreted the 'Action of *Twelfth Night*' as 'that of a Revels, a suspension of mundane affairs during a brief epoch in a temporary world of indulgence, a land full of food, drink, love, play, disguise, and music'. In '*Twelfth Night* and the Morality of Indulgence' (*Sewanee Review*, 1959), Hollander suggested that

The fact that plays were categorized as 'revells' for institutional purposes may have appealed to Shakespeare; he seems at any rate to have analyzed the dramatic and moral nature of feasting, and to have made it the subject of his play. His analysis is schematized in Orsino's opening speech.

The essential action of a revels is: To so surfeit the Appetite upon excess that it 'may sicken and so die.' It is the Appetite, not the whole self, however, which is surfeited: the Self will emerge at the conclusion of the action from where it has been hidden. The movement of the play is toward this emergence of humanity from behind a mask of comic type.

. . . Love, eating, and music are the components of the revelry, then. [And one of the major emphases of Shakespeare's treatment of it is that love is to be regarded] as an appetite. The substance of a feast will always fall into 'abatement and low price' at the conclusion of the feasting, for no appetite remains to demand it. . . . Like Actaeon, [Orsino] is the hunter hunted; the active desirer pursued by his own desires. As embodying this overpowering appetite for romantic love, he serves as a host of the revels.

The other host is Olivia, the subject of his desire. We see almost at once that her self-indulgence is almost too big to be encompassed by Orsino's. . . . 'To season a brother's dead love': she is gorging herself on this fragrant herb, and though she has denied herself the world, she is no true anchorite, but, despite herself, a private glutton. The Duke looks forward to the end of her feast of grief. . . .

. . . Viola is juxtaposed to Olivia here; she is not one to drown her own life in a travesty of mourning. . . . She will serve the Duke. . . . And 'what is his name?' she asks. 'Orsino,' answers the Captain. Orsino – the bear, the ravenous and clumsy devourer. Her own name suggests active, affective music; and the mention of Arion, the Orpheus-like enchanter of waves and dolphins with his music, points up the connotation. Orsino's 'music,' on the other hand, is a static well of emotion in which he allows his own rhetoric to submerge; Viola's is more essentially instrumental, effective, and convincing. . . .

What is most important is that neither Feste, the feaster embodying not the spirit but the action of revelry, nor Malvolio, the ill-wisher (and the *bad appetite* as well), his polar opposite, appears in these introductory scenes. It is only upstairs in Olivia's house (I, v) that the action as such commences. . . . From here on it will be Feste who dances attendance on the revelry, singing, matching wit with Viola, and being paid by almost everyone for his presence. To a certain degree he remains outside the action, not participating in it because he represents its very nature; occasionally serving as a comic angel or messenger, he is nevertheless unmotivated by any appetite, and is never sated of his fooling. His insights into the action are continuous, and his every remark is telling. . . . No one will be revealed in his true dress until he has doffed his mask of feasting. And although neither Feste nor Malvolio will change in this respect, it is for completely opposite reasons that they will not do so.

Every character in the play, however, is granted some degree of insight into the nature of the others. It is almost as if everyone were masked with the black side of his vizard turned inwards; he sees more clearly past the *persona* of another than he can past his own. . . .

. . . Malvolio's 'distempered appetite' results from the fact that he alone is not possessed of a craving directed outward, towards some object on which it can surfeit and die; he alone cannot benefit from a period of self-indulgence. Actually this distemper manifests itself in terms of transitory desires on his part for status and for virtue, but these desires consume him in their fruitlessness; he is aware of the nature of neither of them. This is a brilliant analysis of the character of a melancholic, and Shakespeare's association of the melancholy, puritanic, and status-seeking characters in Malvolio throws considerable light on all of them. . . . For Malvolio's attachment to self-advancement is not being either aristocratically ridiculed or praised as an example of righteous bourgeois opposition to medieval hierarchies. In the context of the play's moral physiology, his disease is shown forth as a case of indigestion due to his self-love, the result of a perverted, rather than an excessive appetite. . . . It is only Malvolio who bears any ill will, and only he upon whom ill will can appear to be directed. He makes for himself a hell of the worldly heaven of festivity, and when Toby and Maria put him into darkness, into a counterfeit hell, they are merely representing in play a condition that he has already achieved.

The plot against Malvolio, then, is no more than an attempt to let him surfeit on himself, to present him with those self-centered, 'time-pleasing' objects upon which his appetite is fixed. In essence, he is led to a feast in which his own vision of himself is spread before him, and commanded to eat it. The puritan concern with witchcraft and the satanic, and its associations of them with madness are carried to a logical extreme; and once Malvolio has been permitted to indulge in his self-interest by means of the letter episode, he is only treated as he would himself treat anyone whom he believed to be mad. . . .

The prank played on Malvolio is not merely an 'interwoven' second story, but a fully developed double-plot. Like the Belmont episodes in *The Merchant of Venice*, it is a condensed representation of the action of the entire play. In *Twelfth Night*, however, it operates in reverse, to show the other side of the coin, as it were. For Mavolio there can be no fulfillment in 'one self king.' His story effectively and ironically underlines the progress toward this fulfillment in everybody else, and helps to delineate the limitations of the moral domain of the whole play. In contrast to Feste, who appears in the action at times as an abstracted spirit of revelry, Malvolio is a model of the sinner. . . .

If Feste's purpose is to serve as a symbol of the revels, however, he must also take a clear and necessary part in the all-important conclusion. *Twelfth Night* itself, the feast of the Epiphany, celebrates the discovery of the 'True King' in the manger by the Wise Men. 'Those wits,' says Feste in Act I, Scene 5, 'that think they have thee [wit] do very oft prove fools, and I that am sure I lack thee may pass for a wise man.' And so it is that under his influence the true Caesario, the 'one self king,' is revealed. The whole of Act V might be taken, in connection with 'the plot' in a trivial sense, to be the other *epiphany*, the perception that follows the *anagnorisis* or discovery of classic dramaturgy. But we have been dealing with the Action of *Twelfth Night* as representing the killing off of excessive appetite through indulgence of it, leading to the rebirth of the unencumbered self. The long final scene, then, serves to show forth the Caesario-King, and to unmask, discover, and reveal the fulfilled selves in the major characters. . . .

As the scene plays itself out, Malvolio alone is left unaccounted for. There is no accounting for him here, though; he remains a bad taste in the mouth. 'Alas poor fool,' says Olivia, 'How have they baffled thee!' And thus, in Feste's words, 'the whirligig of time brings in his revenges.' Malvolio has become the fool, the 'barren rascal.' . . . His business has never been with the feasting to begin with, and now that it is over, and the revellers normalized, he is revealed as the true madman. He is 'The Madly-Used Malvolio' to the additional degree that his own uses have been madness.

For Orsino and Viola the end has also arrived. She will be 'Orsino's mistress and his fancy's queen.' He has been surfeited of his misdirected voracity; the rich golden shaft, in his own words, 'hath killed the flock of all affections else' that live in him. 'Liver, brain, and heart' are indeed all supplied; for both Olivia and himself, there has been fulfillment in 'one self king.' And, lest there be no mistake, each is to be married to a Caesario or king. . . .

At the end of the scene, all exit. Only Feste, the pure fact of feasting, remains. His final song is a summation of the play in many ways at once. Its formal structure seems to be a kind of quick rehearsal of the Ages of Man. In youth, 'A foolish thing was but a toy': the fool's bauble, emblematic of both his *membrum virile* and his trickery, is a trivial fancy. But in 'man's estate,' the bauble represents a threat of knavery and thievery to respectable society, who shuts its owner out of doors. The 'swaggering' and incessant drunkenness of the following strophes bring Man into prime and dotage, respectively. Lechery, trickery, dissembling, and drunkenness, inevitable and desperate in mundane existence, however, are just those activities which, mingled together in a world of feasting, serve to purge Man of the desire for them. . . .

It is the metaphor of the rain that lasts longest, though, and it recapitulates the images of water, elements, and humours that have pervaded the entire play. . . . Humours are also waters. . . . And *waters*, or fluids of all kinds, are continually being forced on our attention. Wine, tears, seawater, even urine, are in evidence from the first scene on, and they are always being metaphorically identified with one another. They are all fluids, bathing the world of the play in possibilities for change as the humours do the body. Feste's answer to Maria in the prison scene has puzzled many editors; if we realize, however, that Feste is probably hysterically laughing at what he has just been up to, 'Nay, I'm for all waters' may have the additional meaning that he is on the verge of losing control of himself. He is 'for all waters' primarily in that he represents the fluidity of revelling celebration. And finally, when all is done, 'The rain it raineth every day,' and Feste reverts to gnomic utterance in a full and final seriousness. Water is rain that falls to us from heaven. The world goes on. Our revels now are ended, but the actors solidify into humanity, in this case. 'But that's all one, our play is done, / And we'll strive to please you every day.'

Through a study of the comic uses of dramatic irony, or what he termed 'discrepant awareness', Bertrand Evans endeavoured to show that 'In the world of *Twelfth Night*, as in the worlds of the comedies just preceding, the spirit of the practiser [deceiver] prevails.' Concentrating on dramaturgical techniques, Evans demonstrated in *Shakespeare's Comedies* (Oxford, 1960) that the playwright frequently contrives to give the audience a perceptual advantage over characters who themselves possess, or think they possess, a perspective superior to that of other characters. Thus,

> Although Feste is either 'in' on most practices or unaffected by them, he, with all Illyria, is ignorant of the main secret of the play, the identity of 'Cesario'. Here, then, even heroine and clown stand below us, and below them the others range down to the bottom, where sit Aguecheek and Malvolio in chronic oblivion. Though also victims of others' practices, neither needs deceiving to be deceived – Nature having practised on them once for all.
>
> But if all are exposed as at some time in ignorance of their situations, yet all but Orsino and Malvolio have compensatory moments when they overpeer others: even Aguecheek, though a fool the while, briefly enjoys advantage over Malvolio. The awarenesses in *Twelfth Night* are so structured that an overpeerer gloating in his advantage is usually himself overpeered by another participant or by us: thus Sir Toby exults in his advantage over 'Cesario', knowing that Sir Andrew is not the 'devil in a private brawl' he would have 'Cesario' believe – but at the same time 'Cesario' holds advantage over him in knowing that 'Cesario' is a fiction; and the last laugh is ours, on Sir Toby, for even he would hardly have made his jest of a duel had he known 'Cesario' truly. From much use of such arrangements, in which a participant's understanding is inferior with respect to some elements of a situation and superior with respect to others, emerge the richest effects of *Twelfth Night* and some of the finest in Shakespeare. . . .
>
> Viola [does] not take up [her] masquerade for the love of mockery. Hers is not a mocking nature. The thing she starts threatens to get out of hand almost at once. Hopelessly wooing Olivia for Orsino, hopelessly loving Orsino, hopelessly loved by Olivia, ignorant that Sebastian is alive to make all right at last, she is caught in what is to her a frightening dilemma such as Rosalind [of *As You Like It*] would never be caught in – for Rosalind is superior to dilemmas. It is in accord with her nature that Viola bears her advantage mercifully in the second interview, and the gap between the pair is exploited tenderly: 'A cypress, not a bosom, / Hides my heart,' Olivia begins, and Viola replies, 'I pity you.' These are not Rosalind and Phebe, the one exuberantly mocking, the other brazen-bold; these are Viola and Olivia, the one bearing her advantage as if it had suddenly become a cross, the other so deeply stricken that laughter at her condition would be gross. . . . Yet the frame of the situation is comic, even grotesque: the reversal of roles, the woman wooing the man, an incongruity in society if not in nature, is a perennial subject of jest; and the fact that

this 'man' is not even a man adds a joke to what is already a joke. . . .

The emotional conflict which rises from this unlaughable treatment of a laughable situation, complex already, is further complicated by the force of the crowning fact in our superior awareness: our knowledge that Sebastian lives and must now be close at hand. If Olivia can love 'Cesario', she can love Sebastian. The 'thriftless sighs' that arouse Viola's pity and prevent us from laughing need not be thriftless; the hand that can free Olivia will also sever the knot that is too hard for Viola to untie. Thus while the laughter implicit in the situation is drowned in the sympathy demanded by the gentleness of both women, the struggle is also flooded with comforting assurance; all is well and will end well. . . .

[One reason for the success of Maria's practice against the overbearing Steward is that Malvolio] is self-deceived before he is deceived. . . . Sir Toby's assurances do not allay Sir Andrew's grave doubts. But Malvolio's fire is the product of spontaneous combustion, and his sense of worthiness is unalloyed by misgivings. Shakespeare makes this fact clear by exhibiting the man's vainglory just before he finds the forged letter. . . . This exhibition of self-deception continues until Malvolio picks up the letter, when deception is welded to self-deception by a gaudy flash of irony: 'What employment have we here?' . . . Exhibiting the seduction of a mind eager to be seduced, the scene surpasses everything resembling it in Shakespeare. . . .

'Observe him, for the love of mockery,' says Maria to her accomplices. Hidden in the box-tree, they hold a triple advantage over Malvolio, in that they watch him when he does not suspect, recognize his self-kindled folly, and, of course, know that the letter which sets him ablaze is forged. Yet the master practiser here is Shakespeare, whose way it is to set participants where they overpeer others while they are also overpeered. The practisers do not suspect, as we are privately reminded when Maria describes Olivia as 'addicted to a melancholy', a disposition which will render Malvolio's smiles intolerable to her. The fact is that Olivia is not now addicted to a melancholy, but is in love with 'Cesario' – and her world has changed. Hence even Maria, knowing nothing of the change, drops below our level. As for Sir Andrew, Shakespeare does not let us forget that the man is a fool all the while he joyously overpeers Malvolio – and that, besides, he is practice-ridden. . . . And while he is most enjoying his advantage over Malvolio, Sir Andrew is made to expose the depth of his congenital unawareness. . . . Maria's invitation to see 'the fruits of the sport' thus carries even higher promise than she intends, since the gullers as well as their gull will, in our perspective, contribute to the fun.

In 'Mistakes in *Twelfth Night* and Their Resolution' (*PMLA:*

Publications of the Modern Language Association of America, 1961), an article that reinforced Evans's thesis about discrepant awareness, Porter Williams, Jr, presented evidence that

> Mistakes control the direction of the action throughout. Viola cannot obtain Orsino's love as long as she is mistaken for Cesario and as long as Orsino mistakes the object of his love; while Olivia, though abandoning one error, that of a seven years' grief, still cannot love Orsino and can never win the disguised Viola. Olivia's other suitors, Sir Andrew Aguecheek and Malvolio, hopelessly deceived into playing the roles of lovers, are fooled each to the top of his bent until unmasked before all by Sir Toby, Maria, and their associates in the subplot. The action reaches its turning point with the cleverest 'disguise' of all and the happiest deception. Sebastian, appearing as himself and hence unwittingly disguised as Cesario, his masked sister, accepts the hand of Olivia, now most truly herself and yet most completely deceived. Only unmasking can follow after this, with the pairing off of the lovers and the dismissal of the thwarted. Feste, the wisest fool of them all, is left alone to frame the action in Time.
>   . . . It is through his mistakes that we can see a character in the play either find or avoid what for him is a right relationship. For example, Olivia's spontaneous love for Cesario, a mistake on most levels, unconsciously prepares her heart for a happy union with Sebastian, just as it also reveals the fallacy of contemplating an unnatural seven years' grief. Likewise, Sebastian, thrust into a world of misconceptions but sensing his own occasion mellow, accepts an offer of marriage in complete ignorance and fully aware only 'That this may be some error' (IV.iii.10).
>   . . . And yet these mistakes are fortunate ones of the mind rather than the heart, even though Olivia thinks that she is marrying Cesario. Intuition, not reason, is at work. Unlike Malvolio, they find happiness because they know what it is 'To be generous, guiltless, and of free disposition' (I.v.89–90). Such impulses can bring tragic disaster, especially if fiery Tybalts or jealous Iagos are about; but given a world this side of tragedy, then the generous impulses of open natures are the surest way to happiness. A willingness to love and, something more, perhaps the gift to recognize a kindred spirit and to risk all, are the touchstones to Shakespeare's serious world of romantic comedy. Olivia's words, 'Love sought is good . . . but given unsought is better' (III.i.158), seem to be the dominant note for those who win happiness in terms of love and friendship, but such giving and receiving must be done without counting the cost or measuring the risk. Viola gives her love unsought to Orsino, while on a more material level a surprising quantity of money and rings is given generously throughout the play, sought and unsought. . . . The secret of true love and friendship,

therefore, is a subtle and delicate relationship, depending upon uncalculating generosity and spontaneous impulses. . . . Shakespeare was particularly adept at underlying the awakening of these spiritual capacities by revealing them while the reason was perplexed with error, with the very mistakes that threatened well laid plans opening the way for intuitive solutions. . . .

No one in *Twelfth Night* entirely escapes the darkness of ignorance, but at least those who come to know generous love and friendship escape time's harshest revenges. Those who escape make it clear why the others suffered, for comedy thrives on poetic justice. Viola is always the touchstone, though Feste may point the moral. Once Viola emerges from the sea, displays her courage and hope, and reveals her generous capacity for love, we have our standard by which to judge the others. Thus Sebastian reaps his fine reward by following his sister's path of openhearted commitment to events. We can expect Antonio, the model of generous friendship, to find generosity in return, as will the Captain who helped Viola, though mistakes have been obstacles to them. . . . [Meanwhile] Malvolio's vanity, Sir Toby's drunkenness and unkindness, and Sir Andrew's foolish limitations, all show how far short they fall in human relationships. . . .

The wise and the generous, then, survive their foolish mistakes, and profit. Most important of all, there has been revealed a kind of wisdom of the heart that flourishes even while the intellect is perplexed. Feste's remark that 'there is no darkness but ignorance' (IV.ii.42–43) achieves its fullest meaning on this deeper or psychological level. It is strange that a study of mistakes, instead of restricting criticism to a discussion of superficial farce, leads directly to the inner life of the play. Every mistake may be a blemish of the mind, but the inner life of the play reveals that only blemishes of the heart destroy. . . .

Among the many excellent recent studies of Shakespearean comedy, one of the most penetrating has been Harry Levin's article 'The Underplot of *Twelfth Night*' in *Shakespeare and the Revolution of the Times* (New York, 1976). Levin begins by noting that

The kind of comedy that was practiced by Shakespeare has repeatedly challenged definition. Though his last comedies have been retrospectively classified as romances, most of their components are equally characteristic of his earlier ones: love, adventure, coincidence, recognition, and occasional pathos. The problem is not simplified by the circumstance that his greatest comic character, Falstaff, was far more impressive in two histories than he is in *The Merry Wives of Windsor*. Traditional definitions of the comic somehow fail to hit the

Shakespearean mark, perhaps because they tend to emphasize the spectatorial attitude of ridicule. Shakespeare's attitude is more participatory; its emphasis falls upon playfulness, man at play, the esthetic principle that Johan Huizinga has so brilliantly illuminated in his historico-cultural study, *Homo Ludens*. Whereas we may laugh at Ben Jonson's characters, we generally laugh with Shakespeare's; indeed, if we begin by laughing at Falstaff or the clowns, we end by laughing with them at ourselves; semantically speaking, they are therefore not ridiculous but ludicrous. . . .

Any speculation about *Twelfth Night* might start with its alternative title, which has no counterpart among the other plays in the First Folio. The subtitle *What You Will* echoes the common and casual phrase that Olivia uses at one point in addressing Malvolio. . . . To designate [the work] by the seasonal dating would have touched off some associations, especially since *Twelfth Night* signalized the grand finale to the Christmas entertainment at Queen Elizabeth's court, and sometimes featured a performance by Shakespeare's company. But the English term seems relatively vague, when contrasted with the overtones of the French and Italian translations. *La Nuit des Rois* almost seems to promise a visitation of the Magi; Shakespeare anticlimactically gives us, instead, the iconological joke about 'We Three' and a clownish snatch of song from Sir Toby, 'Three merry men be we' (II.iii.17, 76–7). *La Notte dell'Epifania* may also hold theological – or at least, in Joycean terms, psychological – connotations. Shakespeare merely seems concerned to promise his audience a pleasant surprise by evoking a winter holiday, even as he did with the opposite season in *A Midsummer Night's Dream*. Festivals are the matrices of drama, and that 'holiday humor' in which the transvested Rosalind invites Orlando to rehearse his wooing sets the prevalent mood for Shakespearean comedy (*As You Like It*, IV.i.69). . . .

. . . Even in the sunniest of Shakespeare's comedies, there are shadows now and then, and it is worth remembering that *Twelfth Night* was probably conceived in the same year as *Hamlet*. The aura of melancholy emanates from Olivia's household, but it extends to Orsino's palace because of his unwelcome suit. . . .

. . . One of the jester's assumed *personae* is that of the Vice, the principal mischief-maker in the old-fashioned morality plays (IV.ii.124). As 'an allow'd fool,' he has the privilege of raillery, which we hear that Olivia's father 'took much delight in' (I.v.94; II.iv.12). Her father's death, which cannot have happened very long before, has presumably added to her brother's in deepening the gloom of the abode where she now finds herself mistress. Shakespeare has gone out of his way to darken the background of the conventional situation among the lovers, possibly reflecting the widespread preoccupation with the theme of melancholia during the early years of the seventeenth century. If so, his ultimate concern was to lift the clouds, to brighten the effect of the picture as a whole by the deft use of *chiaroscuro*, to heighten the triumph of the comic spirit by presenting it under attack. And, of course, with the rise of Puritanism, it was increasingly subject to attackers.

Such considerations may help to explain why Shakespeare went even farther by introducing the character of Malvolio. . . .

. . . As a master of the revels, [Sir Toby] and his fellow revelers embody the forces of life, on the one hand. On the other, the interloping Malvolio represents the force of care, which has usurped a temporary control over once-carefree Illyria. It is not for nothing that his name signifies 'Ill-wisher.' He is the perennial spoilsport, fighting an aggressive rearguard action against a crapulous playboy and his Bacchanalian cohorts. As Olivia's steward, Malvolio's functions are more than ceremonial; he can not only cut off the daily bounties of existence; he can threaten, and he does, to expel the incumbent devotees of good living. After Toby's rhetorical question on behalf of cakes and ale, seconded by Feste's plea for ginger, their prodigal levity takes the offensive against his false dignity. . . . Not only must this non-laugher . . . doff his somber black for yellow stockings and cross-garters, but he must force his atrabilious features into an unremitting smile.

[When Malvolio's comeuppance is complete, we realize that] what we have been watching is a reenactment of a timeless ritual, whose theatrical manifestation takes the obvious form of the villain foiled, and whose deeper roots in folklore go back to the scapegoat cast into the outer darkness. The business of baiting him is not a sadistic gesture but a cathartic impulse of *Schadenfreude* [malicious joy]: an affirmation of Life against Care, if we allow Sir Toby to lay down the terms of our allegory. We could point to an illustration so rich in detail and so panoramic in design that it might prove distracting, if it were not so sharply focused on the conflict before us, Pieter Breughel's *Battle between Carnival and Lent*. . . . Shakespeare loaded his dice on the side of carnival, in that hungover hanger-on, Sir Toby, as against the lenten Malvolio, that prince of wet-blankets. But Shakespeare was writing a comedy – and what is more, a comedy written in defense of the comic spirit. He could commit himself, in this case, to the wisdom of folly and to the ultimate foolishness of the conventional wisdom. But, in his dramaturgy, he was moving onward to care, to death, to mourning, and toward tragedy.

As Karen Greif reads it, 'Like *Hamlet*, but in a comic vein, *Twelfth Night* poses questions about "the purpose of playing" and about whether illusion is perhaps too deeply embedded in human experience to be ever completely separated from reality.'

In her article 'Plays and Playing in *Twelfth Night*' (*Shakespeare Survey*, 1981), Greif asserts that

> Virtually every character in *Twelfth Night* is either an agent or a victim of illusion, and often a player will assume both roles: as Viola is an impostor but also a prisoner of her own disguise, or as Sir Toby loses control of the deception he has contrived when he mistakes Sebastian for his twin. Illyria is a world populated by pretenders. . . .
> . . . The plot contrived to convince the steward of Olivia's passion for him is enacted with deliberately theatrical overtones, and the conspirators employ deception to feed and then expose Malvolio's folly in much the same way that a playwright manipulates illusion and reality upon the stage. Yet Malvolio's enforced immersion in the world of make-believe in no way reforms him. Nor does it enable him to gain a more positive understanding of either his own identity or the ties that bind him to his fellow men. Malvolio remains isolated and egotistical to the end. What is more, the mockers who have seen their own follies reflected in Malvolio's comic performance are no more altered by the experience than he is. . . .
> Maria's letter cleverly exploits Malvolio's conceit, but he himself manufactures his obsession. With only the flimsiest of clues to lead him on, Malvolio systematically construes every detail of the letter to fuel his newly liberated dreams of greatness, never pausing to consider how ludicrous the message really is. . . .
> Malvolio's response to his comic purgatory stirs unresolved questions about the value of playing with reality. Whereas Viola's part in the comedy reveals how the release that playing allows can lead to a renewed sense of identity and human bonds, Malvolio's role exposes the other side of the coin, the realm in which release of imagination leads only to greater isolation and imperception. . . . [But] amusing as Malvolio's surrender to playing is, it raises the most disturbing questions in the play. Can men, in fact, ever distinguish what is real from what is imagined or intentionally spurious? Can they ever come to know the truth about themselves, the identity appearances have concealed from them?
> *Twelfth Night* itself offers no pat solutions. In a comic world devoted to playing and yet mirroring the actual world of being, in which identities are both mistaken and revealed, in which deception can both conceal truths and expose them, and in which bonds have disgraced the words on which men are dependent for communication, no permanent resolution of these ambiguities is ever possible.

Even more unsettling than Karen Greif's analysis of the play is Ralph Berry's. In '*Twelfth Night*: The Experience of the Audience' (*Shakespeare Survey*, 1981), Berry proposes that we

Let the claret which Shakespeare drank, as we know, on expense account symbolize the general experience of *Twelfth Night*. The taste of this play has the same tension between sweetness and dryness, which translates easily into the indulgent reveries of the opening and the realities of rain, ageing, and work, in Feste's final song. . . . The experience of *Twelfth Night* blends our sense of the title metaphor with the growing magnitude of the joke that goes too far, and with it our grasp of the relation between the gulling and romantic actions . . .

. . . There is a certain moral responsibility, even culpability, which the audience assumes in *Twelfth Night*: I don't think the play can be understood without it.

The scene in which Malvolio makes a fool of himself before Olivia (act 3, scene 4) begins to insinuate unease into the audience's consciousness. It is a scene we have been prepared for, and kept waiting for, and it is an unholy delight; yet the thought is emerging that Malvolio has committed an irreversible *bêtise*. The activities of Sir Toby, Fabian, and Maria begin to look like open sadism, and we may make the subliminal connection between Malvolio and bear-baiting, mentioned earlier (1.3.92., 2.5.8). . . . The inexorable line of development holds into the cell scene of act 4, scene 2, and however this is played, the audience is now conscious that the affair is much less funny that it was. The joke has been taken too far, and we know it. Let us hold on to that formulation, and cast back to the beginning of the play. The entire construct prepares us for our realization in the later stages. (One cannot point to a precise moment in act 3, scene 4, when the audience becomes aware of its own queasiness; but it must surely happen.) The hints start, of course, with the title. Twelfth Night is a festival that has already been going on too long. Twelve days and nights of overeating and overdrinking, little or nothing done in the way of useful work: the Elizabethans were not so different from ourselves. By 6 January they were ready enough for one more party, then back to work. The experience of satiety is confirmed in Orsino's opening words. . . .

. . . Whatever one's temperament, there is a time to move off and to bed. Someone else prefers to stay and keep things going, though the fire has died out of the occasion. It is a fault of taste, this failure to judge the natural life of a party, and someone always commits it. . . .

Likeableness, for obvious reasons, is not a critical concept. It looks like an invitation to the untrammelled subjectivities of all readers and playgoers – an abdication of critical decorum. All the same, we need the term here. That is because Shakespeare, as I view it, sets up a design in which we are to begin by liking certain characters and disliking others, and to end with reversing those judgements.

It is all focused on Sir Toby and Malvolio, though other characters can affect matters marginally. . . .

[Sir Toby's] revealed characteristics become steadily less appealing. . . . Stage drunkenness is always an ambivalent affair, for the sufficient reason that it is in real life. A drunk is funny, an alcoholic is not. . . . [W]e warm to [Sir Toby] more in the earlier than the later stages of the acquaintance.

Sir Toby's other characteristics are similarly disenchanting. His relationship with Sir Andrew emerges as contemptuous and exploitative. The comic glow protects his name for a while, certainly. . . . It is in the gulling actions that Sir Toby appears at his least appealing. . . . He pursues the Malvolio affair with a relentlessness that is disturbing. . . . The other matter is the gulling of Sir Andrew and the arranged duel between him and Cesario. Here I stress the force of pattern, so often Shakespeare's way of imparting personality and being. One joke is inconclusive; two suggests a mind obsessively addicted to making sport out of others. . . .

. . . All Shakespeare's plays exhibit some social tensions, if only within the same class. *Twelfth Night*, more than any other comedy of this period, reveals a discreet awareness of these tensions. Three of its personages marry upwards (Sebastian, Viola, Maria), and two seek to (Sir Andrew, Malvolio). This movement upward is caricatured in Malvolio, but the others demonstrate it too. There is a general blurring of social frontiers in Olivia's household, and this contributes to the friction and resentments of the play. . . .

Maria need not be seen and played as the bouncy, vital soubrette of stage history. Her pattern is one of social resentment, a willingness to stir up trouble for others (while usually exiting rapidly from the scene of the crime), and a remorseless drive towards her post-curtain apotheosis: Lady Belch. . . . With Maria, conversations tend to turn into threats to others. Sir Toby is in trouble; Feste may be fired; Cesario should be shown the door; Malvolio will come; Malvolio is mad. . . . Maria endures the classic ambivalences of the lady-in-waiting, above the servants but not ranking with the great. Who is Maria? 'My niece's chambermaid' is Sir Toby's description, in her presence. It is not what we should term an introduction: Sir Toby is speaking to Sir Andrew, presumably just out of earshot of Maria. The editorial glosses are unanimous in their assurance that 'My niece's chambermaid' means 'lady-in-waiting' or 'lady's maid'. But the *OED* does not confirm this certitude. The fact is that *chambermaid* did also, at this time, mean (as we should expect), 'female servant', roughly the usage of today. . . . I suggest that the 'servant' sense is present, and in Maria's mind; which is why Sir Toby does not speak the word to Maria's face. . . .

The cell scene is crucial. On the one side, we begin to detach ourselves from the sustained animosity of Feste, and from the self-interested sadism of Sir Toby. On the other, we recognize a 'different' human being emerging from the darkness. It is a rebirth, almost. . . . What happens to Malvolio has nothing to do with pathos. It is a matter of human identity emerging, and it is all in the words. . . .

. . . The identity which Malvolio discovers for himself in the cell, and which he imparts to us, is the backing for his promise: 'As I am a gentleman.' Not, be it noted, 'steward'. The identity of functional authority is rejected in favour of a term whose core of meaning lies outside, as well as within, social rank. . . . *Gentleman*, of all social terms, casts the widest net. The word contains the ideas of birth, education, wealth, behaviour, and values; yet it allows no single aspect to dominate, nor can any element insist on its presence. *Gentleman*, that uniquely English invention, is at bottom the principle of 'tolerance' within the social structure, the moving part that takes the strain of fixed relationships. . . . Not 'fellow', that socially ambivalent word Malvolio mistook from Olivia, but fellowship, is Malvolio's discovery. The man who would be 'Count Malvolio', fantasy's alternative to 'Steward', now founds himself on the truth of 'gentleman'. . . .

Hence the way is paved for Malvolio's entry [in the concluding scene], and his climactic statement of injury. The tone and quality of that last speech are obvious to all. What matters formally is that the speech is in verse. For the first time in the play, Malvolio speaks in the language of the rank to which he had aspired. It is his ultimate irony that in the moment of humiliation and disgrace he speaks in the tongue of social elevation and human dignity.

That final speech, leading to the appalling 'I'll be reveng'd on the whole pack of you', is the climax of everything that happens in *Twelfth Night*. The experience must be confronted, and neither denied nor indulged. 'Malvolio: a Tragedy' is a sentimentalization of this play. But equally, one is struck by the large number of critics who, on this issue, seem bent on repressing instincts which, outside the theatre of *Twelfth Night*, they would surely admit. . . . Most certainly [Malvolio] is to be expelled, if *Twelfth Night* is a 'free-and-easy festive comedy'; but supposing the intruder belongs in the play, what then?

How can one explain this critical imperviousness to the ending? One comes to view the critics here as a representative sampling of the human mind. They *want*, as we all do, a comedy; they do not want a disturbance to the agreeable mood created in *Twelfth Night*. . . . They seek a formula that helps to suppress the disquiet one inevitably feels. In this they faithfully embody certain tendencies within the mind, and thus – as Shakespeare well knew – of his audience. . . .

. . . . [I]t is only necessary to extend the thought an inch further, and ask: was it not Shakespeare's intention to 'spoil the effect of the comedy', and was not that the goal to which the entire dramatic enterprise was directed? Why not? Where is it laid down that a dramatist may not build into his design a threat to its own mood?

In its final stages, that threat all but destroys the mood of *Twelfth Night*. The minor action bids to overwhelm the major. The Illyrian world of fulfilled romance, genial comics, and harmless pranks metamorphoses into an image of the real world, with its grainy texture, social frictions, and real pain inflicted upon real people. Malvolio must bear the burden of the real world, as he did its festive release. The disposable person of part one has become the victim of part two, and thus the agent for showing up the festive spirit itself. . . .

'*I'll be reveng'd on the whole pack of you*.' The theatrical dimension of the line is all-important, and we need the historical imagination to grasp it. At *pack*, the subliminal metaphor discloses itself. It is a bear-baiting. The audience becomes spectators, Malvolio the bear. The theatrical voltage of the shock is immensely increased if we accept that bear-baiting actually occurred within the same auditorium. . . . The essential point is that the original audience would have witnessed enough bear-baitings, whether in the specific theatre of *Twelfth Night* (Globe), in other theatres such as the Hope, or elsewhere. The connections between theatre, bear-baiting, and festivity were well established. And the awareness of those connections would have governed the audience's experience of Malvolio. So would the delivery of the line. We see a Malvolio who must address his stage tormentors, roughly at right angles to the sight lines of the audience. He is addressing Orsino and company, not us. Imagine a Malvolio in the centre of the platform stage, addressing others downstage: he is surrounded on three (or all) sides by tiers of spectators, who are still perhaps jeering at him, and turns on his heel through at least 180 degrees to take in 'the whole pack of you'. That way the house, not merely the stage company, is identified with the 'pack'. It is theatre as blood sport, theatre that celebrates its own dark origins. That, too, is 'festive' comedy. What the audience makes of its emotions is its own affair. I surmise that the ultimate effect of *Twelfth Night* is to make the audience ashamed of itself.

Through a witty variation on Ralph Berry's discussion of the audience's response to Malvolio, Stephen Booth suggests that the play tempts us to *become* the over-eager Steward. In an article entitled '*Twelfth Night*: 1.1: The Audience as Malvolio', in *Shakespeare's 'Rough Magic'*, a collection edited by Peter Erickson and Coppelia Kahn (Newark, Del., 1985), Booth 'sets out to demonstrate that the first scene of *Twelfth Night* is nonsense – demonstrable nonsense, but (since it has made, and presumably always will make, perfectly good sense to its audiences), nonsense that is *merely* demonstrable'. He goes on to argue that

> nonsense is often not only a valuable, but the vital, ingredient in the greatest literary works – that nonsense can be the physical means by which our minds approach metaphysical experience – the experience of phenomena *like* the metaphysical phenomena we know exist but cannot ordinarily know except by arbitrary and diminishing metaphor. Although the particulars I talk about are small and thus clearly different from the large ones that C. L. Barber talked about when he wrote about *Twelfth Night*, this essay too is finally concerned with a holiday aspect of *Twelfth Night* – or more particularly, with a holiday aspect of its first scene. I suggest that to experience that scene is to be given a small but metaphysically glorious holiday from the limitations of the ordinary logic by which sentences determine what they will be understood to say and that that holiday is a brief and trivial but effectively real holiday from the inherent limitation of the human mind. . . .
>
> [Consider lines 9–14 of Act I, Scene i.] This sentence . . . is effortlessly assimilable by a listener. Only the Folio printer – who starts a new independent clause with *Nought* in line 11 – seems to have been disturbed by it. (The Folio punctuation could make *Receiveth* an error for 'Receivest'; it suggests that the first of the Folio's two sentences be understood as 'O spirit of love, how quick and fresh art thou that – notwithstanding thy capacity – receiveth as the sea.' Or – by retaining the full stop after *sea* in line 11, but ignoring the logic implied by the comma after *capacity* at the end of the previous line – one could isolate the word *notwithstanding* and leave *capacity* the receiver: 'O spirit of love, how quick and fresh art thou that – notwithstanding [that is, even though thou art quick and fresh] – thy capacity receiveth as the sea.') A case could be made for the Folio punctuation and the inflectional revision it demands, or for the modification by which *notwithstanding* stands logically alone as an elliptic reference to the preceding exclamation, but – for the moment at least – they are irrelevant to my concerns here. It is the effectively standard, all-but-universal editorially punctuated reading I care about: that is the one that has satisfied – seemed right to – generations of scholars, critics, and audiences ever since Nicholas Rowe emended the punctuation in 1714. This is the traditional punctuation as adapted in the New Arden edition (ed. J. M. Lothian and T. W. Craik [London, 1975]). . . .

> O spirit of love, how quick and fresh art thou,
> That notwithstanding thy capacity
> Receiveth as the sea, nought enters there,
> Of what validity and pitch soe'er,

> But falls into abatement and low price,
> Even in a minute.

Notwithstanding the ease with which it is assimilated, the repunctuated sentence is a chimera. Its head is an exclamation: *O spirit of love, how quick and fresh art thou.* As the words are heard, *quick* has to mean 'lively' – 'sprightly', in fact – and *fresh* has to mean practically the same thing: 'vigorous,' 'youthful.' The trunk of the sentence starts out to be its tail: the word *that* obviously means 'who' or 'which' and introduces a justification of the exclamation. However, the forward progress of the sentence is delayed by an ostentatiously logical reservation: *notwithstanding thy capacity receiveth as the sea.* *Notwithstanding* is a logical gesture, but its action is ultimately illogical. Up to this point, the modification meshes with the logic of the clause it interrupts: '. . . . how quick and fresh art thou, who, though you are sea-like in one respect. . . .' The modification has, however, altered the senses of *quick* and *fresh*: the notion of capacity recurs to the food metaphor and activates the senses 'keen' and 'hungry' for *quick* and *fresh*. The change in the senses of *quick* and *fresh* thus asserts an extralogical pertinence of this sentence to the preceding lines. A second later the word *sea* invokes the senses *quick* and *fresh* have as 'water' words, words indicating the quality of water – specifically, water that is not saline, is not sea water; and – since the essential question is between *the spirit of love* and *the sea* – the simile suddenly but perfectly contradicts the now relevant aqueous sense of *how quick and fresh art thou*. The semantic meanderings of *quick* and *fresh* thus at once give a sound of rightness to the sentence *and* render it nonsensical. . . .

What is more to the point here, the action of perceiving a sentence as two things at once – what is there and what the listener perceives to be there – recurs throughout the play. Take, for example, the subscription of the Maria–Olivia letter: 'She that would alter services with thee' (2.5.157–58). That subscription has, as far as I know, never been glossed. It needs no gloss. *Why* it needs no gloss, however, is fascinating. Considering our everyday, working assumptions about the relationship of language and understanding, it is amazing that this obviously simple assertion *is* obviously simple. Try to make another sentence in which 'to alter' and 'to exchange' are synonyms. Just try. 'She that would alter services with thee' is made meaningful by its context, informed by a context relevant to 'an altar' – an altar in a church – sustained by the relevance of both the liturgical and sexual senses of 'service,' and smoothed over by an implied logic that says that, since 'to exchange' and 'to change' are synonyms, and 'to alter' and 'to change' are synonyms, 'to exchange' and 'to alter' must also be synonyms. . . . After scene 1, disjunctions between what is signified and what is understood from the signal become common on the stage. The audience is often conscious that a character ignores obvious signals in the words he hears. . . .

The relation of what I have said about an audience's – about our – superiority to the 'hard' evidence of the language in *Twelfth Night* relates so obviously to the behavior of the characters in the story that there is little need to illustrate the parallel. . . . I suspect that the intended implications of 'The Audience as Malvolio' are now clear. . . . My title singles out Malvolio as the preeminent example of a character who mistakes evidence. What is most interesting in this context is that many audiences, some students, and even some scholarly critics see Malvolio's self-delusion as a contributing factor in his acceptance of the forged letter and its contents. The credentials of and in that letter are awfully convincing. The letter gives Malvolio plentiful and persuasive evidence that Olivia loves him – much stronger evidence than Viola has when she says 'She loves me sure . . . I am the man' (2.2.21–24). Viola just happens to be correct. Sherlock Holmes himself would accept Maria's letter as a love letter from Olivia to Malvolio. Malvolio's self-delusion is a factor in our initial acceptance of the justice of the deception, but, when he later makes a fool of himself, he does so because he has been made a fool *of*, tricked, not because he is a fool. Malvolio, however, *is* a self-deluded fool, and that fact colors and confuses our understanding of cause and effect in the letter scene. Similarly, we are inclined to think it ridiculous that Malvolio should even imagine that Olivia might love a self-important servant. On the other hand, although we may find Olivia ridiculous in loving a woman dressed as a boy, we accept the idea that she could be infatuated with a genuine Cesario – with a self-important servant. (The parallel between Malvolio and Cesario is, in fact, carefully spelled out in 3.1.97–124.)

If one wanted to draw a lesson from *Twelfth Night* the one to draw would be the one Viola and Sebastian – and only Viola and Sebastian – seem to learn in the course of the play: do not let overpowering evidence overpower you – the lesson they could be said to respond to when they perform their minuet of supportive evidence in 5.1.224–51 (*My father had a mole upon his brow / And so had mine*) – supporting evidence for a truth self-evident to us, a truth we are impatient to hear them acknowledge. If one drew that moral, then the relationship between the characters in *Twelfth Night* and their audience, which so often listens to context rather than content, would be like that between 'the picture of we three' (a picture of *two* donkeys or – sometimes – a picture of *two* fools), and its beholder.

But I do not want to draw that moral (or, for that matter, any moral). I do not want to draw that moral because that moral does not yield itself up; it must be drawn. To draw that moral one would have to be a jackass.

Audiences of *Twelfth Night* do not, and therefore should not, feel like fools looking at fools, or jackasses looking at jackasses. . . . I submit that, although common sense says that the reason *Twelfth Night* is a joyous and liberating play is that so many of its characters and events are joyous and free, common sense is wrong. I submit that much of our joy in *Twelfth Night* derives from triumphant mental experiences like our modest but godlike achievement in comprehending scene 1. The processes the language of scene 1 sets free are not unusual to ordinary verbal experience. Take, for example, the current American idiom 'I could care less,' meaning 'I could *not* care less.' The triumph of understanding that idiom is of the same sort as those evoked by the various comparable but more complex constructions I have talked about. What is special about the mental triumphs that the language and the action of *Twelfth Night* enable us to perform is their number, their concentration, and their variety. If the act of comprehending 'I could care less' is comparable to doing a mental somersault from the high trapeze, then our easy, graceful, matter-of-fact acceptance of the two-and-a-half-hour experience of *Twelfth Night* is comparable to doing the triple over all three rings of a three-ring circus at once and being one's own catcher.

In another interrogation of *Twelfth Night*'s effects upon its audiences – 'Fiction and Friction', in *Shakespearean Negotiations* (Berkeley, 1988) – Stephen Greenblatt asks:

What if Olivia had succeeded in marrying Orsino's page Cesario? And what if the scandal of a marriage contracted so far beneath a countess's station were topped by a still greater scandal: the revelation that the young groom was a disguised girl? Such a marriage – if we could still call it one – would make some sense in a play that had continually tantalized its audience with the spectacle of homoerotic desire: Cesario in love with 'his' master Orsino, Orsino evidently drawn toward Cesario, Antonio passionately in love with Sebastian, Olivia aroused by a page whose effeminacy everyone remarks. But how could the play account for such desire, or rather, since an account is neither called for nor tendered, how could the play extricate itself from the objectification of illicit desire in a legal marriage? . . .

. . . To be matched with someone of one's own sex is to follow an unnaturally straight line; heterosexuality, as the image of nature drawing to her bias implies, is bent. Shakespeare's metaphor is from the game of bowls; the 'bias' refers not only to the curve described by the bowl as it rolls along the pitch but also to the weight implanted in the bowl to cause it to swerve. Something off-center, then, is implanted in nature – in Olivia's nature, in the nature that more generally governs the plot of the comedy – that deflects men and women from their ostensible desires and toward the pairings for which they are destined.

. . . An enacted imbalance or deviation is providential, for a perfect sphere would roll straight to social, theological, legal disaster: success lies in a strategic, happy swerving. The swerving is not totally predictable because the bowl will encounter obstacles, or 'rubs,' that will make its course erratic; if sometimes frustrating, these rubs are also part of the pleasure and excitement of the game. Licit sexuality in *Twelfth Night* – the only craving that the play can represent as capable of finding satisfaction – depends upon a movement that deviates from the desired object straight in one's path toward a marginal object, a body one scarcely knows. Nature is an *unbalancing* act.

Swerving is not a random image in the play; it is one of the central structural principles of *Twelfth Night*, a principle that links individual characters endowed with their own private motivations to the larger social order glimpsed in the ducal court and the aristocratic household. The play's initiatory design invites the audience to envisage the unification of court and household through the marriage of their symbolic heads, Orsino and Olivia. This uniting, at once a social and psychological consummation, is blocked only by a vow that must be broken in the interest of both the political and the natural order of things. To intensify the narrative pressure behind this design, the play insists upon the perfect eligibility of Olivia: she is not only a great heiress but, in the wake of the deaths of her father and only brother, the sole ruler of her fortunes. . . . The lady richly left was a major male wish-fulfillment fantasy in a culture where the pursuit of wealth through marriage was an avowed and reputable preoccupation. . . .

The maid, however, is strong-willed and refuses perversely to submit to the erotic dance that would lead to the legitimate male appropriation of her person and her 'dirty lands' (2.4.82). Indeed she appears to enjoy ruling her household – controlling access to her person, taking pleasure in her jester, managing her manager Malvolio, dispensing rewards and punishments. . . .

Swerving in *Twelfth Night* . . . is at once a source of festive surprise and a time-honored theatrical method of achieving a conventional, reassuring resolution. No one but Viola gets quite what she or he consciously sets out to get in the play, and Viola gets what she wants only because she is willing to submit herself to the very principle of deflection: 'I am not that I play' (1.5.184). She embraces a strategy that the play suggests is not simply an accident of circumstances but an essential life-truth: you reach a desired or at least desirable destination not by pursuing a straight line but by following a curved path. This principle underlies Sebastian's explanation of Olivia's mistake: 'Nature to her bias drew in that.'

Sebastian glosses his own image with the comment, 'You would have been contracted to a maid' (5.1.262); that is, he invites Olivia to contemplate what would have happened had nature *not* drawn to her bias. . . . Only by not getting what she wants has Olivia been able to get what she wants and, more important, to want what she gets.

Nature has triumphed. The sexes are sorted out, correctly paired, and dismissed to bliss – or will be as soon as Viola changes her clothes. And nature's triumph is society's triumph, for the same clarification that keeps marriage from being scandalized by gender confusion keeps it from being scandalized by status confusion: no sooner has Sebastian explained to Olivia that he is both a maid and man than Orsino adds, as if he were in no way changing the subject, 'Be not amaz'd, right noble is his blood.' . . . Now, through the magical power of the name of the father, we learn that the threat to the social order and the threat to the sexual order were equally illusory. All's well that ends well. . . .

[But despite its comforting conclusion,] *Twelfth Night* may not finally bring home to us the fundamental distinction between men and women; not only may the distinction be blurred, but the home to which it is supposed to be brought may seem less securely ours, less cozy and familiar, than we have come to expect. . . .

At least since the time of Galen it had been widely thought that both males and females contained both male and female elements . . . the predominance, rather than the exclusion, of one or the other helped, along with the original position of the seed in the womb and other factors, to determine sexual identity and to make possible a harmonious accord between sex and gender. Predominance was never – or at least rarely – absolute, nor, in the opinion of most, was it established in final and definitive form in the womb. On the contrary, virtually all males experienced a transition during childhood from a state close to that of females – indeed often called 'effeminate' – to one befitting an adult man. Conversely, if less frequently, the predominance of the appropriate female characteristics could take some time to establish itself. Where the female elements were dominant but still insufficiently strong, the woman would be a virago; similarly, a man in whom male seed was weaker than it should be was likely to remain effeminate. And in those rare cases . . . where the competition between male and female elements was absolutely undecided, a hermaphrodite could be formed.

. . . Proper individuation occurred as a result of the successful resolution of the friction between the competing elements. . . . One peculiar consequence of this view was that normal women had to submit to the weaker internal principle, to accept a certain debility, in order to achieve full female identity, an identity that itself entailed submission to a man; women were *by definition* the weaker sex. A further consequence is that women had momentarily to overcome their inherent defect, and hence their female nature, to produce the seed necessary for generation. Not surprisingly, this overcoming was thought to be difficult; accordingly, the medical texts prescribe extended foreplay as an integral part of sexual intercourse and, for cases where caresses and lascivious words fail, provide recipes for vaginal douches designed to 'heat' women beyond their normal bodily temperature.

But if the Galenic heritage brought with it the notion that human singleness was achieved out of an inherent doubleness, it also brought with it a very different notion: since Galen it had been believed that the male and female sexual organs were altogether comparable, indeed mirror images of each other. . . .

To be sure, this exact homology implies a difference that derives from the female's being colder, and hence less perfect, than the male. This defect keeps the female genitals from being born, as it were. . . . [And] not only are the female genitals an inverted version of the male genitals, but they are also like the perfectly formed but functionally useless eyes of the mole, which are in turn like the blind eyes of creatures that have not yet emerged from the womb. By invoking birth the metaphor implicitly acknowledges the functional utility it is intended to deny, and this paradox, far from embarrassing Galen, enables him to sustain a double vision of the female body, at once defective and perfectly suited to its function, a vision that endured for centuries. . . .

. . . . At least in the Galenic thought that dominated sixteenth- and seventeenth-century medicine, female ejaculation was at the center of the homology between the sexes, for as [Ambroise] Paré declared, 'generation or conception cannot follow without the concourse of two seeds, well and perfectly wrought in the very same moment of time'. . . . Everything in the process of conception hinges on sperm, which is the sole generative principle in a world without eggs, and sperm cannot be produced by either sex without intense sexual delight. . . .

The link . . . is heat: through heat the struggle between the male and female seed is determined, and again through heat the genital structure of the male [the clitoris, commonly depicted as a female counterpart to the penis] emerges from its hidden place [in the female's vulva], and again through heat ejaculation and orgasm are produced. . . .

[According to Jacques Duval and other Renaissance medical authorities,] seed is produced and emitted by the concoction, or cooking, of blood; this cooking is accomplished through erotic friction between men and women. Hence the recurrent images in the medical literature of what a seventeenth-century English gynecologist calls 'the *Fervour* of a very *Libidinous Tickling*.' . . .

The medical texts that we have been examining suggest that the generative power of nature centers on fruitful, pleasurable chafing, and I want to propose that this notion . . . resonates in the fashioning of Shakespearean characters, particularly in comedy. The theatrical representation of individuality is in effect modeled on what the culture thought occurred during sexual foreplay and intercourse: erotic chafing is the central means by which characters in plays like *The Taming of the Shrew*, *A Midsummer Night's Dream*, *Much Ado about Nothing*, *As You Like It*, and *Twelfth Night* realize their identities and form loving unions.

The enemies of the Elizabethan and Jacobean theater charged that the playhouse was 'Venus' Palace,' a place of erotic arousal. For all its insistence on the solemn ceremony of marriage, Shakespearean comedy curiously confirms the charge, not only by gesturing forward to the pleasures of the marriage bed but also by the staging of its own theatrical pleasures. . . .

. . . Shakespeare realized that if sexual chafing could not be presented literally onstage, it could be represented figuratively: friction could be fictionalized, chafing chastened and hence made fit for the stage, by transforming it into the witty, erotically charged sparring that is the heart of the lovers' experience. . . .

Moreover, for Shakespeare friction is specifically associated with verbal wit; indeed at moments the plays seem to imply that erotic friction *originates* in the wantonness of language and thus that the body itself is a tissue of metaphors or, conversely, that language is perfectly embodied. . . .

[As illustrated by the dialogue between Viola and the Clown at the beginning of Act III in *Twelfth Night*,] dallying with words is the principal Shakespearean representation of erotic heat. Hence his plots go out of their way to create not only obstacles in the lovers' path but occasions for friction between them. . . .

Why should that fashioning be bound up with cross-dressing (Rosalind, you will recall, is pretending to be a boy named Ganymede)? In part, I suggest, because the transformation of gender identity figures the emergence of an individual out of a twinned sexual nature. That emergence, let us recall, begins in the womb, but it never results in the absolute exclusion of the other seed, and the presence of both genders remains evident through adolescence.

Shakespeare's most ingenious representation of this twinned gender identity, which must have empowered the transvestite performances of his company's boy actors, is in *Twelfth Night*, with its fiction of male and female individual twins who are at the border of adulthood. . . . With a change of a few conventional signals, the exquisitely feminine Viola and the manly Sebastian are indistinguishable: hence, perhaps, the disquieting intensity of Antonio's passion for Sebastian and the ease with which the confused Olivia is 'betroth'd both to a maid and man' (5.1.263). . . .

Though Shakespeare characteristically represents his women characters – Rosalind, Portia, Viola – as realizing their identities through cross-dressing, this whole conception of individuation seems to be bound up with Renaissance conceptions of the emergence of male identity. Viola in disguise is said to look like one whose 'mother's milk were scarce out of him' (1.5.161–62); in effect a boy is still close to the state of a girl and passes into manhood only when he has put enough distance between himself and his mother's milk. If a crucial step in male individuation is separation from the female, this separation is enacted inversely in the rites of cross-dressing; characters like Rosalind and Viola pass through the state of being men in order to become women. Shakespearean women are in this sense the representation of Shakespearean men, the projected mirror images of masculine self-differentiation. . . .

One consequence of this conceptual scheme – 'For that which man hath apparent without [a penis and a scrotum], that women have hid within [a clitoris and a womb]' – is an apparent homoeroticism in all sexuality. Though by divine and human decree the consummation of desire could be licitly figured only in the love of a man and a woman, it did not follow that desire was inherently heterosexual. The delicious confusions of *Twelfth Night* depend upon the mobility of desire. And if poor Antonio is left out in the cold, Orsino does in a sense get his Cesario. I should add as a corollary to this set of exchanges and transformations that men love women precisely *as representations*, a love the original performances of these plays literalized in the person of the boy actor.

. . . The open secret of identity – that within differentiated individuals is a single structure, identifiably male – is presented literally in the all-male cast. Presented but not represented, for the play – plots, characters, and the pleasure they confer – cannot continue without the fictive existence of two distinct genders and the friction between them.

One of the issues now being debated among scholars of Tudor and Stuart drama is whether theatres such as the Globe were agents of social and political change. Among those who have written most eloquently on this topic is Jean E. Howard, and in a recent article, 'Crossdressing, the Theatre, and Gender Struggle' (*Shakespeare Quarterly*, 1988), she notes that

> Discussion of androgyny, or of the erasure of sexual determinacy, always centers with regard to [*Twelfth Night*] on the figure of Viola. Yet the first thing to say about her crossdressing is that it is in no way adopted to protest gender inequities or to prove that '*Custome* is an idiot.' Viola adopts male dress as a practical means of survival in an alien environment and, perhaps, as a magical means of keeping alive a brother believed drowned, and of delaying her own entry into the heterosexual arena until that brother returns. In short, for her, crossdressing is not so much a political act as a psychological haven, a holding place. Moreover, and this is a key point, from the time Viola meets Orsino in I.iv there is no doubt in the audience's mind of her heterosexual sexual orientation or her properly 'feminine' subjectivity. As she says when she undertakes to be Orsino's messenger to Olivia, 'Whoe'er I woo, myself would be his wife' (I.iv.42). She never wavers in that resolve even while carrying out the task of wooing Olivia in Orsino's name. The audience always knows that underneath the page's clothes is a 'real' woman, one who expresses dislike of her own disguise ('Disguise, I see thou art a wickedness' [II.ii.271]), and one who freely admits that she has neither the desire nor the aptitude to play the man's part in phallic swordplay. The whole thrust of the dramatic narrative is to release this woman from the prison of her masculine attire and return her to her proper and natural position as wife. Part of the larger ideological consequence of her portrayal, moreover, is to shift the markers of sexual difference inward, from the surface of the body and the apparel which clothes that body, to the interior being of the gendered subject. The play shows that while crossdressing can cause semiotic and sexual confusion, and therefore is to be shunned, it is not truly a problem for the social order if 'the heart' is untouched, or, put another way, is not accompanied by the political desire for a redefinition of female rights and powers and a dismantling of a hierarchical gender system. . . . It is fair to say, I think, that Viola's portrayal, along with that of certain other of Shakespeare's crossdressed heroines, marks one of the points of emergence of the feminine subject of the bourgeois era: a woman whose limited freedom is premised on the interiorization of gender difference and the 'willing' acceptance of differential access to power and to cultural and economic assets.

Just as clearly, however, the play records the traditional comic disciplining of a woman who lacks such a properly gendered subjectivity. I am referring, of course, to Olivia, whom I regard as the real threat to the hierarchical gender system in this text, Viola being but an *apparent* threat. . . . At the beginning of the play [Olivia] has decided to do without the world of men, and especially to do without Orsino. These are classic marks of unruliness. And in this play she is punished, comically but unmistakably, by being made to fall in love with the crossdressed Viola. The good woman, Viola, thus becomes the vehicle for humiliating the unruly woman in the eyes of the audience, much as Titania is humiliated in *A Midsummer Night's Dream* by her union with an ass. Not only is the figure of the male-attired woman thus used to enforce a gender system that is challenged in other contexts by that figure, but also, by a bit of theatrical handy-dandy, the oft-repeated fear that boy actors dressed as women leads to sodomy is displaced upon a woman dressed as a man. It is Viola who provokes the love of Olivia, the same-sex love between women thus functioning as the marker of the 'unnatural' in the play and a chief focus of its comedy. . . .

What then can we say, in conclusion, about female crossdressing on the Renaissance stage? I think that, often, female crossdressing on the stage is not a strong site of resistance to the period's patriarchial sex-gender system. Ironically, rather than blurring gender difference or challenging male domination and exploitation of women, female crossdressing often strengthens notions of difference by stressing what the disguised woman *cannot* do, or by stressing those feelings held to constitute a 'true' female subjectivity.

SUGGESTIONS FOR FURTHER READING

Many of the works quoted in the preceding survey, or excerpts from those works, can be found in modern collections of criticism. Of particular interest are the following titles:

Baker, Herschel (ed.), *Twelfth Night* (Signet Classics edition), New York: New American Library, rev. edn, 1985.

Billington, Michael (ed.), *Approaches to 'Twelfth Night'* (Directors' Shakespeare), London: Hern, 1990.

Bloom, Harold (ed.), *William Shakespeare's 'Twelfth Night'* (Modern Critical Interpretations), New York: Chelsea House, 1987.

Charney, Maurice (ed.), *Shakespearean Comedy*, New York: New York Literary Forum, 1980. (See the entries below for Carroll, Lamb, and Siegel.)

Cookson, Linda, and Bryan Loughrey (eds), *Critical Essays on 'Twelfth Night'* (Longman Literature Guides), Harlow, Essex: Longman, 1990.

King, Walter N. (ed.), *Twentieth Century Interpretations of 'Twelfth Night'*, Englewood Cliffs, NJ: Prentice-Hall, 1968.

Palmer, D. J. (ed.), *'Twelfth Night': A Casebook*, London: Macmillan, 1972.

Wells, Stanley (ed.), *'Twelfth Night': Critical Essays*, New York: Garland, 1986.

Other studies of Shakespeare that include valuable discussions of *Twelfth Night*:

Astington, John H., 'Malvolio and the Dark House', *Shakespeare Survey*, 41 (1989), 55–62.

Bamber, Linda, *Comic Women, Tragic Men: A Study of Gender and Genre in Shakespeare*, Stanford: Stanford University Press, 1982.

Barnet, Sylvan, 'Charles Lamb and the Tragic Malvolio', *Philological Quarterly*, 33 (1954), 177–88.

Barton, Anne, '*As You Like It* and *Twelfth Night*: Shakespeare's Sense of an Ending', in *Shakespearian Comedy* (Stratford-upon-Avon Studies 14), ed. Malcolm Bradbury and D. J. Palmer, London: Edward Arnold, 1972.

Belsey, Catherine, 'Disrupting Sexual Difference: Meaning and Gender in the Comedies', in *Alternative Shakespeares*, ed. John Drakakis, London: Methuen, 1985.

Bradbrook, Muriel C., *The Growth and Structure of Elizabethan Comedy*, rev. edn, Baltimore: Penguin, 1963.

Brown, John Russell, 'Directions for *Twelfth Night*', in *Shakespeare: The Theatrical Dimension*, ed. Philip C. McGuire and David A. Samuelson, New York: AMS Press, 1979.

—— *Shakespeare and his Comedies*, London: Methuen, 1957.

Carroll, William C., 'The Ending of *Twelfth Night* and the Tradition of Metamorphosis', in *Shakespearean Comedy*, ed. Maurice Charney (see above).

Charlton, H. B., *Shakespearian Comedy*, London: Methuen, 1938.

Dickey, Stephen, 'Shakespeare's Mastiff Comedy', *Shakespeare Quarterly*, 42 (1991), 255–75.

Dollimore, Jonathan, 'Subjectivity, Sexuality, and Transgression: The Jacobean Connection', *Renaissance Drama*, NS 17 (1987), 53–81.

Donno, Elizabetha Story (ed.), *Twelfth Night* (New Cambridge Shakespeare), Cambridge: Cambridge University Press, 1985.

Draper, John, *The 'Twelfth Night' of Shakespeare's Audience*, Stanford: Stanford University Press, 1950.

Dusinberre, Juliet, *Shakespeare and the Nature of Women*, New York: Macmillan, 1975.

Erickson, Peter, *Patriarchal Structures in Shakespeare's Drama*, Berkeley: University of California Press, 1985.

Everett, Barbara, 'Or What You Will', *Essays in Criticism*, 35 (1985), 294–314.

Freedman, Barbara, 'Separation and Fusion in *Twelfth Night*', in *Psychoanalytic Approaches to Literature and Film*, ed. Maurice Charney and Joseph Reppen, Rutherford, NJ: Fairleigh Dickinson University Press, 1987.

Goldsmith, R. H., *Wise Fools in Shakespeare*, East Lansing: Michigan State University Press, 1955.

Gregson, J. M., *Shakespeare: 'Twelfth Night'* (Studies in English Literature 72), London: Edward Arnold, 1980.

Greif, Karen, 'A Star is Born: Feste on the Modern Stage', *Shakespeare Quarterly*, 39 (1988), 61–78.

—— 'Plays and Playing in *Twelfth Night*', *Shakespeare Survey*, 34 (1981), 121–30.

Hartman, Geoffrey, H., 'Shakespeare's Poetical Character in *Twelfth Night*', in *Shakespeare and the Question of Theory*, ed. Patricia Parker and Geoffrey Hartman, London: Methuen, 1985.

Hartwig, Joan, 'Feste's "Whirligig" and the Comic Providence of *Twelfth Night*', *ELH: English Literary History*, 40 (1973), 501–13.

Hayles, Nancy, 'Disguise in *As You Like It* and *Twelfth Night*', *Shakespeare Survey*, 32 (1979), 63–72.

Heilbrun, Carolyn, *Toward a Recognition of Androgyny*, New York: Knopf, 1973.

Jardine, Lisa, *Still Harping on Daughters: Women and Drama in the Age of Shakespeare*, Totowa, NJ: Barnes and Noble, 1983.

Jenkins, Harold, 'Shakespeare's *Twelfth Night*', *Rice Institute Pamphlet 45*, no. 4 (January 1959), 19–42.

Jones, David, 'Twelfth Night' in *Shakespeare in Perspective*, vol. 1, ed. Roger Sales, London: Ariel Books (British Broadcasting Corporation), 1982. (Also see the remarks on *Twelfth Night* in the same volume by Dorothy Tutin.)

Jorgens, Jack J., '*Twelfth Night*', in *The Shakespeare Hour*, ed. Edward J. Quinn, New York: New American Library, 1985.

Kermode, Frank, 'The Mature Comedies', in *Early Shakespeare*, ed. John Russell Brown and Bernard Harris (Stratford-upon-Avon Studies 3), London: Edward Arnold, 1961.

Kimbrough, Robert, 'Androgyny Seen Through Shakespeare's Disguise', *Shakespeare Quarterly*, 33 (1982), 17–33.

King, Neil (ed.), *Twelfth Night* (Longman Study Texts), Harlow, Essex: Longman, 1989.

Lamb, M. E., 'Ovid's *Metamorphoses* and Shakespeare's *Twelfth Night*', in *Shakespearean Comedy*, ed. Maurice Charney (see above).

Lawry, J. S., '*Twelfth Night* and "Salt Waves Fresh in Love"', *Shakespeare Studies*, 6 (1970), 89–108.

Leech, Clifford, '*Twelfth Night*' *and Shakespearean Comedy*, Toronto: University of Toronto Press, 1965.

Leggatt, Alexander, *Shakespeare's Comedy of Love*, London: Methuen, 1974.

Levine, Laura, 'Men in Women's Clothing: Antitheatricality and Effeminization from 1579 to 1642', *Criticism*, 28 (1986), 121–43.

Lewis, Cynthia, ' "A Fustian Riddle"? Anagrammatic Names in *Twelfth Night*', *English Language Notes*, 22 (1985), 32–37.

Logan, Thad Jenkins, '*Twelfth Night*: The Limits of Festivity', *Studies in English Literature*, 22 (1982), 223–38.

Lothian, J. M., and T. W. Craik (eds), *Twelfth Night* (The Arden Shakespeare), London: Methuen, 1975.

McLuskie, Kathleen, 'The Act, the Role, and the Actor: Boy Actresses on the Elizabethan Stage', *New Theatre Quarterly*, 3 (1987), 120–30.

Mahood, M. M. (ed.), *Twelfth Night* (New Penguin Shakespeare), Harmondsworth: Penguin, 1968.

Malcolmson, Cristina, ' "What you will": Social Mobility and Gender in *Twelfth Night*', in *The Matter of Difference: Materialist Feminist Criticism of Shakespeare*, ed. Valerie Wayne, Ithaca, NY: Cornell University Press, 1991, pp. 29–57.

Markels, Julian, 'Shakespeare's Confluence of Tragedy and Comedy: *Twelfth Night* and *King Lear*', *Shakespeare Quarterly*, 15 (1964), 75–88.

Montrose, Louis Adrian, ' "Shaping Fantasies": Figurations of Gender and Power in Elizabethan Culture', *Representations*, 1 (1983), 61–94.

Nevo, Ruth, *Comic Transformations in Shakespeare*, London: Methuen, 1980.

Novy, Marianne, *Love's Argument: Gender Relations in Shakespeare*, Chapel Hill: University of North Carolina Press, 1984.

Osborne, Laurie E., 'The Texts of *Twelfth Night*', *ELH: English Literary History*, 57 (1990), 37–61.

Palmer, D. J., '*Twelfth Night* and the Myth of Echo and Narcissus', *Shakespeare Survey*, 32 (1979), 73–78.

Park, Clara Claiborne, 'As We Like It: How a Girl Can Be Smart and Still Popular', in *The Women's Part: Feminist Criticism of Shakespeare*, ed. Murray M. Schwartz and Coppelia Kahn, Urbana: University of Illinois Press, 1980.

Petronella, Vincent F., 'Anamorphic Naming in Shakespeare's *Twelfth Night*', *Names*, 35 (1987), 139–46.

Potter, Lois, *Twelfth Night* (Text and Performance Series), London: Macmillan, 1983.

Schleiner, Winfried, 'Orsino and Viola: Are the Names of Serious Characters in *Twelfth Night* Meaningful?', *Shakespeare Studies*, 16 (1983), 135–41.

Scragg, Leah, ' "Her C's, Her U's, and Her T's: Why That?" A New Reply for Sir Andrew Aguecheek', *Review of English Studies*, 42 (1991), 1–16.

Siegel, Paul N., 'Malvolio: Comic Puritan Automaton', in *Shakespearean Comedy*, ed. Maurice Charney (see above).

Sinden, Donald, 'Malvolio in *Twelfth Night*', in *Players of Shakespeare*, ed. Philip Brockbank, Cambridge: Cambridge University Press, 1985.

Slights, Camille Wells, 'The Principle of Recompense in *Twelfth Night*', *Modern Language Review*, 77 (1982), 537–46.

Slights, William E., ' "Maid and Man' in *Twelfth Night*', *Journal of English and Germanic Philology*, 80 (1981), 327–48.

Turner, Robert K., 'The Text of *Twelfth Night*', *Shakespeare Quarterly*, 26 (1975), 128–38.

Ungerer, Gustav, 'The Equinoctial of Queubus', *Shakespeare Studies*, 19 (1987), 101–10.

—— ' "My Lady's a *Catayan*, We are Politicians, Maluolios a Peg-a-Ramsie" ', *Shakespeare Survey*, 32 (1979), 85–104.

—— 'Sir Andrew Aguecheek and his Head of Hair', *Shakespeare Studies*, 16 (1983), 101–33.

—— 'The Viol da Gamba as a Sexual Metaphor in Elizabethan Music and Literature', *Renaissance and Reformation*, 8 (1984), 79–80.

Warren, Roger, ' "Smiling at Grief": Some Techniques of Comedy in *Twelfth Night* and *Così fan Tutte*', *Shakespeare Survey*, 32 (1979), 79–84.

Welsford, Enid, *The Fool: His Social and Literary History*, London: Faber and Faber, 1935.

Wentersdorf, Karl P., 'The "Passy Measures Panyn" Crux in *Twelfth Night*: Is Emendation Necessary?', *Shakespeare Quarterly*, 35 (1984), 82–86.

Wikander, Matthew H., 'As Secret as Maidenhead: The Profession of the Boy-Actress in *Twelfth Night*', *Comparative Drama*, 20 (1986), 349–63.

Williamson, Marilyn, *The Patriarchy of Shakespeare's Comedies: The Plays in History*, Detroit: Wayne State University Press, 1986.

Woodbridge, Linda, *Women and the English Renaissance: Literature and the Nature of Womankind, 1540–1620*, Urbana: University of Illinois Press, 1984.

Yearling, Elizabeth M., 'Language, Theme, and Character in *Twelfth Night*', *Shakespeare Survey*, 35 (1982), 79–86.

Background and general critical studies and useful reference works:

Abbot, E. A., *A Shakespearian Grammar*, New York: Haskell House, 1972.

Allen, Michael J. B., and Kenneth Muir (eds), *Shakespeare's Plays in Quarto: A Facsimile Edition*, Berkeley: University of California Press, 1981.

Andrews, John F. (ed.), *William Shakespeare: His World, His Work, His Influence*, 3 vols, New York: Scribners, 1985 (articles on 60 topics).

Barroll, Leeds, *Politics, Plague, and Shakespeare's Theater*, Ithaca: Cornell University Press, 1992.

Bentley, G. E., *The Profession of Player in Shakespeare's Time, 1590–1642*, Princeton: Princeton University Press, 1984.

Berry, Ralph, *Shakespeare and Social Class*, Atlantic Highlands, NJ: Humanities Press, 1988.

Blake, Norman, *Shakespeare's Language: An Introduction*, New York: St Martin's Press, 1983.

Bullough, Geoffrey (ed.), *Narrative and Dramatic Sources of Shakespeare*, 8 vols, New York: Columbia University Press, 1957–75 (printed sources, with helpful summaries and comments by the editor).

Calderwood, James L., *Shakespearean Metadrama*, Minneapolis: University of Minnesota Press, 1971.

Campbell, O. J., and Edward G. Quinn (eds), *The Reader's Encyclopedia of Shakespeare*, New York: Crowell, 1966.

Cook, Ann Jennalie, *Making a Match: Courtship in Shakespeare and His Society*, Princeton: Princeton University Press, 1991.

—— *The Privileged Playgoers of Shakespeare's London*: Princeton: Princeton University Press, 1981 (an argument that theatre audiences at the Globe and other public playhouses were relatively well-to-do).

De Grazia, Margreta, *Shakespeare Verbatim: The Reproduction of*

Authenticity and the Apparatus of 1790, Oxford: Clarendon Press, 1991 (interesting material on eighteenth-century editorial practices).

Eastman, Arthur M., *A Short History of Shakespearean Criticism*, New York: Random House, 1968.

Gurr, Andrew, *Playgoing in Shakespeare's London*, Cambridge: Cambridge University Press, 1987 (an argument for changing tastes, and for a more diverse group of audiences than Cook suggests).

—— *The Shakespearean Stage, 1574–1642*, 2nd edn, Cambridge: Cambridge University Press, 1981 (theatres, companies, audiences, and repertories).

Hinman, Charlton (ed.), *The Norton Facsimile: The First Folio of Shakespeare's Plays*, New York: Norton, 1968.

Muir, Kenneth, *The Sources of Shakespeare's Plays*, New Haven: Yale University Press, 1978 (a concise account of how Shakespeare used his sources).

Onions, C. T., *A Shakespeare Glossary*, 2nd edn, London: Oxford University Press, 1953.

Partridge, Eric, *Shakespeare's Bawdy*, London: Routledge & Kegan Paul, 1955 (indispensable guide to Shakespeare's direct and indirect ways of referring to 'indecent' subjects).

Rabkin, Norman, *Shakespeare and the Common Understanding*, New York: Free Press, 1967.

Righter, Anne, *Shakespeare and the Idea of the Play*, London: Chatto & Windus, 1962.

Schoenbaum, S., *Shakespeare: The Globe and the World*, New York: Oxford University Press, 1979 (lively illustrated book on Shakespeare's world).

—— *Shakespeare's Lives*, 2nd edn, Oxford: Oxford University Press, 1992 (readable informative survey of the many biographers of Shakespeare, including those believing that someone else wrote the works).

—— *William Shakespeare: A Compact Documentary Life*, New York: Oxford University Press, 1977 (presentation of all the biographical documents, with assessments of what they tell us about the playwright).

Spevack, Marvin, *The Harvard Concordance to Shakespeare*, Cambridge, Mass.: Harvard University Press, 1973.

Van Doren, Mark, *Shakespeare*, New York: Henry Holt, 1939.

Vickers, Brian (ed.), *Shakespeare: The Critical Heritage, 1623–1801*, 6 vols, London: Routledge & Kegan Paul, 1974–81.

Whitaker, Virgil K., *Shakespeare's Use of Learning*, San Marino, Cal.: Huntington Library, 1963.

Wright, George T., *Shakespeare's Metrical Art*, Berkeley: University of California Press, 1988.

PLOT SUMMARY

I.1 In his palace in Illyria, Orsino, the Duke, discusses his love for Olivia, a countess, with his gentlemen attendants. One of them, Valentine, has just returned from Olivia's household with the news that the Countess has gone into mourning for the death of her brother.

I.2 Viola arrives in Illyria, having narrowly escaped drowning when her ship sank. She managed to reach the boat launched by the crew, but her brother did not. The Captain describes the country, and Viola decides to try to gain a place at Orsino's Court.

I.3 At Olivia's house, her gentlewoman, Maria, unsuccessfully urges Sir Toby Belch, the uncle of Olivia, to moderate his behaviour. As well as drinking excessively, he has brought into the house Sir Andrew Ague-cheek, a foolish knight who wishes to be Olivia's suitor.

Sir Andrew enters and, after Maria leaves, is persuaded to continue with his suit by Sir Toby.

I.4 At his palace, Orsino asks Viola, who is now disguised as Cesario, to go to Olivia and convince her of his love. 'Cesario' agrees, though Viola would rather marry Orsino herself.

I.5 In Olivia's house, Maria tells Feste, a clown, that to avoid being dismissed he needs to justify his previous absence. Olivia enters and Maria leaves him to defend himself.

Feste wins Olivia's good favour again with his jests. This upsets Malvolio, Olivia's steward, who dislikes clowns generally and Feste in particular.

Maria returns and announces the arrival of a young man; Olivia tells Malvolio not to let him in if he comes from Orsino. Sir Toby, drunk, briefly enters and then exits. Olivia sends Feste to look after him.

Cesario, who has refused to leave, is allowed to enter. Alone with Olivia, he describes the intensity of Orsino's love for the Countess. Olivia says that she cannot love Orsino, but asks Cesario to return to tell her how Orsino reacts to this reply. Alone, she admits that she finds Cesario attractive. She sends Malvolio to return to Cesario a ring which she pretends he left and to pass on the message that she will explain her refusal if Cesario returns the next day.

II.1 On the shore of Illyria, Sebastian, Viola's twin, explains to

Antonio, the captain of the vessel that rescued him, who he is and how he lost his sister at sea. Now he sets off for Orsino's Court. Antonio resolves to follow him, although he has many enemies at Court.

II.2 Not far from Olivia's house, Malvolio gives the ring and message to Cesario. Cesario guesses that Olivia loves him.

II.3 That night at Olivia's, Sir Toby and Sir Andrew banter, and are soon joined by Feste, who sings. Maria enters, asking for quiet, and is soon followed by Malvolio. He warns Sir Toby that he may be turned out of the house, and is mocked and abused until he leaves.

Maria manages to calm Sir Toby by describing a trick she plans to play on Malvolio. She will write love-letters and leave them for the steward. As Maria's writing is like Olivia's, and as Malvolio is very vain, he will assume that Olivia desires him.

II.4 Orsino, in his palace, has Feste sing. When the clown has finished, the Duke dismisses everyone but Cesario, whom he asks to urge his suit with Olivia again.

II.5 In the garden of Olivia's house, Sir Toby, Sir Andrew and Fabian, another servant of Olivia's, hide in a tree while Maria drops a letter for Malvolio to find.

She conceals herself, and Malvolio enters, day-dreaming of being married to Olivia. He finds the letter, and convinces himself that it is a declaration of Olivia's love for him. He resolves to follow its instructions about how he should dress and act in Olivia's presence.

When he has left, Maria discusses the success of her trick with the others.

III.1 Elsewhere in the garden, Cesario talks to Feste, who leaves to announce Cesario's arrival to Olivia. Olivia, when she comes, dismisses the others who have entered. She asks Cesario if he loves her, and he says that he does not. She asks him to come again, in case he might persuade her to love Orsino.

III.2 Inside the house, Sir Andrew, who has noticed Olivia's affection for Cesario, is about to leave. Sir Toby and Fabian persuade him that Olivia was trying to make him jealous. He agrees to their plan to challenge Cesario to a duel, and so gain a reputation for valour in Olivia's eyes. He leaves to write the challenge.

Maria enters, and takes them to see Malvolio, now behaving as the love-letter instructed.

III.3 In a street in Illyria, Antonio finds Sebastian. Antonio explains that he is in danger and, giving Sebastian his purse, arranges to meet him later at an inn.

III.4 Olivia, feeling depressed, asks Maria to send for Malvolio. Unusually he smiles constantly and points out his yellow cross-gartered stockings. Olivia thinks him mad and, before

going to see Cesario whom she has had called back, tells Maria to look after him.

Sir Toby, Maria and Fabian treat Malvolio as if he were possessed by a devil and he leaves in disgust. Sir Andrew enters with his challenge. Sir Toby reads it out and undertakes to give it to Cesario. Sir Toby sends Sir Andrew to wait for Cesario in the orchard.

When Olivia and Cesario enter, the others withdraw. Olivia again presses her love on the unwilling Cesario and urges him to return the next day. Olivia leaves.

Sir Toby enters, with Fabian, and issues a verbal challenge on Sir Andrew's behalf to Cesario. Cesario wishes to leave, but is prevented by Sir Toby who, leaving him with Fabian, goes to Sir Andrew. Sir Toby returns with Sir Andrew, explaining to him what an excellent swordsman Cesario is.

Sir Toby brings them together (promising each that the other has promised not to hurt him). Antonio enters and, mistaking Cesario for Sebastian, offers to fight on his behalf. Sir Toby draws. Officers arrive and arrest Antonio.

Antonio asks Cesario for the purse (which he had given to Sebastian) and becomes upset when Cesario denies any knowledge of either it or him. After the officers have led Antonio away, Cesario realizes that he has been mistaken for his brother, and leaves. Sir Andrew, Sir Toby and Fabian go after him.

IV.1   Feste, having found Sebastian in a street, asks him to return and speak with Olivia. Sir Andrew enters and, similarly mistaking Sebastian for Cesario, strikes him and is struck back. Sir Toby and Sebastian draw their swords.

Olivia enters and, seeing Sir Toby about to fight, as she believes, Cesario, orders her uncle to leave. She leads Sebastian off to her house.

IV.2   Inside the house, Maria disguises Feste as a curate. Watched by Sir Toby, he goes to question Malvolio, who has been locked in a dark room. Through the door, Malvolio declares that he is sane and begs to be released. Feste refuses and returns to Maria and Sir Toby.

Sir Toby asks Feste to go back to Malvolio and find out if the steward will seek to be revenged on his captors if he is released. Undisguised, Feste speaks with Malvolio, who asks him to fetch a light and paper, which he goes to do.

IV.3   Olivia, with a priest, comes out to Sebastian, who has been waiting in her garden. (She still believes him to be Cesario.) They leave to be married.

V.1   In front of Olivia's house, the Duke and his company meet Feste and Fabian. Feste goes to fetch Olivia. Officers bring Antonio

before the Duke, and Antonio denounces Cesario, whom he believes to be Sebastian.

Olivia enters with her attendants, and rejects Orsino's profession of love. The Duke tells her she will never again see Cesario, whom he knows she loves. Cesario goes to leave with Orsino, which distresses Olivia. She has the priest fetched and he confirms her recent marriage to Cesario.

The Duke is disgusted with Cesario's apparent dissembling. Sir Andrew enters bleeding from blows received when he and Sir Toby attacked Cesario. Cesario denies hurting anyone. Sir Toby enters injured, and Olivia orders both of the knights to be taken away and looked after.

Sebastian enters and apologizes to Olivia for having hurt her relatives. All are amazed that there should be two Cesarios. Viola reveals who she is, and gradually the general confusion is resolved. Orsino offers to marry Viola and she accepts.

Feste reads out a letter he has brought from Malvolio. Olivia sends Fabian to release the steward, and invites Orsino to celebrate the recent events at her house. He accepts.

Malvolio enters, complaining of his treatment. He shows the love-letter to Olivia, who realizes that it was written by Maria. Fabian explains what has happened and asks that the tricksters be excused, adding that Sir Toby has married Maria. Malvolio leaves in anger.

After the others leave to organize the various celebrations, Feste sings an epilogue.